ABOUT FACE

American Society of Missiology Monograph Series

THE ASM MONOGRAPH SERIES provides a forum for publishing quality dissertations and studies in the field of missiology. Collaborating with Pickwick Publications—a division of Wipf and Stock Publishers of Eugene, Oregon—the American Society of Missiology selects high quality dissertations and other monographic studies that offer research materials in mission studies for scholars, mission and church leaders, and the academic community at large. The ASM seeks scholarly work for publication in the Series that throws light on issues confronting Christian world mission in its cultural, social, historical, biblical, and theological dimensions.

Missiology is an academic field that brings together scholars whose professional training ranges from doctoral-level preparation in areas such as scripture, history and sociology of religions, anthropology, theology, international relations, interreligious interchange, mission history, inculturation, and church law. The American Society of Missiology, which sponsors this series, is an ecumenical body drawing members from Independent and Ecumenical Protestant, Catholic, Orthodox, and other traditions. Members of the ASM are united by their commitment to reflect on and do scholarly work relating to both mission history and the present-day mission of the church. The ASM Monograph Series aims to publish works of exceptional merit on specialized topics, with particular attention given to work by younger scholars, the dissemination and publication of which is difficult under the economic pressures of standard publishing models.

Persons seeking information about the ASM or the guidelines for having their dissertations considered for publication in the ASM Monograph Series should consult the Society's website—www.asmweb.org.

Members of the ASM Monograph Committee who approved this book are:

Michael A. Rynkiewich, Arbury Theological Seminary
Judith Lingenfelter, Biola University
Roger Schroeder, SVD, Catholic Theological Union

PREVIOUSLY PUBLISHED IN THE ASM MONOGRAPH SERIES

David J. Endres, *American Crusade: Catholic Youth in the World Mission Movement from World War l through Vatican ll*

W. Jay Moon, *African Proverbs Reveal Christianity in Culture: A Narrative Portrayal of Builsa Proverbs Contextualizing Christianity in Ghana*

E. Paul Balisky, *Wolaitta Evangelists: A Study of Religious Innovation in Southern Ethiopia, 1937–1975*

Auli Vähäkangas, *Christian Couples Coping with Childlessness: Narratives from Machame, Kilimanjaro*

About Face

Rethinking Face for 21st-Century Mission

CHRISTOPHER L. FLANDERS

American Society of Missiology
Monograph Series

VOL. 9

◆PICKWICK *Publications* • Eugene, Oregon

ABOUT FACE
Rethinking Face for 21st-Century Mission

American Society of Missiology Monograph Series 9

Copyright © 2011 Christopher L. Flanders. All rights reserved. Except for brief quotations in critical publications or reviews, no part of this book may be reproduced in any manner without prior written permission from the publisher. Write: Permissions, Wipf and Stock Publishers, 199 W. 8th Ave., Suite 3, Eugene, OR 97401.

Pickwick Publications
An Imprint of Wipf and Stock Publishers
199 W. 8th Ave., Suite 3
Eugene, OR 97401

www.wipfandstock.com

ISBN 13: 978-1-60899-523-3

Cataloging-in-Publication data:

Flanders, Christopher L.

About face : rethinking face for 21st-century mission / Christopher L. Flanders

x + 312 p. ; 23 cm. Includes bibliographical references and index.

American Society of Missiology Monograph Series 9

ISBN 13: 978-1-60899-523-3

1. Interpersonal relations—Religious aspects. 2. Interpersonal communications—Religious aspects. 3. Interpersonal conflict—Religious aspects. 4. Missions. I. Title. II. Series.

BV601.8 F45 2011

Manufactured in the U.S.A.

Books published in the American Society of Missiology Monograph Series are chosen on the basis of their academic quality as responsible contributions to debate and dialogue about issues in mission studies. The opinions expressed in the books are those of the authors and are not represented to be those of the American Society of Missiology or its members.

To Cara

Contents

List of Figures and Tables / ix
Introduction / 1

PART 1: The Loss of Face

1 Cultural Disconnect and the Foreignness of Thai Christianity / 15

2 Sources of Prosopagnosia (Loss of Face): The Modern Western Self / 44

3 Sources of Prosopagnosia (Loss of Face): The Misconstrual of Honor, Guilt, and Shame / 57

PART 2: Recovering Face

4 Face and Facework Theory / 75

5 Theoretical Reflections on Thai Face / 103

6 A Description of Thai Face / 117

Part 3: Preserving Face

7 Theological Anthropology and a Christian Understanding of Face / 163

8 A Theological Framework to Orient Face / 190

9 Reconceiving the Soteriological Task / 210

10 Salvation in the Context of Thai Face / 242

11 Conclusions and Recommendations / 263

Appendix A: Interviewee Demographic Information / 273
Appendix B: Thai Facework Terms / 275
Appendix C: Reasons for Avoiding Face Loss / 277
Appendix D: Positive Ways of Gaining Face / 279
Appendix E: Positive Consequences of Face / 282
Appendix F: Characteristics of a Face Person / 284
Appendix G: Characteristics of a Person with Honor / 286
Appendix H: Characteristics of a Person with Dignity / 289
Appendix I: Metaphors of Face / 291

Bibliography / 293
Index / 307

Figures and Tables

Table 1: Characteristics of Guilt and Shame / 61

Table 2: Characteristics of "Face People" / 121

Table 3: Characteristics of Face, Honor, and Dignity / 139

Figure 1: Prototype Face Scenario / 151

Introduction

FOR THAIS, FACE IS a fact.[1] Indeed, the issue of face represents a basic concern for many, perhaps most Thai people.[2] Even Thais who self-consciously resist playing the face "game"[3] still must live their lives in a society that remains profoundly attached to face. Face, however, constitutes a problematic, particularly for Thai Christianity. Such a problem rests in the fact that Thai Christians and non-Thai missionaries alike have generally failed to engage the issue of face. Yet face, as a critical and central issue in Thai culture, demands such an engagement.

During ten years as a missionary in Thailand, I increasingly became aware of this fact, noting a disturbing tendency of missionaries who would inevitably underestimate the importance of face and face-related issues in Thai culture. Given the critical importance face holds for many Thais, this lack of awareness was alarming. Some seemed nearly oblivious to Thai face

---

1. By face, I do not mean the physical body part, but the use of the term as a metaphor representing a type of interpersonal social honor and identity projection—"the claimed sense of self-respect or self-dignity in an interactive situation" (Ting-Toomey 1994:3).

2. Thai social psychologist Suntaree Komin contends that face and face-related concerns form the core of Thai culture and personality (1991). Ranking the ten most central Thai cultural values, her nationwide survey research placed the issue of Thai face (what she alternately terms "ego orientation") as primary for the Thai personality. Indeed, so central was this preeminent concern for face that nine of the remaining ten most basic cultural values all functioned as mechanisms to uphold and maintain the Thai face. My own interaction with Thai culture and people has continually demonstrated how central such face issues are for the Thai people.

3. By "game" I do not imply a lack of seriousness. Indeed, for many, face is a profoundly significant concern. That Thai face exhibits rules, patterns, goals, and involves multiple "players" makes the use of the game metaphor quite appropriate.

issues and certainly unaware of the salience of face in everyday Thai life. Yet, even those more aware of the importance of face in Thai culture held unhelpful postures. Such attitudes often took the shape of either uncomfortable ambivalence about, or at times, outright hostility toward, face.

This might not have been so troubling if simply a missionary deficiency. Yet, even Thais, who as a whole are profoundly occupied with face, did not appear to reflect on this issue in a substantive way. Such neglect was apparent in Thai Christian literature. One looked in vain to find any critical discussion or reflection upon the topic, either by missionaries or by Thai Christians. Also, in classes, sermons, and informal discussions with Thai Christians, the issue of face did not seem to constitute an area of focal attention.[4] Even when addressed, the topic paralleled the more negative assessment of the missionary community. Thai believers did not make face a point of explicit and intentional engagement from a Christian perspective.

Thus, whether in theology, evangelism, or issues involving sin, salvation, or atonement, Thai Christians and missionaries alike seem either uninterested in or possibly incapable of addressing issues related to face. This glaring incongruity between the value of face for Thais and the lack of intentional engagement within the Thai Christian community is deeply troubling.

Surely, such a lack of careful attention to face is a dangerous posture. Uncritical views of face, furtively attaching to the theology of the Thai church, are potentially detrimental for its life and mission. Such seems to be an unavoidable situation without proper attention to face. Additionally, to ignore face is to run the risk of missing valuable cultural resources, implicit in the Thai experience of face, for the critical task of authentic Thai theological reflection.

This lack of engagement with face raises critical issues with which we must wrestle. How is it that such a central sociocultural issue has not been a more significant part of the Thai Christian vocabulary or experience? How pervasive are these negative attitudes regarding face? What lies behind them? Might this lack of self-conscious engagement with face have any relationship to the persistent Thai perception of Christianity as a foreign, Western religion? How should Christians understand this notion of face and how it relates to the ways we understand and proclaim the gospel?

4. A close friend also doing research on Thai face preached a sermon about face in an established Thai church in Southern California. He noted after the sermon how several (many who had been Christians for a considerable time) remarked that this was the first time they had ever heard a sermon in church about face.

In this book, I contend that this lack of adequate attention to face illustrates a significant dimension of a cultural disconnect between the life of the Thai church and the broader cultural context in which it exists. That face has not been on the theological "radar screen" in Thailand is attributable partly to missionaries who have often been oblivious of or significantly averse to face. This has had the effect, I believe, of engendering the same type of lack of concern for face among Thai Christians. The theological concerns of missionaries, which Thai Christians subsequently adopted, did not contain a place for face and thus ultimately subverted face questions. It seems a Western theological agenda has subtly but effectively inoculated the Thai church against face.

In an unpublished monograph written nearly three decades ago, Joseph R. Cooke (1978) suggested that the Thai Christian community was not connecting deeply with Thai culture, particularly in the ways missionaries and Thai believers articulated soteriology. He proposed that the way forward was, partly, to pay greater attention to honor and shame, two issues that are central to the experience of face. Inherent in face and honor issues, Cooke contended, was atonement in a relational mode, a more fruitful notion upon which to base gospel presentation. My suspicion is that Cooke was correct in his assessment and recommendations. Here I want to contend that it is imperative for the ongoing life and witness of the Thai church to understand more fully the importance of face and honor in Thai culture and its relevance for Thai Christian theological reflection.

Goals

The title of this book involves an intentional double entendre. On one level, this study is simply research into the area of Thai face and face-related behavior. It involves cultural and theological discussions "about" the issue of face. Yet, the title also suggests more than a neutral examination of face, as if a simple phenomenological description would suffice. The issue of face demands inclusion as a legitimate category for theological and soteriological reflection within the Thai context. This second sense of "about face," then, points to the need for a reorientation of face, a fundamental shift in the way we view face. This shift must involve a fundamentally different assessment of a phenomenon traditionally viewed with ambivalence and negative regard. Such a shift requires a new theological framework within which Thai Christians and missionaries might more appropriately frame the issue of face.

I claim that an adequate cultural and theological study of Thai face will reveal a fruitful cultural resource for orienting authentic contextualized theologizing in the Thai context, particularly for a contextually appropriate soteriology. This project works toward several specific goals to substantiate this central claim:

- Document the disconnect of the gospel with Thai culture, specifically in the areas of soteriology and face
- Develop a cultural model of Thai face that illustrates the meaning and function of face in Thai culture
- Explore Thai face as a theological issue, seeking to discern its implications for theology and missiology
- Investigate theoretical perspectives that will enlarge the understanding of face and face-related concepts within the missiological community
- Provide a framework for understanding the nature and task of contextual soteriology

The ultimate goal of this work, however, must be to assist the Thai church to enlarge its theological vocabulary, thus providing "legs" for the Thai theological project and the contemporary witness of the Thai church. Thus, my attempt at the reorientation of thinking concerning face is directed toward theological, soteriological, and missiological purposes.

Significance

I submit this project holds potential significance in four areas: face in Thai culture, face and facework theory, soteriology, and missiology.

Face in Thai Culture

Many academic treatments of Thai culture reference face as a pervasive cultural trait, yet frequently gloss over face issues in pursuit of other theoretical agendas. Regarding this tendency, Clark perceptively notes that the

> . . . literature which has spoken to the subject generally has devoted a paragraph or two, hardly enough to give a summary . . . Needless to say, Thai face has rarely been discussed as an extensive and cohesive component of culture and behavior. (Clark 2000:19)

Through ethnographic interviews with Christian and non-Christian Thais, this study will contribute to a more robust understanding of this underspecified, yet important dimension of Thai culture.

Face and Facework Theory

Anthropologist Michael Herzfeld, in a significant article on social honor, makes a notable observation. That is, the English term "honor" (and shame as well) is an "inefficient gloss" that covers an extremely wide variety of indigenous terminological systems (Herzfeld 1980:339). In reality, there is no such thing as honor, but only culturally specific "honors." Scholars, however, often proceed as if the definition of such terms is self-evident. Such obscures the important emic dimensions such terms invariably exhibit.

What Herzfeld suggests is true of honor also seems equally the case regarding face. That is, the specific term "face" covers an incredibly wide variety of phenomena. Researchers, however, often naively subsume such diverse experiences under the single rubric of the English term "face" without attention to specific emic features. Theorists assume the meaning of face without adequate attention to the particular shape face may take in diverse cultural contexts. Indeed, to assume a universal notion of face and proceed from such an a-contextual and generalized concept, not only represents inadequate research but, more seriously, a subtle form of ethnocentrism. Though the study of face and facework is a growing area of academic focus, there continues to be a need for culturally specific, linguistically nuanced face research.

Such prompts face researchers Tracy and Baratz to eschew generalized notions of face, arguing for careful, contextually specific face research.

> Theories of facework, we argue, must be built from the ground up. We must avoid prematurely developing abstract general theories to insure that we capture what is most important and interesting about the interactions studied. (Tracy and Baratz 1994:303)

They continue that we presently need "to build middle-range, domain-specific theories if we are to advance our understanding of face and facework" (1994:303). H. Chang and R. Holt note that it is

> ... precisely because of this (cultural) variation, face needs to be explored in situ within its "home" system of cultural meanings to assess how members of a given culture choose to regulate their interpersonal lives. (Chang and Holt 1994:96)

Additionally, it is imperative to study face in native languages to understand properly this culturally specific dimension of human behavior we term face (Ting-Toomey and Cocroft 1994:334). These scholars concur regarding a critical need for face studies that explore emic understandings of face and culturally specific facework strategies in specific contexts, cultures, and languages. This project represents such a linguistically nuanced, culturally specific analysis of emic dimensions of face for a particular (viz. Thai) context.

Soteriology

Proposing face as an integrative motif for Thai theological reflection on the meaning of the cross is in keeping with a growing trend in contemporary theological studies to conceive theology as fundamentally relational. Such a theological research program assumes metaphors of relationality, connection, and connectedness as "a solid basis for a creative and fruitful re-articulation of theological ideas and methods today" (Haers 2003:2). A relational account of the theological task highlights the proper *telos* of true theological formulation. That is, fundamentally, theology is *sapientia*, not *scientia* (Crutcher 2003:549). Proper theological formulation then is not just for increasing understanding but also about forging healthier modes of relationality. Reconsidering the Thai Christian belief mosaic, particularly the area of salvation, within a face/honor framework fits in well with such a research program and may indeed play an important constructive role in such a relational theology.

Missiology

Missiologists have also neglected face and face-related concerns. Some (Lienhard 2000, 2001; Müller 1996) mention face obliquely, subsuming it under the rubric of so-called "shame cultures" and "honor cultures." Yet, to date there exists no substantive missiological treatment of this critically important topic. This study aims to raise awareness of the ubiquity and importance of the issue of face and attempts to begin filling in this gaping lacuna in contemporary missiology. The theoretical issues I engage will further clarify the features of face and face-related notions, both generally but also for the Thai context. Explicating a cultural model of Thai face may serve as a tangible example for the missiological community of the critical importance for building understandings of terms and concepts from "the ground up." It also aims to highlight how the missiological community often misunderstands face and undervalues what actually holds great potential for theological and missiological reflection.

This project, I believe, is significant for the Christian community in Thailand. It is the judgment of many (Cohen 1990; Cooke 1978; Gustafson 1987; Hughes 1982, 1996; Keyes 1993; Swanson 2003) that the shape of much Thai Christianity remains conspicuously foreign. This book will, I hope, stimulate creative and contextually appropriate theological and soteriological work among both Thai and non-Thai Christian workers in Thailand. It is my hope that a constructive engagement with this basic Thai cultural value of face will contribute to reducing foreignness and encourage a more culturally authentic Thai theology.

Limitations

Since my primary purpose is to highlight the positive value of a proper understanding of face, I offer only an oblique critique of the negative dimensions of face. This dark side of face is clearly an important issue that deserves serious study and reflection. Such, however, lies outside the purview of this work. My immediate agenda is to highlight the nature of Thai face and legitimate face as an area of theological importance. Additionally, I limit this project to the context of Thai Protestantism, understanding that the contexts of Thai Catholicism and the more recent phenomenon of Thai Pentecostalism may yield differing accounts. Finally, the cultural model of Thai face that I present I construct from a relatively homogenous grouping of Thais (i.e., younger, educated, urban Thais). Thus, the specific shape this model takes may not be generalizable to the broader context of Thai culture.

Assumptions

Following Booth, Colomb, and Williams (1995), I contend that good research should assume the proper end of changing the way people think. Moreover, to change thinking demands effective argumentation and rhetorical acumen, that is, making and demonstrating a good case. Because this is so, I wish to highlight the basic assumptions upon which this books proceeds and to anticipate some potential objections readers may raise regarding the ideas I offer.

First, I argue for the salience of face in Thai culture. For this, I offer a generalized cultural model of Thai face that places face possession at the center of the Thai psyche and relationality. Additionally, I discuss several academic studies that acknowledge this basic importance of face in Thai culture.

I also propose a more robust understanding of face than many (e.g., Western missionaries) typically assume. For this, I engage contemporary discussions of the self that illustrate the ubiquity and essential function of face for all human relationality. In addition, I examine face from a biblical-theological perspective, which I contend provides scriptural warrant for a renewed appreciation of face and face-related issues. Some might object that since face is essentially a negative cultural trait, a disconnect with Thai culture is actually proper. Though face can indeed be negative, I will argue that face is something all of us do all the time. Face forms a critical and necessary dimension of the human self and all social relations. There is room to explore not only negative dimensions of face but also potentially positive and healthy dimensions as well.

What if the Thai church itself also critiques face as negative and problematic? My claims stand, I believe, as long as such critiques operate out of a skewed, uncritical, or a reductionist understanding of face. That is, outsiders (Western missionaries) may have unduly influenced (possibly continuing to influence) the perspectives of insiders (viz., Thais).

Regarding the disconnect between the Thai Christian community and its cultural surroundings, I provide historical anecdotes from missionary history, contemporary missionary attitudes to salvation and face, and a description of the narrative logic of face. Such an account runs counter to the Western logic that lies behind the penal substitutionary model of atonement, the version of atonement dominant among modern Western Protestant Christians and missionaries.

Some might contend that I overstate this disconnect between the Thai Christian community and the surrounding culture. To those who do not recognize this disconnect I can only answer that it is quite real but generally understated and regularly obscured by a universalizing theological agenda that presses Western concerns and categories upon all theology. Others might note that the Thai church might have worked out a relevant understanding of face, albeit a tacit "folk" theology of face. Perhaps. Yet, I believe this project is critical as long as any Thai theological understanding of face remains merely tacit and not subject to explicit theological reflection.

It is possible some may contend that the lack of attention to face forms only a small, and therefore inconsequential, part of the larger problem. Yet, the goals of this project are legitimate, I maintain, as long as we accept that the Thai church can only solve the problem of disconnect incrementally, issue by issue. It is true that face represents only one of the myriad issues the Thai church must address regarding this cultural disconnect. If my assessment is correct, however, this one issue of face is actually a principal contributor to this disconnect.

Some might wonder how an increased understanding of face might matter for the task of theology in the Thai context. My proposals for the nature of the theological task assume key cultural issues to be proper objects of explicit theological attention and discernment. Indeed, that our cultural contexts invariably shape this process of theological discernment is not something to fear. Thus, if all forms of human relationality, particularly those in the Thai context, require something like that which we term face, then this surely must form an area of focus for intentional theological inquiry.

I note recent discussions (Driver 1986; Fiddes 1989; Green and Baker 2000; Gunton 1989; McClendon 1994) that demonstrate how New Testament images of salvation themselves are contingent and culturally specific. This results in "unhooking" the notion of atonement from any one particular theory (e.g., penal substitution) and establishes the task of soteriological construction as a fundamentally contextual project. Soteriology, as an inherently contextual task, must of necessity rest upon culturally salient metaphors and specific narrative logic. Those who fail to recognize the importance Thai face holds for contextually theology or soteriology may be embracing a "their theology should look like our theology" approach, misunderstanding the contextual nature of all theological descriptions, including those concerning soteriology and atonement.

Some, missionaries and Thais alike, would no doubt wonder whether there is a need to "improve" upon the penal substitution theory of atonement to which so many in the Thai Christian community apparently subscribe. Does this view not describe the essence of what "really happened" at the cross? For these, other notions (e.g., face, honor/shame) might serve soteriology in illustrative ways but cannot constitute the "essence" of atonement. Taking exception to that viewpoint, I proceed upon the assumption that our theories of atonement are contextual attempts to describe in relative ways the effects of the life, death, and resurrection of

Jesus. A comprehensive explanation of the mechanics of atonement is not present in the New Testament (which rather provides a series of images) and lies outside the limitations of metaphorical language. Even putting aside for a moment the issue of whether the penal substitutionary theory of atonement itself represents a biblically faithful and theologically coherent description of salvation, given the contextual nature of soteriological description, all theories of atonement and soteriological description may only provide a relevant model for specific contexts.

Others may point to a Thai church that has perhaps adapted quite happily to modern Western forms of atonement thinking. Yet, as long as the Thai church fails to recognize the missional nature of all soteriological construction and atonement theory, it will forfeit the opportunity to frame the work of God's salvation in ways that resonate more deeply with the broader cultural context within which the Thai church exists. Thus, to be content with its theology or soteriology in a legitimate fashion requires that the Thai Christian community base its understandings upon its own culturally specific theological and soteriological voice.

Some may suggest that in the end this project does not materially contribute to greater church growth. That is, as one Thailand missionary noted to me in a conversation, non-contextualized churches seem to grow just as well as supposedly contextualized ones. The validity of this project stands, however, as long as we realize the primary goal of authentic contextual theology and soteriology is not immediate numerical church growth but an authentic incarnational expression of God's truths.

Another potential objection to this project would challenge my place, as a non-Thai, to offer suggestions for what might constitute authentic Thai theology or soteriology. This concern is misplaced, however, as I am not dictating the terms of what might constitute authentic Thai theology. Rather, what I offer here are provisional suggestions as orienting motifs, designed to spur on the Thai Christian community to more engaged theologizing. I conceive of my role, then, more as a *provocateur* instead of an architect. The building of Thai theology and soteriology is a task that properly belongs to the Thai church as it works out its uniqueness within the context of the historical church universal.

Overview of the Argument

When people experience loss of face they often engage in various types of strategies to regain, reclaim, or redeem face. If successful, they subsequently endeavor to maintain face and to avert further face loss. The conceptual organization of this work follows this tripartite face pattern. Thus, I structure my treatment of Thai face and its soteriological value from this flow of face-loss → face-redemption → face-maintenance.

Section 1 documents historically how it is that a theological engagement with the issue of face is missing in the Thai Christian community. This I term "The Loss of Face." Such involves understanding the extent and sources of Western missionary inattention to face and how this has led to a parallel loss in the Thai church. Section 2 deliberately attempts to reclaim a healthy view of face. Thus, I title this section "Redeeming Face." Finally, section 3, "Maintaining Face," presents the theological and soteriological value of face for the Thai context. The development of this argument constitutes an attempt to engage face in a theologically healthy fashion, thus upholding the issue of face.

Therefore, I summarize the flow of my argument in this way. Face is a ubiquitous dimension of all human relationality. Specifically, face represents a complex, linguistically explicit, and culturally salient component of Thai society. This fact should necessitate the issue of face to form a critical component for the theological project of the Thai Christian community. This clearly, however, is not the case. Face continues to suffer inattention from the Thai Christian community. When some do demonstrate awareness of face, this often takes the form of puzzlement or aversion.

Close attention to the nature of face reveals a valuable cultural resource for Thai theology and soteriology. This connection between face and soteriology is not arbitrary. The issue of soteriology in the Thai context represents one significant dimension of the broader cultural disconnect that plagues contemporary Thai Christianity. Face offers a nexus of images and concerns that draws together issues of relational atonement, acceptance, honor, and shame. Specific face logic in Thai culture contrasts significantly with the Western cultural and legal logic that underwrites the soteriological understandings of a large segment of the Thai Christian community (Thai Christians and foreign missionaries included). This leads me to contend that the notion of face may provide a culturally compelling narrative logic upon which to construct a more adequate Thai soteriology.

Andrew Walls (1996) discusses what he sees as the proper role of mission studies in contemporary scholarship. Because of the growing recognition that the center of the Christian faith no longer resides in the Western world, Walls argues for a "renaissance of mission studies" demanded by this new situation. Walls expounds on the characteristics of this new type of mission studies, noting that such

> ... will require not just rigorous scholarship, but *depth* of scholarship.... It will require integrated scholarship, which engages with all the existing theological disciplines and in doing so enriches them. It will need to bring to the task a range of disciplines and sources of which most even of the best theologians are innocent. It will need to demonstrate learning and professional competence in the phenomenology and history of religion and in the historical, linguistic, and social sciences too, for those disciplines also need the renaissance of mission studies. (1996:151)

Such an approach requires a missiology that recognizes the critical importance of integrative, cross-disciplinary research. This project strives toward this best sense of interdisciplinary research as it integrates historical research, biblical-theological reflection, and social-scientific investigation. It remains for the reader to judge whether I have attained to such a lofty goal.

Upon learning about this research project, a Thai Christian remarked to me that she hoped I could help the Thai church "solve the problem" of face. By this, I think, she was reflecting on the negative dimensions of face and hoped I could hopefully discover a way to rid the Thai church of face or face-related problems. What I offer here, however, is not a "solution" to the face "problem." Rather, I hope to demonstrate that there are important dimensions of Thai face about which we know little but which, if we take time to learn, will help the Thai Christian community deal with face in a more biblically faithful, theologically coherent, and contextually relevant fashion.

PART I

The Loss of Face

1

Cultural Disconnect and the Foreignness of Thai Christianity

A MARKED FOREIGN SHAPE has defined Christianity throughout its short history in Thailand. This story is unquestionably a complex one, involving a great number of factors. Though not every cause is evident, commentators from various disciplines have observed this persistent feature of Thai Christianity. Many have offered thorough and eloquent treatments.[1] Indeed, this disconnect between Christian expressions and the Thai culture has been so deep that for many Thais, the notions of Christian and Thai stand as mutually exclusive, antipodal points.

I recount this story of cultural disconnect between the gospel and Thai culture through the dual lenses of soteriology and face. That is, I will illustrate this disconnect from the vantage point of the theology of salvation of the Thai church and also how missionaries interacted with Thai culture in the area of face. In doing so, I will offer only a short account establishing this foreign shape since a fuller discussion would extend far beyond the more modest scope of this project. I will then probe the sources of this disconnect and illustrate how we can see such through soteriology and face.

---

1. See for example Cohen (1990), Cooke (1978), Ek Thabping (1974), Gustafson (1987), Hughes (1982, 1984a, 1984b, 1994, 1999), Keyes (1993, 1996), Koyama (1974), Swanson (1984, 1991, 2003), Wisely (1984).

An anecdote from a prominent historian of the Thai church illustrates well the tension and disconnect between Christian and Thai identity.

> I have often told the story of a young boy I met while on a search for a particular home: he said to me, "A lot of Christians live around here." Just to make a little conversation with this young boy, I asked him, "And what about you, youngster? Are you a Christian?" He replied, "No, I'm a Thai." (Swanson 1984:164)

The personal anecdote Swanson offers points to this basic polarity that exists for many between being Christian and being Thai.

Throughout the history of Thai Protestantism,[2] missionaries have continued to create and cultivate a continuing dependency on foreign religious expressions, in particular, those of a Western conservative evangelical kind (Swanson 1999:xix). Early missionaries demonstrated a stark rejection of Thai culture, questioned the validity and depth of Thai conversions, and generally distrusted the ability of Thai Christians to control the affairs of their own churches. Because of this disconnect, missionaries could "not surrender the reins" (Acocella 2001:xvi). This pervasive foreignness was not a problem about which most were aware until the 1930s (Maen 1979:386). Therefore, for more than one hundred years, there was no substantive attempt to counteract or reduce this foreignness of Thai Christianity (1979:387). Even when there were efforts to work against this foreignness, it was frequently a surface-level solution. The occasional appeal for acculturation actually was often "merely a modification of the institutional Church regulations by which Thai Christians could participate in Thai cultural activities" (1979:387–88).

---

2. There has existed in Thai Protestant Christianity an essential homogeneity in missionary theology, particularly as it involves issues of salvation. The vast majority of Protestant missionaries to Thailand have been American Presbyterians, the dominant missionary force in Thailand until after WWII (Swanson 2003:2). Thai Protestant churches, many of which have been Thai-governed entities for quite some time, have essentially duplicated the practices, forms, and theology of these earlier missionaries. After WWII, Thai Protestantism became increasingly complex with an influx of various agencies and new denominations. This surface-level diversity, however, masked a remarkable uniformity in theology and approach. Despite denominational and organizational differences, there existed such a continuity of underlying attitudes and theological commitments that Thai church historian Herbert Swanson could remark that it was "still possible to treat Protestantism in Thailand as a single entity" (Swanson 1999:xix). This has possibly changed to some degree with the recent rise of Pentecostal churches in Thailand. As Zehner has observed, particularly regarding notions of supernatural power, Thai Pentecostalism is an amalgam of Protestant theology and local cultural impulses (Zehner 1991, 1996, 2003).

The Zimmerman Report

A 1928 conference initiated by John R. Mott and held in Bangkok was a pivotal event for the eventual formation of the Siamese National Christian Council. One outcome of this conference was the recruiting of Harvard sociologist Carle Zimmerman to produce a national survey of the church in Thailand. Although his major task was a comprehensive national agricultural survey, which the Thai government commissioned, Zimmerman's report on the status of the Thai church offers an important window into Thai Protestant Christianity, one hundred years after its inception.

This 1931 document, the "Zimmerman Report,"[3] noted two specific concerns. First, it lamented the fact that the Christian church in Thailand was not growing as it should numerically. Second, in sometimes cutting language, the report highlighted the serious disjuncture that existed between the Thai Christian communities and the surrounding culture, this some one hundred years after missionary activity had first begun.

The report noted how Christianity had come as essentially a Western cultural enterprise. Western expansion went hand in hand with church growth as the missionaries "did not create a Siamese Christian church but made the converts members of a Western church" (Zimmerman and McFarland 1931:19). That there were likely "thousands of fine spirits" who accepted the doctrines of Christianity and even followed Christian ethics to some degree but could not join such a "foreign" religion was an indictment of the profoundly Western shape of the Thai church. This meant that becoming a Christian essentially required local Thais to become "almost completely de-nationalized and de-culturalized from (the convert's) own social system" (1931:14). As the report noted, "the man who joins the church must inevitably 'lose face'" (1931:16).

Though there have been changes in recent practice (e.g., a more prominent role granted to Thai leaders in the church), the philosophical and theological assumptions of the missionaries from this early period continue to circumscribe the organizational structures, practices, and theology of Thai churches. Even recent well-intentioned attempts to contextualize the gospel have often been unconscious efforts to adapt a Western missionary religion to Thai social and cultural realities (Swanson 2002a:40).

---

3. The report also listed missionary Bertha McFarland as coauthor. McFarland's precise role in the construction of the report is unclear though it does seem certain that Zimmerman was the main contributor.

Anthropologist Charles F. Keyes, for example, notes that until quite recently Christianity "has never been able to shed its mantle of 'foreignness.'" So much is this the case that "even those Thai who have faced profound crises of power have not found in Christianity a vision of a moral community that could be Thai" (Keyes 1993:277). Another anthropologist, who has focused upon missionary interaction with Thai culture, argues that until very recently the difference between the worldviews of Thai and missionary constitutes "an unbridgeable chasm" (Cohen 1990:341). Though perhaps overstated, such illustrates a fundamental truth. Even in northern Thailand, where early missionaries met with the greatest numerical success, Christianity continued to be decidedly foreign at many levels (Swanson 2003:177). Maen notes that "not a single missionary has really been criticized of having 'Siamized' or Buddhistized' Christianity as the early Church apologists were of having 'Hellenized' it" (Maen 1979:163).

Contemporary missiologists also concur, lamenting the essentially Western structure of Thai Christianity. The Thai church continues as a struggling religious minority marked by a continual wrestling with its "westernity" (Wisely 1984:163; Gustafson 1987). As recently as 1997, research showed that because of strongly anti-syncretistic perspectives, attitudes among missionaries in Thailand toward appropriating Thai culture in Christian witness often bordered on antipathy (Nantachai 1997:314). Many continue to believe that Thai culture, as a Buddhist culture, is essentially satanic, evil, and corrupted (1997:314–15).

Admittedly, there does seem to be some moderation in recent years. There have been "subtle accommodations," yet these fall short of constituting any fundamental change (Cohen 1990:343, 347). It is also increasingly clear that there exists a tacit Thai "folk" theology at work among Thai churches in spite of much foreignness and continuing missionary influence.[4] Yet, in many ways, present-day missionaries still display many of the ideas and attitudes of those of earlier generations. Despite some encouraging modulations, Thai Christianity has yet to lose this pervasive foreign face.

This disconnect has yielded serious consequences. Clearly, such has been at the heart of the general lack in the contemporary Thai church of authentic Thai theology. Thai churches, to this day, have developed no

---

4. Recent research done by anthropologist Edwin Zehner demonstrates how Thai evangelicalism, in mostly unrecognized and surprising ways, has appropriated certain local religious impulses reconfigured into the schema of acquired Christian notions (Zehner 1991, 1996, 2003).

self-conscious Thai theological tradition. Rather, Thai Christians seem content simply to repeat the theology of their missionary founders. "The conservative missionary mentality absolutely forbids dialogue with the culture, therefore the church has never gained the ability to reflect on what it wants to take, wants to eschew, wants to put aside for further reflection" (Swanson 2002b). Foreign missionaries continue to hold almost complete control over theological development and efforts of indigenization (Kim 1980:209). Christian bookstores in Thailand carry the latest translated versions of the works of contemporary evangelical authors such as Peter Wagner, James Dobson, and Max Lucado, yet there continues to be a dearth of Thai-produced theological material.

This disconnect also appears to have had a material effect upon church growth. That is, such foreignness continues to be, at least in part, an obstacle that keeps Thais from following Jesus. Based upon a limited survey sample, Philip J. Hughes discovered that among those who had formerly been Buddhist, the greatest obstacle to becoming a Christian was that Christianity was "not Thai" (Hughes 1996:6).

Missionary Theories of Culture

In 1887, pioneer missionary Daniel McGilvary was speaking with a group of northern Thai people. Another missionary who was also present, W. Clifton Dodd, recounted in a letter how the missionary teacher McGilvary engaged these unknowing, "heathen" students in discussion. Talk in generalities eventually turned to the topic of religion. As McGilvary began to converse more pointedly about the Christian faith, a profound shift in communication dynamics occurred. "Soon," Dodd remarked in approving tone, "the conversation became a monologue" (Dodd 1888:493). This observation by Dodd encapsulates perfectly the missionary approach characteristic not only of the early period of missionaries, as Dodd and McGilvary represent, but also of many who would follow. Underlying this missionary "monologue" were notions of culture, the gospel, and missionary practice that would ultimately lead to quite unintended consequences. Dodd's remark was both lamentably prescient and tragically ironic. The missionary "monologue" of which he spoke signaled a deep disconnect with Thai culture, the effects of which the Christian church in Thailand would continue to struggle against, even to this present day.

This change of dynamic from a conversation to monologue was ironic precisely because the mono-directional transfer of an "eternal" and "unchanging" gospel was, in Dodd's mind, a good thing. For Dodd, McGilvary, and other missionaries of their day, the contemporary discussions of gospel and culture would likely have seemed completely perplexing, if not patently dangerous. The missionary was the bearer of God's eternal and unchanging message. The possession of such a treasure made it incumbent upon these mission workers to maintain the integrity of the gospel, particularly against the distorting influence of heathen, non-Christian cultures. Thai people and Thai culture had nothing to contribute to the gospel message. A monologue, from such a perspective, was appropriate and necessary.

Modern missionary engagement with Thai culture has assumed a specific theory of culture. Dominant among Protestant missionaries during the eighteenth and nineteenth century, this approach toward other cultures did not arise directly from the pages of the Bible. In profound ways, evangelical Protestantism was a product of the Enlightenment (Bebbington 1989:74). It was this post-Enlightenment nexus of philosophical and theological ideas that formed the conceptual framework within which Protestant missionary activity took place (Stanley 2001:8). David Bosch is surely correct in contending that "the entire western missionary movement of the past three centuries emerged from the matrix of the Enlightenment" (Bosch 1991:274). The particular missionary theory of culture that formed most missionary activity traded upon post-Enlightenment ideas that emerged from this matrix. Here, we must investigate further the Enlightenment strain that had the most influence on English-speaking evangelicalism and the modern missionary movement, that is, the Scottish Enlightenment (Stanley 2001:17).[5]

The Scottish Enlightenment and Common Sense Realism

A major component of Scottish Enlightenment influence was the empirical inductivism of Francis Bacon. This approach was "scientific," focusing on discrete facts, understood through an inductive process. Above all else, Baconism was a thoroughly rational approach that exalted the human mind in all types of inquiry. Such thinking became the conventional

---

5. Just as surely as the missionary movement was borne out of Enlightenment currents is the sometimes-overlooked fact that there were multiple responses to these Enlightenment influences. Scholars increasingly recognize what we term "the Enlightenment" is in fact, a series of interrelated phenomena that defy singular descriptions. There were several "enlightenments" during the eighteenth century, each with common features as well as distinctive qualities (Stanley 2001:16).

approach not only in science but also in religion. That Baconism was a singularly dominant influence in early American theology is clear from the words of conservative Calvinist theologian Samuel Tyler, who stated in 1844 that "the Baconian Philosophy is emphatically the philosophy of Protestantism" (Holifield 2003:174).

The Scottish philosopher Dugald Stewart and theologian Thomas Reid utilized this Baconian approach in their philosophy and theology. These two, credited with being the fathers of the school of thought often termed Scottish Common Sense Realism, had a profound impact on American religion. It was through their influence that American Protestantism, and American evangelicalism in particular, thoroughly embraced the moral philosophy of common sense, especially in its Baconian-inspired Scottish form (Noll 2002:102).

Common Sense Realism was a philosophy designed to combat the radical empiricist skepticism of David Hume. It assumed that the proper operation of the human mind, through its regulative functions and an ability to discern its own internal operations, "ensured knowledge of things as they really were" (Holifield 2003:177). This "knowing" could be done directly, without intermediate help from any non-rational source. Such knowledge was certain and perspicuous. It rested upon an inductive accumulation of ìfactsî readily apparent and available to any fair-minded, objective, rational mind. Such thinking viewed abstract concepts or speculations not empirically verifiable with great suspicion. Those who held such "common sense" notions viewed them as axiomatic, that is, as self-evident principles grounded in human experience that no "rational" person could reasonably doubt. Such were the foundational ideas of the Common Sense approach (2003:177).

In America, the most articulate advocates of these ideas were not philosophers but rather Protestant educators and ministers. Timothy Dwight, speaking at Yale, contended that common sense was in fact "the most valuable faculty . . . of man" and that "our Saviour treats every subject in the direct manner of Common Sense" (Noll 2002:233). Scottish Common Sense Realism, underwritten by a thoroughgoing Baconism, was a philosophical movement that exerted an unparalleled influence on early American theology (Holifield 2003:175).

Of particular importance, however, was the influence of these notions upon a methodology for establishing truth claims. The common sense approach asserted that strict induction from experience and the "facts" (in this case data from the Bible) was the only legitimate approach to establish truth, including religious truth (Noll 2002:234). This induction from the biblical "facts" was a process the rational mind could accomplish unimpeded. Anyone could understand truth clearly and indubitably. For the Common Sense project, entertaining the possibility that truth could be mediated through authorities or sources outside "correct thinking" was simply not allowable. The rational human mind was the supreme authority and arbiter of truth. Properly aware, all people could understand truth without mediation and completely eschew influence from all "external" (i.e., non-rational) forces. This meant that Common Sense proponents could discard with cavalier abandon constructs such as tradition, human perception, and human culture. Such "non-rational" influences could only cloud the mind and impair the rational quest for true understanding. Thus, as an approach to truth, Common Sense Realism did not simply view culture and human tradition with suspicion; it was, in fact, an extreme anti-culture approach, providing the basis for a profoundly a-contextual theological and missional orientation.

Common Sense Realism tended to be blind to its own assumptions and philosophical commitments. It lacked a sense of historicity, of being a product of a certain time and cultural context. Commenting on this hidden danger of the combination of common sense notions with American religion, James Marsh lamented that the intermingling of these two was so intimate and complete that "by most persons they are considered as necessary parts of that same system" (Noll 2002:248). A common sense approach necessarily collapsed its own perception of the world with what it thought represented "reality" or "truth." The interpreters' religion, the way they saw things according to "common sense," was the way things truly were. The result was a religious system that denied its own location in history. In essence, Common Sense Realism operated as a view "from nowhere." This a-historical, a-cultural position inherent in Common Sense Realism then led to a naive universalizing tendency. It was because of this a-historical position together with its own bias against any form of human mediation that made the Common Sense approach incapable of entertaining questions of contextuality. These Enlightenment-inspired commitments resulted in a theory of culture that was essentially a-cultural and universalizing.

Applied to the Christian faith, this had dramatic effects. Through the application of human rational power mediated by "common sense," one could "know" what the gospel was. Such would be clear to any "rational" person who properly induced from the data of the Bible. Thus, not only was it unnecessary to think explicitly about the ways local culture might positively influence theological reflection or our understanding of the gospel, such considerations were in fact potentially heretical. Tradition and human cultures blinded the natural powers of the rational human mind. Such could only obscure the "pure gospel." Christianity, in this vein, rested upon revelation and rejected "lesser" alternatives such as tradition and culture (Hardy 2001:216). Daniel Hardy aptly summarizes the effect of such a notion regarding the "allowable" influence culture, that is, "the lesser alternative."

> All beliefs need to be tested and accepted by reason, not because of "authorities," whether texts, traditions, or "divinely appointed" priests or leaders. This would fulfill, even perfect, the natural rationality and goodness of humanity. Such in turn constituted a universal standard: through reason, all might be free and equal in society. The universal superseded local prejudices and practices. (2001:206)

Rationality, configured in Scottish Common Sense mode, necessarily trumped the local, irrational vagaries of non-Christian cultures. Yet, ironically, the gospel advocated by Common Sense–influenced proclaimers was in fact a specific cultural configuration itself, that is, the specific cultural form of Western evangelical Protestantism. Missionaries operating in Common Sense mode, however, would not likely be aware of these notions. The gospel as they saw it, though profoundly influenced by their own Western culture and ideas, seemed self-evident. It was true, while other cultures and differing perspectives were necessarily false.

Enlightenment Views of Culture

The impact of such a view becomes important for discussions of missionary activity since "the same Scottish intellectual tradition that gave birth to common-sense philosophy also exercised a disproportionate influence on mission theory" (Stanley 2001:17). Missionary theory and practice were, according to Hardy, "formed, controlled, and checked" by these Enlightenment orthodoxies (Hardy 2001:215). The a-contextuality required by Common Sense Realism would affect in profound ways missionary work among non-Western cultures. Adamant resistance to local cultures, traditions, and religions would characterize such. Missionaries advocating the "common sense gospel" would naturally highlight the incompatibility of these non-Western cultures with the gospel. Resistance of this kind, combined with their own lack of ability to reflect upon and discern the influence of their own Western culture on the way they framed the gospel, would lead missionaries to operate with a "cut and paste" approach. Such an approach involved "cutting out" the "truth" from the missionary context and "pasting" it in unmodified form into completely different cultural contexts. Walls describes the same theological approach among the early British missionary movement. For these missionaries, "Theology was a *datum* to be explained and demonstrated in the new cultural setting, not something which would develop in it" (Walls 1996:197). Disdaining "mediations" that were present in non-Western cultures, this approach of missions would necessarily lead to simple reproduction of Western ideas and theology.[6]

Several factors (e.g., confessional tradition, organizational ethos, missionary culture, personality) might influence the particular form this clash would take. That such disconnect would occur, however, was to a large degree predetermined. This inevitability was the result of a particular theory of culture inherently incapable of appropriating culture or context in a meaningful way. These various theological and philosophical commitments yielded a theory of culture that was intrinsically hostile to local cultures, traditions, and values. Culture itself was the villain, the main thing to avoid, and an element that missionaries had to extract from the native converts. Change in theological formulation that considered cultural issues, as is suggested in more recent discussions of contextual

---

6. Besides the general a-contextual nature of these Enlightenment ideas, Stanley notes five other features common to Enlightenment-influenced mission activity (Stanley 2001:8). First, there was a general notion that all non-Western peoples were "heathen" and thoroughly lost in darkness and sin. Second was a corresponding perspective that viewed all non-Christian religion as "heathen idolatry," devoid of any trace of the grace of God. Third, there existed a confidence that civilization in its Western form was inherently superior to other cultural manifestations, particularly in terms of rationality and technology. Fourth, there was an equally unwavering confidence in the ability of human rational powers and ability to lead to knowledge of God and, ultimately, regeneration. Fifth, there was a prevalent orientation to address the gospel to individuals, calling each person to an identifiable and self-conscious experience of conversion. Though only the last two characteristics are arguably due exclusively to Enlightenment factors, the Enlightenment was responsible for the ways in which missionary activity expressed these patterns (Stanley 2001:8). Together, these characteristics would provide the ingredients for a significant clash with local cultures.

theology, could only be viewed as anathema, since it would call into question the sufficiency of the entire epistemological and theological infrastructure upon which the missionaries and their faith stood. The vagaries of culture itself were the central problem. Culture was an unfit vessel for theology. The lost condition of heathen non-Christian nations formed a chasm that culture could not help span. Missionaries affected by such were "immunized" against culture.

Mixed together the antipathy of Common Sense Realism toward the mediating influences of tradition and culture, the Common Sense-inspired self-evident universal gospel the missionaries possessed, and the propensity to dismiss carte blanche all non-Western cultures as fundamentally void of redeemable elements, provided a powerful ideological cocktail that, in fundamental ways, "inoculated" the missionaries against non-Western cultures. Missionaries, by virtue of their tacit theory of culture, were predestined for disconnect with local cultures. Such philosophical and cultural commitments predetermined the monological approach of the missionaries.

Impact on Missionary Activity

The ways this a-contextual and universalizing theory of culture affected missionary activity were both pervasive and deep. As a way to investigate this impact, the framework provided by Daniel Hardy is helpful. Hardy proposes that we should conceive of mission in terms of intervals, that is, the conceptual space that exists between one's own situation and that of another (Hardy 2001:215). Such a conceptualization contains two basic dimensions. The first dimension is the construal of the missional space between missioners and the missionized, that is, what shape such space represents. The second dimension involves the various strategies used to bridge this missional space. Hardy makes the point that different Enlightenment orthodoxies variously influenced the ways missionaries construed these two missional dimensions. Thus, a particular response to Enlightenment currents determines both "difference" (i.e., how to conceptualize the shape of space between the missionary and those to whom they go) and "responsibility" (i.e., how to navigate such space) (2001:217). For most evangelical Protestants, and particularly those involved in the missionary movement, the philosophy of Common Sense Realism essentially dictated the responses given these two dimensions.

Difference

First was the tendency to conceive of missional space primarily as difference. Missionaries from this period, as Stanley mentions, were profoundly dualistic in their conception of non-Western peoples. In contrast to Christianized Western cultures, those in foreign lands were "heathens" living in radically deficient cultures. Such a view, however, is not the exclusive property of Enlightenment thinking. Within the history of Western Christianity, the notion of the outside world as pagan or heathen dates back at least to Tertullian and was strongly reinforced by dualism inherent in Augustinian theology (Stanley 2001:9).

The Enlightenment, however, shaped this idea of heathenism is new ways. The notion of radical difference between "Christian" and "non-Christian" cultures rested upon the even more basic notion of the unity of all humankind. Eighteenth-century Enlightenment thinking directly engendered such a tendency to conceive of the entire world as one human race. The differences, then, which existed between the heathen and Christian were not essential qualities of different races, but the results of various environmental factors. The processes of rationalizing and Christianizing the heathen peoples could overcome, in principle, these factors the environment produced (Stanley 2001:11).

For most missionaries of this period, there also existed a tenacious belief in the superiority of modern "Christian" civilization, namely, that culture that characterized the modern Western world. Missionaries during this period essentially collapsed the gospel and Western civilization into one neat package. Difference between the modern "Christian" world and the heathen "non-Christian" world, then, was not only due to a lack of the gospel. Any cultural differences with non-Christian peoples indicated a deficiency of both true religion as well as "proper culture," that is, "civilized" Western culture. In practice, this resulted in missionary attitudes and practices that collapsed the distinction between expansion of Western culture and the propagation of the Christian faith (Stanley 2001:10). These two projects were essentially one and the same.

Asymmetry

The second dimension of Hardy's missional space is the strategy used to navigate such space. If missionaries conceived of the space primarily as difference, then given their view of culture the proper way to maneuver through this difference was naturally asymmetrical. This asymmetry produced a mono-directional flow of resources and influence; essentially, this produced a system characterized by a "we give, they receive" dynamic. To admit another option would be to call into question the fundamental truthfulness of the gospel as they conceived it. The Baconian approach, filtered through Scottish Common Sense Realism, demanded that we already know the truth. If people properly exercise their God-given rationality, this truth would be "obvious."

A set of Christendom assumptions also supported this notion. Western culture was a "Christian culture," where the gospel and Christian influence had shaped language and thought forms over several centuries. A turn to heathen culture, for instance that of Thailand, for mediating notions would amount to a tacit admissiaon that the missionaries had not gotten it right. To admit Thai cultural considerations into the theological equation would be to undercut notions basic to the legitimacy of the West as a Christian culture and civilization. Such was a move no Western missionary was likely prepared to make.

We can see this asymmetry clearly in two specific ways. First, the prevalent attempt to essentially de-culture local peoples was profoundly asymmetrical. As already mentioned, the Enlightenment contributed a new sense of unity of humanity with differences explained in terms of environment (e.g., non-Western cultures or non-Christian religion) (Stanley 2001:11). If people do not respond appropriately to the gospel (as all rational and logical people, should respond), this must result from the influence of false tradition, culture, and religion. If the environment was the basic problem, the solution was to remove the local people from the corrupting influence of that environment, that is, their language, culture, and religious context. Often, this deculturalization took the form of education in missionary institutions. Missionaries assumed that an intentional process of education could change such a situation. In missionary-directed schools, local people could receive "proper" instruction in culture, mores, and values. Such schools could serve as an alternate environment, "unpolluted" by the surrounding heathen culture. Such would lead to a dual strategy of education (in Western mode) together with the preaching of the gospel.

A second asymmetrical strategy involved the way missionaries framed the message of the gospel. The superiority of Western Christendom culture was not the only given. The very gospel the missionaries purveyed was thought of as a fixed, unchanging set of truths. The missionaries had the true gospel, while the contaminating influence of tradition and culture endangered the purity and truthfulness of that gospel. Because of this, any self-conscious reflection, vis-à-vis new cultural contexts, was at best unnecessary, at worst a great danger to the very truth of the Christian message. Because of this, the missionary gospel would be of a "cut and paste" kind, simply a copy of that which came out of the cultural context of the missionaries. The important point is that such an approach was itself a necessary extension of the Common Sense perspective most missionaries held. Because of this, missionaries had to reproduce the gospel in an undifferentiated form. Thus, the very conceptualization of the gospel message, based upon Common Sense notions, forced the missionaries into an asymmetrical transaction of proclamation. Ultimately, this asymmetry only reinforced a dominant Western configuration of the good news.

These strategies missionaries most frequently utilized were ones that positioned the missionaries as "bringers" and the non-Christian strangers as "receivers" (Hardy 2001:218). This was especially the case regarding the bringing of an already predetermined and set gospel and the impartation of Western culture. As Hardy notes, whether such postures could ever allow foreign cultures to be "the field of God's prevenient activity is a matter of question" (2001:218). Such a situation assumed an asymmetrical and universalizing one way "monologue" as the proper way to navigate the distance between missionaries and local peoples.

It is not an exaggeration to state that missionaries who operated within this Enlightenment-laden tradition of Scottish Common Sense Realism were generally incapable of engaging non-Western cultures in positive ways. Some have contended that if these early missionaries had simply taken the time to acquire a deeper understanding of local cultures, their approach would have been significantly different (Nantachai 1997:129). It is undeniable that missionaries during this period often exhibited a frightening disregard for and lack of deep understanding of local cultures.

Yet, it is questionable whether such deeper cultural awareness would have led to meaningful differences in approach. Deeper cultural understanding likely would not have been able to counteract the more dominant power of their philosophical and theological commitments. Their own strategies were, in fundamental ways, a result of their Enlightenment programming. Such programming resulted in the chasm of difference that missionaries could navigate only by asymmetrical strategies. Missionaries viewed the local people as passive receptors of the missionary gospel. "The missionaries were not expected to 'learn' anything from the natives, nor to adjust or accommodate their own construction of reality in any way" (Cohen 1990:340).

This missionary approach characterized by Enlightenment-inspired difference and asymmetry would ultimately bring about tremendous conflict and disconnect with local cultures. Several different factors (e.g., confessional tradition, organizational ethos, missionary culture, and personality) would influence how this difference and asymmetry would shape this disconnect. That such disconnect would occur, however, was to a large degree predetermined by the missionaries' Common Sense theory of culture.

The Thai Case

Understanding this philosophical and theological background prepares us to examine in more depth how and to what extent these Enlightenment-inspired tendencies were a part of missionary activity in the Thai case. Upon examination, the Thai sources reveal these very same ideas and strategies characteristic of the broader Protestant missionary movement.

The same dualistic worldview that grew out of Scottish Common Sense Rationalism profoundly influenced American Presbyterianism, the religious tradition with which the majority of Protestant missionaries though World War II associated themselves. Such an absolutist attitude could admit "no middle ground" between the world of darkness and that of light (Swanson n.d.). And, like many Enlightenment-influenced missionaries, this resulted in an acute sense of difference between the missionaries and the Thai people.

In the minds of the missionaries, Thai culture was radical deficient. This extreme antipathy towards what they conceived of as a heathen, tainted culture resulted in exceedingly unflattering images. These consisted, for example, of missionary notions of Thai society "being like a valley of dry bones, vain, idolatrous, irreverent, angry and wicked wolves, morally degraded, helpless, ignorant, lonely, and dead" (Swanson 2003:87). Such caricature was not limited to the realm of religion. For missionary Dan Beach Bradley, the Thai government was purely heathen as were the Thai children (W. Bradley 1981:72).

Missionaries felt alienated from northern Thai society and characterized such in terms of radical difference. The subsequent strategies of mission similarly alienated their converts from that society (Swanson 1984:22). The asymmetry in such approaches was quite marked. One area that such asymmetry was particularly dominant was that of the gospel itself. Rev. Egon Wachter, a Presbyterian missionary, believed strongly that the "pure gospel" could not be in any way altered or adapted. It came from God and missionary success depended entirely upon the ability to keep this message untainted (Wachter 1888, as quoted in Swanson 1991:13).

The Zimmerman Report conceded that the Edinburgh Conference of 1910 had changed a non-indigenous orientation to some extent. Contemporary (at that time) missionaries were becoming more aware of the difference between Westernization and Christianization. Also, there was more favor for allowing nationals the opportunity to direct their own affairs (Zimmerman and McFarland 1931:15). This growing awareness was, in fact, the very engine driving the push for a national leadership and a national church. Still, despite such progress, psychological ownership of the church remained weak (1931:12).

This was particularly troubling in light of the real danger such might bring about. The report makes it clear that a non-indigenous type of church posed a serious threat, especially in light of a potential rise in nationalism or a corresponding surge in anti-Western sentiment. "Psychologically, (the church) is not yet a national institution." If the present course continued, a church "nine-tenths a western institution" would not fare well. If, however, it could be reversed and become "nine-tenths Siamese" then such troubled waters could likely be navigated and possibly emerge even stronger than before (Zimmerman and McFarland 1931:20).

The report cites other weighty problems, which illustrate the general missionary asymmetry. There existed a serious lack of indigenous Christian apologetic and Christian literature (1931:18). It critiqued quite explicitly missionaries who did not demonstrate any awareness of the Thai social system (1931:19). The report references the tendency of Western missionaries who try to change the basic social structures of Siamese society. "The new convert finds that his old order of life is destroyed. He is freed from the old social controls and he does not have as yet a new system" (1931:21). Also problematic were the controlling attitudes and practices of many missionaries. Instead of teacher, wise father, or other non-dominating role, missionaries often operated as the

> ... older brother who insists at all times upon giving unasked-for advice, sure he is right and all others wrong. The attitude became that of antagonism rather than of sympathetic Christian service. The policy of permitting a national to "save his face" in silence was too seldom adopted. (1931:19)

In summary, the Zimmerman Report offered a prophetic critique of a Thai church that was profoundly Western. In various ways, it highlighted the serious disjuncture that existed between the Thai Christian communities and the surrounding culture—a disjuncture that, to a large degree, was formed by the missionary modes of difference and asymmetry.

The Thai case demonstrates many of the pervasive characteristics of Enlightenment-influenced Protestant missionary attitudes and activities. The missionary antipathy toward Thai culture precluded any positive assessment of Thai culture as resources for the life of the church. In fact, the missionaries not only viewed Thai culture with a negative eye but also attempted to extract, as completely as possible, the church and its converts from their cultural context. These missionaries resisted a contextualized or indigenous Christian movement in Thailand.

Disconnect and the Gospel

The most basic soteriological idea among Protestant theology of this period was the doctrine of penal substitution, a theory that had become the quasi-orthodox theory among most Western Protestantism beginning in the mid-sixteenth century. In the penal view, Jesus' death on the cross provides the solution to the dilemma of human separation from God. Jesus experiences this accursedness and punishment on our behalf. He, in effect, takes upon himself the punishment humankind deserved. By doing so, he satisfies the wrath of God and exhausts divine punishment that humankind deserved because of sin. Jesus, as sinless God-man, assumes our punishment, absolving us of our moral guilt. Since Jesus' death satisfies the demands of God's retributive justice (i.e., someone has been punished, so guilt is removed) humans are free once again to enter into relationship with God. God and humankind can once again have fellowship. Salvation, then, becomes primarily forgiveness of transgression and release from guilt. It is no exaggeration to state that for much Protestant theology, personal guilt and salvation from sin have come to function symbiotically, existing in a theological tandem at the core of much evangelical soteriology. An examination of the records indicates that the theological approaches to salvation and conversion that Protestant missionaries brought to Thailand, with minor variations, parallel those typical of eighteenth- and nineteenth-century American Protestantism.

Hughes summarizes the message of early missionaries in northern Thailand as presenting the basic human problem of sin, salvation as the forgiveness of those sins, and release from despair and a new state of joy and happiness resulting from this salvation (Hughes 1982:12–13).

An entry from the journal of Bradley, dated August 14, 1837, noted his writing of a tract that was

> ... designed to give a full account of the natural and moral attributes of Jehovah. I feel that it is the time to expose to the eyes of the people the horrors of idolatry, and charge home the conviction of sin and guilt upon them by all possible and laudable means. (Feltus 1936:45, as quoted in Nantachai 1997:124)

Daniel McGilvary, pioneer missionary to northern Thailand and a dominant figure during his fifty-three years of missionary service, in like fashion summarized that the gospel was a message of pardon for the sin-sick soul (McGilvary 1912:99). McGilvary's awareness that the people "readily admit that there is no pardon in Buddhism" corresponded well with his deep conviction that "no subject has such constraining power over men who are conscious of their guilt and sin as the Cross of Christ" (McGilvary 1894:373). Sin was the problem. Such brought about guilt that was resolved by the pardon that resulted from the work of Jesus upon the cross. In similar vein, Dodd summarizes the gospel message for the northern Thai as a claim to grant pardon of sin and offer a better heaven than Nirvana (Dodd 1888:492).

McGilvary recounted their early experience upon arrival in the northern city of Chiang Mai.

> While the mass of our visitors came from curiosity, some came to learn ... whatever was their object in coming to see us, we soon gave every crowd, and nearly every visitor, to understand what we had come for. We had come as teachers-primarily as teachers of a way of salvation for sinners. And we never addressed a crowd of thoughtful men or women who did not readily confess that they were sinners, and needed a saviour from sin. (McGilvary 1912:79)

What stood out for McGilvary was the explicit awareness the people supposedly exhibited regarding their own sinfulness. Explicit self-awareness of personal sin and guilt, in the mind of McGilvary, was apparently not limited to his Thai audience. So universal and pervasive a human predicament was guilt that he projected such upon the Buddha himself, writing that "the Buddha groaned under his own load of guilt" (1912:181). One sees how the presumption of a universal human nature combined with Western Protestant soteriology were thrust upon even an Indian philosopher from the sixth century BC. How precisely McGilvary thought he knew this, we cannot be sure. Likely, he would have referred to the universal state of humankind as culpable sinners. Since he assumed the antidote the universal gospel provided came in the form of "pardon," McGilvary, like his peers, diagnosed the disease as guilt. The radically anachronistic idea of projecting such upon someone from a foreign culture living more than two millennia earlier was, in all likelihood, unintelligible for someone steeped in the universalistic theology and philosophy of the times.

Additional anecdotes illustrate these pervasive tendencies. It was McGilvary's contention that salvation from sin and the notion of pardon was in fact that which attracted Thais to Christianity. Interest among Thais resulted from "pardon freely promised to all who believe in Him . . . (which) is the final argument that wins these people" (McGilvary 1912:328). Once, after McGilvary had preached in public, the larger crowd dispersed, and those who were more "thoughtful" stayed for further discussion. These, McGilvary noted with confidence, stayed because of the heart of his message, "this doctrine of salvation from sin" (1912:328). Another, this time an abbot of Umong monastery with whom McGilvary had what he termed a "deep-rooted friendship" (1912:188), also showed interest. Characteristically, McGilvary notes that for him "the sense of sin weighed heavily" since the Buddhist monk knew that there was no opportunity for pardon in Buddhism (1912:82).

In an 1887 report to the board published in *Church at Home and Abroad,* Dodd provided an account of McGilvary's teaching. He noted that the reception was remarkable, and "without exception these Buddhists confessed at the outset, or were soon brought to concede, the immeasurable superiority of Christianity." He then goes on to note that "the sense of sin is universal, so too is the insufficiency of the works of merit. Many sad souls confessed that they had long been dreading the penalty for sins for which they feared that 'merit-making' could not atone" (Dodd 1888:493). This presupposition that the gospel is to be configured around the issue of pardon of sin combined with the assumption that the human heart universally seeks for a resolution to the existential guilt produced by sin to form the foundational soteriological notion in early Protestant missions in Thailand.

Unfortunately, however, there was not always such a pleasant fit between the missionary expectations and ideas with the local response. This message of guilt, contrition, and promise of pardon seemed to yield frustratingly little positive effect. If the records are any indication, more often than not these expectations were seriously frustrated. The Thai people, in general, did not show the level of regret and sin-consciousness the missionaries deemed appropriate. There were those, of course, who were scornful of the entire religious system. McGilvary mentions a Siamese commissioner who administrated Siamese interests in Chiang Mai. McGilvary comments that this man, Praya Tep Worachun, actually encouraged Christianity. This was not because the Christian message moved him in any way. Rather, he accepted that it offered a respectable morality yet saw neither a reason nor possibility for "atonement for sin" (McGilvary 1912:194).

This frustration was not because of a lack of interested inquirers. Indeed, there seemed to be considerable interest among the local people. Neither was it a result of any lack of exposure to the missionary message. Missionaries were active in preaching as multitudes heard their message. Bradley comments,

> . . . many have read all our publications in course, and now earnestly seek for more. Many can repeat large portions of their contents. Some seem to be inquiring the way of salvation with considerable earnestness. We indulge trembling hopes that a few of those with whom we are acquainted have given their hearts to God. We tremble for these, because they do not give us clear evidence of sorrow for sin which we much desire to see. (1841a:202)

Bradley again weighs in on this perceived deficiency:

> There appears to be no special convictions of sin among all these millions of polluted heathen. Scarcely even will one of them inquire with deep felt solicitude, What shall I do to be saved? The way of the Spirit seems not yet to be prepared among them. (1841b:176)

Such a lack of "moral sensitivity," some thought, came from a defect in the Thai personality. Missionaries could characterize this bewildering lack of expected contrition and guilt simply as a lack of a moral conscience. Such a bald appraisal comes from Jesse Caswell. "From this it may be seen, how almost impossible it is for a Siamese to possess a conscience that shall speak in a distinct tone on the subject of right and wrong." This is because the "conscience of a Siamese is indeed a chaos. Actions are reckoned right or sinful, not because they are perceived to be so, but because they have been so labeled by religion or public sentiment" (Caswell 1848:16). If the consciences of the local people were unable to properly understand the difference between "right and wrong," they were then hopelessly limited in ability to respond to the missionaries' message of forgiveness.

For many of these missionaries, the primary defect was in Thai culture itself. Caswell notes that the Thai mind was "peculiarly unfitted for understanding and embracing the doctrine of the forgiveness of sin through an atonement" (1848:16). He explained this by associating blood sacrifice as uniquely formative for engendering the notion of sinfulness and guilt. According to Caswell, the major purpose of the Old Testament sacrificial system was to engender among people a yearning for such forgiveness. Cultic blood sacrifice was "an expression of (people's) hope that (their) sin might be forgiven on account of the sufferings of another being" (1848:16). Yet, Thai Buddhism contained no such notion of blood sacrifice for forgiveness. It contained no equivalent doctrine to that of penal substitutionary atonement. The Thai people seemed little burdened by a heavy sense of guilt from sin. It was because of this that Buddhism, in Caswell's eyes, was "from beginning to end . . . irreconcilably at enmity with the idea of mercy, or gratuitous favor" (1848:16).

Frustration that resulted from preaching and not getting an adequate response seemed to have been a rather widespread phenomenon. Such was in stark contrast to the general flow of conversion experience among Americans, that is, conversions based upon the specific expectations provided by the theological underpinnings of penal substitution, guilt, and pardon. These ideas were not immediately compelling to most Thai listeners. "The real difficulty," Meakin concluded,

> . . . is to make an impression on the lethargic minds of the people, whose impassive inactivity is never more marked than in connection with religion. None but those who have tried it know what it means to address a crowd or a succession of individuals without an objection being raised, but without the least signs of an impression having been made. (1896:43)

He continues, quoting an unnamed missionary who stated that preaching to the Thai people was

> . . . like bombarding an earthwork . . . one's shots are buried and nothing is seen. It would be a relief even if one hearer 'got mad' about it. There is a point to which the Siamese will yield, as if they would do so to any extent, but when you get to the important moment of all you find a dead wall. (1896:43)

This "important moment" was in all probability an appeal to accept the gospel of guilt and pardon. In part, this lack of explicit reaction, a "dead wall," was a response to a Western message predicated upon quite Western ideas and expectations.

The 1931 Zimmerman Report also commented extensively on evangelism and conversion. For example, it noted that the typical Western approach to conversion discussed above was not simply an occasional phenomenon propagated by a few missionaries. These Western ideas and concerns permeated the life of the Thai church. Evangelistic methods in the Thai church were in fact Western methods. This meant that first, one must "train the people in the full realization of the Christian ethic; the second is to furnish a psychological release to all those mental cares" (Zimmerman and McFarland 1931:17). This surely involved the program of inculcating feelings of moral culpability, which produces guilt and the suitable amount of demonstrable remorse. The psychological release likely refers then to the resolution of this guilt by release because of pardon of sin. Such clearly indicates that the Western gospel focus upon sin, continued to be a dominant mode of mission through 1931.

What is especially intriguing, however, is that the report does not single out missionaries as the primary focus of critique. The report instead levels its scathing rebuke at the structures and life of the entire Thai church. The work of an earlier generation of missionaries had now embedded foreignness in the Thai church itself. When conversion is predicated upon such thoroughly foreign experiences and ideas it comes as no surprise that, as the report mentions, there existed a lack of a truly indigenous Christian apologetic or Thai-authored Christian literature (Zimmerman and McFarland 1931:18). All that was necessary was to translate "orthodox" theology from the Western church into the Thai language.

The Western message of forgiveness of sins and release from guilt through Christ's death on the cross produced extremely limited results. In part, this was likely due simply to its excessively foreign and Western shape. Hughes aptly summarizes the level of foreignness these ideas likely represented to the Thai mind.

> The idea that Jesus Christ suffered the consequences of Thai people's sins, committed two thousand years later in time, and four thousand miles away in space, and bearing those consequences in such a way that has implications for our bearing the consequences, is not so easily assimilated. These ideas are based on presuppo-

sitions about the nature of sin as being a universal condition of which actions are only symptomatic, and about sacrifices which can take the place of oneself in bearing the consequences of this universal condition. The amount of accommodation which this requires in the concept of demerit as it is used for sin in northern Thailand and the presupposition of schemas for dealing with sin is enormous. (1984b:254)

Lack of response was not for lack of interest or willingness to hear the gospel. The message missionaries preached took as basic certain experiences that were not a salient feature of the Thai psyche. Thais did not seem burdened by a guilty conscience. The idea of Jesus dying to pay for human sin was perhaps intelligible but apparently not compelling for most Thai people.

Inspired by the Enlightenment, Protestant Evangelicals went to Thailand with a theory of culture that contrasted unfavorably Thai culture with "Christian" culture. Their mission strategies were fundamentally asymmetrical. The gospel was the Western message of salvation from sin and release from guilt.

This specific type of disconnect continues. As the earlier generations of missionaries perplexed with the Thai lack of response to the gospel, so too a majority of contemporary evangelical missionaries experience the same types of frustration in their witness to Thais (Nantachai 1997:21). They believed both that their ministry was to assist Buddhists in understanding the concept of sin and benefits of a relationship with Christ, and that Buddhists, upon understanding this, would come to Christ (1997:309, 311). In particular, the fixity of contemporary evangelical notions of witness and a frequently unbending certainty that their approach is the correct one had led to an approach unable to utilize Thai culture (1997:310).

Cooke notes that the Thai language lacks a satisfactory word for the Western notion of guilt or guiltiness. Not surprisingly, it seems that few Thais ever seem to become Christian believers because of a crushing burden of guilt due to wrongdoing. "There is little or no anguish over the guilt of sin, or longings to be washed clean, or religious hunger for forgiveness" (Cooke 1978:4). The missionary community, however, generally sought to inculcate and then relieve such feelings with the gospel. Cooke tersely notes, "whether or not this Godward feeling of guilt is always worth sharing with the Thai world, even if we could, is open to question" (1978:8).

Contemporary missiological discussions do not seem to have advanced this discussion much further. Almost every missiological study of note regarding Thai Christianity frames issues of gospel and evangelism in terms of strategy and methods (Davis 1993; Kao 1990; Kim 1980; Smith 1982; Virat 1990; Wisley 1985). Often, the discussion centers on indigenous forms (e.g., drama and music) and communication issues. Rarely, however, does discussion about the proper content of the message exist. Even those who do attempt to formulate a message more in terms of Thai culture ultimately offer only new husks within which the essential evangelical kernel of remission of sins and relief from guilt may be more effectively wrapped. To this day, it seems that there is little attention to how Thai culture may help frame the message of the gospel.

A prominent missionary in Thailand notes that conservative evangelicals "have been so intent on bringing about the conversion of the Thai that they have not stopped to ask whether they are pushing for conversion to Christ or to western Christianity" (Gustafson 1987:1). Though those that do convert often are characterized as having done so based upon guilt and the desire for forgiveness of sin, such is likely not usually the case. Research by Hughes on motivation for conversion and the function of religion among Thais confirms this. He concludes, "There are few people who respond to the Gospel because of its message of salvation as the forgiveness of sin, even though this continues to be a common theme in evangelistic campaigns" (Hughes 1982:46).

Disconnect and Face

Interestingly, though perhaps not surprisingly, there is little explicit reference to issues of face in the missionary literature. Prior to contemporary discussions in the social sciences, face had not existed as a discrete area of attention in interpersonal behavior. Thus, rather than simply look for the term "face" in missionary records, it is more profitable to seek the missionary stance toward face in anecdotes that illustrate an implicit, though a readily discernible, view of Thai face. Three specific areas seem to stand out as exemplars of missionary face attitudes. These are the various ways missionaries conceived Thai customs, the Thai character or personality, and Thai religion. What a historical examination of these three areas indicates is that face-oblivion and face-aversion were common, perhaps dominant modes of Western missionaries in Thailand.

Thai Customs

In complex ways, Thai face was interwoven with the Thai social hierarchy. Thai face produced communication strategies that involved indirectness, a complicated series of linguistic honorifics, and general sensitivity to refrain from giving offense to others. In particular, such concerns were encoded into specific Thai customs. A brief examination of historical anecdotes illustrates certain missionary stances toward these face-related customs.

An entry in Bradley's journal dated August 31, 1851, mentions a revealing incident (Feltus 1936:142, quoted in Nantachai 1997:128). There were a small number of Buddhist priests traveling in a boat through one of Bangkok's many canals. Bradley was standing on the bridge above preaching. The priests asked the missionary to move off so they could pass under, reflecting the general custom of not standing above another person, particularly not elevating one's feet above another's head. Bradley himself mentions in his account that in the hierarchical culture of Thailand it was a great cultural sin to be above monks. The American missionary flatly refused to move, however, notifying the priests that he did not "believe in such foolishness." After a brief exchange, the priests paddled on through.

An early mission in Bangkok accepted certain resolutions regarding missionary practice. The second of the four resolutions prohibited missionaries from using Thai titles in addressing royalty because it implied Lordship over others. As Lord notes, "their misguided sense of democracy shown by their refusal to accept and use Thai titles, was not democratic-it was just plain rude" (Lord 1969:139). Such a Western egalitarian impulse resisted tenaciously a key component of the Thai face "game," that is, the use of honorifics to designate face-laden status.

Another pioneer missionary, Daniel McGilvary, describes an event he terms a "scene that defied description," which reveals much regarding his attitude about face (McGilvary 1912:396). During a New Year festival, a band playing loud music surrounded McGilvary and would not desist playing until he gave them money. This he refused to do until they finally wore down his resistance and he gave them a very small amount. Characterizing the experience, McGilvary notes that they would likely not have finally left "without something to save their face." Whether McGilvary's reading of the situation as one involving face was correct, it is certain from his pejorative, almost mocking description that he viewed the issue of saving face as a negative one.

McGilvary records other incidents that illustrate these same tendencies. Upon visiting the home of a local northern Thai lord (a "Chao Fā") in the city of Chiang Rung, an attendant requested McGilvary to take off his shoes. He answered that such was not their custom and proceeded to enter regardless of an officer presiding at the door who seemed perturbed at their insistence (McGilvary 1912:357).

A wife of a prominent early missionary in Bangkok had access to the women of the king's palace. She narrates two incidents that reveal strongly antagonistic face attitudes. First, she describes meeting a woman of high rank in the halls. Though those accompanying her bowed low as the woman passed, Mrs. Mattoon stood upright. The same thing occurred upon a chance meeting with the king himself. Mattoon, explaining why she did not bow low in royal presence, noted simply, "Oh, I am an American; our customs are different from yours" (Mattoon 1884:329). Her fundamental orientation toward Western egalitarian ways prejudiced her attitudes toward such face deference. "Little by little," she notes, "are such miserable customs worn away by persistent Christian effort" (1884:329).

Bradley's approach was a challenging, aggressive approach that did not first rely upon relationship (Nantachai 1997:131). The a-relational nature of his work is clear from his personal goal to spend no more than fifteen to thirty minutes on each presentation of the gospel (1997:130). What Nantachai does not do is define more specifically the dimensions of relationality that he implies in his critique. That is, for most Thai, a significant component of interpersonal effectiveness is being sensitive to the face of the other in interactive contexts.

Perhaps there was a fundamental lack of understanding that these sorts of customs were intimately connected with face. Certainly, these were not the only customs that missionaries resisted. Yet, these specifically relate to issues of face and face giving. It is clear that many missionaries maintained a face-averse position, often even recklessly so.

Characterization of Thai Personality

We may also see missionary attitudes toward face in the ways they characterized the Thai personality. George McFarland noted regarding Thai communication style, "The Siamese are certainly the worst and most helpless people. Deception is so natural among them, they cannot speak or act the truth" (Maen 1979:48). The indirectness and hesitancy to speak forthrightly prevalent in Thai communication, it seemed to McFarland, was immoral and conniving.

Missionaries also conceived such public deference as being fearful. Caswell mentions as an obstacle a "general fearfulness, which renders public preaching, in the true sense of the term, almost impracticable, and hinders men from so much as entertaining the question of a change of religions." This fearfulness, rather than an occasional trait of certain people, is "an essential element of Siamese character, so that without it a man ceases to be a Siamese." The results of such were inconsistency in attendance at public preaching and few "who dare seriously to entertain the question of a change of religion" (Caswell 1848:17).

Missionaries perceived this lack of engagement in argumentation as passivity. Thus, the 1909 annual report of the Siam Mission notes that the Siamese hardly ever offer opposition to the Christian preacher. They will not argue, and are usually courteous, at least in the presence of the missionary; "but in the art of passive resistance they are hard to beat. The process of spiritual growth seems to be slower in them than in other races." (Siam Mission 1909:21).

> It is seldom that a Laos Buddhist priest, these days, will stand up in an argument for his religion. We wish they were more ready to do so. This unwillingness is due, in part to their passive, indifferent nature; in part, to the consciousness that their sacred books are illogical and will not bear comparison with the Christian Scriptures. Whatever the cause, it would be both easier and more productive of results, if we could get at their inward thoughts and ascertain their difficulties in embracing Christianity. It is a pleasure therefore, occasionally to find a priest who boldly states and defends his doctrines. (McGilvary 1904:109)

Missionaries thought that such lack of aggressive public engagement with issues relating to religion reflected fear and passivity. Clearly, however, these issues related to the local people's attachment to their own face as well as sensitivity toward others' face. And, just as clearly, missionaries did not hold to attitudes that could accommodate such face orientation.

In fact, such may relate more to the missionary penchant for direct, confrontational preaching and teaching that pushed and demanded. Such caustic missionary communication strategies likely resulted in such face threat or potential face loss that people simply did not come back.

It is clear to any perceptive observer of Thai culture that what missionaries characterized as deceptive, lacking conviction, passive resistance, indifferent, were, at least in part, due to Thai modes of face and facework. Of course, it would be pointless to deny that there were Thais who had false motives or were outright deceptive. Yet, it is tempting to venture that much of what Western missionaries perceived as false or deceptive were products of facework rather than a putative Thai weakness of sin.

Attitudes Toward Thai Religion

We see missionaries express this same frustration in their discussions of Thai religion. It is evident that most missionaries took a quite unfavorable position toward Thai religion. This went well beyond the level of conceptual notions of truth and falsity. We might characterize the various ways the missionaries spoke about the Thai religion as combative aggression rather than any sort of moral suasion.

Thus, missionaries often expressed quite starkly their disdain for Thai religion. H. R. H. Prince Damrong noted in his account of early Thai interaction with missionaries, that the missionaries "took pains to show contempt for the religion of the land, and thus created the natural impression that their schools were opened for the ultimate purpose of teaching the youths of the country to despise the faith of their father" (G. McFarland 1999:13). Here is a Thai royal, one who had frequent interaction with early missionaries, characterizing this missionary approach with the terms "contempt" and "despise."

Two reports substantiate that such social effrontery was indeed a serious problem. A 1929 report notes, "preaching should only exalt Christ. It should not disparage other religions" (Christian Conference Committee 1929:16). Such likely was to counter the face-threatening methods of many missionaries, which contradicted the Thai penchant for avoiding direct, face-threatening activity, even when disagreements existed.

The Zimmerman Report noted that missionaries often took the position of "older brother who insists at all times upon giving unasked-for advice, sure he is right and all others wrong. The attitude became that of antagonism rather than of sympathetic Christian service. Such social effrontery disallowed opportunities for Thais to "save face" while frequently placing them in face-compromising situations (Zimmerman and McFarland 1931:19).

In the section entitled "The Religious Psychology," the report discusses the issue of assertive missionary tendencies. "There are a great many missionaries who feel it their duty to rush at these problems like Don Quixote at his wind-mills. They want people to make decisions." The report suggests that unless there is change, such "aggressive crusading type of Christianity, only failure can be expected" (Zimmerman and McFarland 1931:16f.). The report mentions what it terms the psychological "problem of 'saving face.'" It points to "thousands of fine spirits" who accept the doctrines of Christianity and even follow Christian ethics to some degree. Yet, because "the man who joins the church must inevitably 'loose face,'" few actually ever become Christians (1931:16). Clearly, this type of face loss resulted from an institution that was in its formal characteristics decidedly foreign. It is also likely that such face loss resulted from the aggressive ethos of the missionary brand of Christianity. To associate with such a face-oblivious or face-averse community likely resulted in great psychological stress.

Summary

This brief excursion into the interaction of missionaries and Thai culture is a critical building block for the argument of this project. The missionary disconnect, which their theory of culture and theological approach necessitated, led to both a lack of cultural connection in soteriology and the area of face. These twin points of disconnect form the foundation for the subsequent chapters of this study.

2

Sources of Prosopagnosia (Loss of Face): The Modern Western Self

THAT WESTERNERS OFTEN HOLD a face-oblivious or face-averse posture is both interesting and important. Yet, an issue of even greater significance is to explain exactly why such attitudes prevail. It is this issue, the sources of these attitudes, upon which this chapter focuses.

An important matter that at first glance may seem to have little to do with a discussion of face involves a peculiar neurological illness. In his well-known work *The Man Who Mistook His Wife for a Hat*, Oliver Sacks (1998) discusses a condition where

> due to a lesion in the right occipital cortex, patients become unable to recognize faces as such, and have to employ an elaborate, absurd, and indirect route, involving a bit-by-bit analysis of meaningless and separate features. (1998:209)

The proper term for this type of visual neurological deficit is prosopagnosia (1998:21), a combination of the Greek terms for deficit (*agnosia*) and face (*prosopon*). Essentially, this is a disorder of face perception, that is, an inability to properly distinguish human faces.

Sacks highlights the case of one Dr. P. This man had full possession of normal human faculties except for one—he could not perceive faces. "A face, to us, is a person looking out-we see, as it were, the person through his persona, his face. But for Dr. P., there was no persona in this sense-no outward persona, and no person within" (Sacks 1998:13). What is particularly interesting is though Dr. P. had this debilitating neurological disorder, he was wholly unaware that he had lost this ability to recognize faces. It was not something that bothered him or over which he agonized, as might happen with many neurological disorders. Besides being unable to recognize a face, he was also oblivious that this was in fact his situation.

The same dynamic of neurological deficit that forms the condition of prosopagnosia also occurs, I contend, as a cultural and theological malaise. What I mean is that a failure to properly recognize the prevalent human phenomenon of face constitutes a type of prosopagnosia no less devastating than the neurological kind. Such a form of prosopagnosia may exist in either the face-oblivious form or one of face-aversion. Prosopagnosia of the face-oblivion kind occurs when one simply does not recognize face or face-related behavior. Such people may live in contexts where face occupies a central and explicit role in social intercourse. Yet, they fail to see this for what it is. Likewise, face-oblivious people may not be at all aware of the critical importance of either face or face-related issues in their own cultures, naively assuming face is something that people do "over there."

Even those who possess an awareness of face, however, may also be prone to a version of prosopagnosia. This occurs when one acknowledges face yet holds a decidedly face-averse posture. It is surely acceptable to argue that certain behavior related to face is improper. The face-averse posture to which I refer here, however, does not offer such a nuanced account of face. Rather, it often takes the form of a categorical rejection of face, thus offering a global evaluation of face as simply wrong.[1] In effect, such a negative and totalizing account of face results from not recognizing the full number of dimensions that actually constitute face. This face-aversion form of prosopagnosia results not from denying face but from gravely misunderstanding it. Certain cultural and theological commitments force upon these chronically face-averse sufferers of prosopagnosia a skewed understanding of what face is, predisposing them to view face from a mono-dimensional and essentially negative viewpoint. For either kinds

---

1. Such is apparent in conversation I had with a veteran Western missionary to Hong Kong who was pursuing an advanced degree in missiology. When I asked him about his experience with face, he reacted passionately. "For me," he exclaimed, "face is simply a lie!" He proceeded to illustrate what he termed a "black" area of Chinese culture though eventually admitted that at a certain level he had acquiesced to the issue of face (and associated issues such as honor and shame). Such a begrudging acceptance, he concluded, was necessary since he otherwise could not carry out ministry in the Chinese context. Ministry pragmatics kept him in the face "game," as it were, but it was patently clear that this was neither a game he wished to play nor one he thought consistent with Christian faith.

of cultural and theological prosopagnosia, the basic issue is that of a failure to recognize face. Yet, it is with this cultural or theological prosopagnosia that many in the West suffer.

In this chapter, I contend that there exist two primary sources of this cultural and theological prosopagnosia. First, a lack of adequate appreciation of face is connected, in complicated ways, to a particular understanding of another pivotal cultural phenomenon, viz., the self. I discuss this notion of the self to highlight the ways the modern Western configuration of self inherently resists face and face-related issues. Second, a great degree of face oblivion and face aversion results from misunderstanding regarding issues of shame and guilt. This seems particularly acute in the missiological community. I thus address the notions of shame and guilt, and the associated issues of honor cultures and justice cultures.

The Self and Face

The modern Western notion of the self, no matter how self-evident such might seem, is in fact a historically conditioned entity that did not emerge overnight. Primarily a product of modernity, the configuration of the self most familiar to the Western mind is the result of centuries of historical and cultural forces, with certain sources stretching at least as far back as Augustine. This notion then of a discrete individual self that lies at the core of our humanness is indeed "both peculiarly Western and historically perishable" (Gergen 1971:239). Clifford Geertz, in a now famous characterization, notes how this Western self is "a rather peculiar idea within the context of the world's cultures" (Geertz 1984:126). This Western notion of self is a

> . . . bounded, unique, more or less integrated motivational and cognitive universe, a dynamic center of awareness, emotion, judgment and action organized into a distinctive whole and set in contrast both against other such wholes and against its social and natural background." (1984:126)

This Western self is a "solitary self-communicating self, radically independent of relationships with anyone or anything else in this world" (Kerr 1986:72). It is a "self-assured, self-sufficient, centered self that constituted a stable identity in the midst of a chaotic world" (Grenz 2001:97).

It seems likely that every language provides avenues for self-reference and descriptions of reflexive thought, action, and attitude. This is not, however, the same as abstracting something called a "self" and making it into a formal notion, preceded by a definite or indefinite article (e.g., "the" self or "a" self). Such usage reflects something important which is peculiar to our modern sense of the self as a personal agent (C. Taylor 1989:113).

My contention here is that the Western conceptions regarding face I mentioned above are in fact misconceptions that derive directly, though not entirely, from this prevalent modern Western configuration of the self. To put it another way, the dominant Western version of the self inherently resists face and face concerns. To understand how this is, we must first understand the modern Western conception of self and how it has come about. Among the sociohistorical and moral factors that produce this Western conception, I wish to focus on five such "sources of the self" that are central to the story of the development of the modern Western self. These five, in different ways, form critical components to the ultimate shape the Western self has taken.

The Essential Self

In the Western world, a critical question in the discussion regarding the self has been what constitutes the substance of the person. The landscape of this discussion of relational versus essentialist interpretation in philosophy and theology is both tortuous and highly contentious. To even begin such a review would go far beyond the boundaries of this project. We may, however, reasonably assert some things regarding the general impact of this line of thinking regarding the self.

Dominating this discussion have been two primary issues, that is, the quality and quantity of substances that comprise the human self, and the number and hierarchical ordering of the faculties of the soul (Shults 2003:172). This driving concern is in part traceable to Greek philosophical perspectives. For Aristotle, "relation" is an accident of "quantity" (2003:14). In such a view, how a thing is related to other things, its "towardness," is not properly constitutive of what a thing truly "is." Relatives are accidental and less "real."[2] What is ultimate is the "substance" of a thing, that is, what something is in its essence. In the Greek philosophical tradition, this essence, however defined, did not involve the relations a thing had outside of itself. Such substance metaphysics naturally leads to the question of how many substances properly constitute the human person and what these substances or essences are (2003:184). The important point here, however,

   2. For a fuller treatment of this, see Gunton 1997:38–42; Shults 2003:11–22; Ury 2001:62–79.

is that there exists in this approach a categorical priority privileging substance over against relation.[3]

This notion is applied subsequently not only to things such as rocks, trees, and chairs, but also to thinking beings. As Ury notes, this ontological assertion applied to God (that "God is substance," or the search to understand an essence of the Divine) is the point of departure of "a maze of tortuous options still unresolved" (Ury 2001:62). Western thinking has often over-simplified this problem of the proper nature of God by identifying substance with abstract and static notions or sometimes a more general category such as "stuff." In the end, this starting point for theological reflection inevitably moves the discussion of God toward categories that are static and monadic (2001:62).

These same static and monadic categories come to influence how we view the self. "So we naturally come to think that we have selves the way we have heads or arms" (C. Taylor 1989:112). Selves become discrete "things" that possess some fundamental substance that is characteristic of the self qua self. The human self becomes a thing that exists in relationship with other selves but whose existence is not constituted by or necessarily linked to those relationships.

Such a static and essentialist version of the self is problematic for in the end it is reductionist, forcing a sort of "lowest common denominator" approach upon reflection about what it is to be a self. This self can exist as itself without qualification from other entities. The effect of such thinking was to minimize the importance of relationality to being and, by extension, to the human self. Without ultimately pointing a "non-relational finger" at any one particular influence, what does seem clear is that the overall effect of thinking about the human self in terms of essence or substance has yielded a Western legacy that conceives of the self as "a thing in itself, unattached, or unaffected by another thing" (Ury 2001:76).

The Inward Self

Taylor notes how our general notion of the self in the Western world is structured by the language of "inside" and "outside," that is, our thoughts,

---

3. In this discussion, there is often an uncritical conflation of Platonic ontology with that of Aristotle. Indeed, Aristotle's conception of substance does admit a notion of *telos* and thus the possibility of growth and development that does not obviate its essential characteristics (Ury 2001:74). It does seem, however, that the Western appropriation of both Platonic and Aristotelian ontology has yielded a strong type of substance ontology where relationality is of less consequence to being than is a thing's putative essence.

ideas, and feelings as mental states internal to us and the things to which these refer as external objects in the world. Thus, our thinking about our self grants a basic reality to "inner depths the way we have hearts or livers, as a matter of hard, interpretation free fact" (C. Taylor 1989:112). Such a self, again, proves to be a self peculiarly characteristic of modern Western provenance.

Modern interpreters more or less accept that Augustine was primarily responsible for the introduction of "the inwardness of radical reflexivity" to Western thought (C. Taylor 1989:131).[4] The inward Augustinian turn was a decisive turn toward the rational. Augustine emphasized an elevation of rationality or *cogito* as fundamental to what it means to be human. This elevation of the status of the rational aspect of the self provided the substance of his radical inward turn (Grenz 2001:61).

In Augustine, this fundamental emphasis on internal rationality works in concert with Platonic dualism. For Augustine, the immaterial and immortal soul was the primary "stuff" of the person. This soul dwelled in and used the material body, but the true essence of a person was located in this interior soul. In turn, human rational capacities existed as a function of this inner, non-material soul (Shults 2003:168). By essentializing the self as internal rationality, this Augustinian account ultimately precludes relationality or outwardness as being constitutive of the self. Certainly, Augustine was not intentionally undermining an other-orientation. His emphasis on

---

4. There is debate as to whether the theological position of Augustine was more relational than many scholars have acknowledged. Ury, for example, questions whether Augustine "botched the job handed him by the Cappadocians" to the extent that many suggest (2001:145). That he did show ambivalence toward the word "person" should not preclude accepting that his language about the divine nature was often dynamic and relational (2001:143). For example, along with the Cappadocians, Augustine did not view the divine substance as a hypostatic monad (2001:159) and there appears to exist a somewhat dynamic relational dimension the Augustinian notion of substance and person. "For all the passages which can be taken to support the conception that it was he who first internalized spiritual reflection with the strong simplicity resident in the analogy of memory, understanding, and will, there are other corresponding passages which propose an equally dynamic relationality" (2001:159). Yet it was through a hesitancy to fully apply the notion of relationality to "person" that Augustine lost much of the conceptual power of the relational concept of God that had existed in many previous Christian thinkers (2001:220). Therefore, even though there does exist scholarly debate about the exact role Augustine plays in the move toward the self as an isolated monad, the present consensus seems to be that the notion of substance as mediated through the Western church has adversely affected in significant ways the earlier Christian notions of relationality and personhood (2001:272).

the internal was more a response to the chaos in society and in his own self, and provided a way of ordering such fragmentation (Grenz 2001:64).

Yet, the unintended consequences of his emphasis are quite apparent. Regarding such, LaCugna observes that the notion of the person

> . . . in the Augustinian tradition has mainly to do with individual consciousness and its internal differentiations. The journey of the soul toward God is a journey inward. The process by which the soul comes to the deepest knowledge of itself and of its God is introspection and self-reflection. This makes the social, communal, toward-another character of personhood rather difficult to see. (1991:247)

This inward turn is also evident in the way Augustine modeled his metaphors of Trinitarian relations on the human individual. In his profoundly influential work *De Trinitate*, Augustine argued that since God created humankind in his image, there are "vestiges" of the Trinity in our selves that function analogically to God's own self. Thus, Augustine draws upon several images to demonstrate the essence of the Trinity. Human love (i.e., a self that loves, that which is loved, and love itself) and the human mind (i.e., a mind that remembers, that knows, and that loves) were two of the most influential (Grenz 2004:9). What is important to notice is how Augustine utilized the resources contained within the single human self rather than drawing upon images that are relational or social. In effect, this Augustinian individualizing and internalizing began the process that contributed significantly to a rational, individualized notion of the self.

The Rational Self

Augustine's influence on subsequent thinking regarding the self is clear in perhaps the best-known Western theological definition of a human being, that of Boethius (Shults 2003:225). For Boethius, a person is an individual substance of a rational nature (*persona est naturae rationalis individua substantia*) (Boethius 1847:1371D). Such a definition rests solidly upon the presuppositions of substance ontology, the discrete individual self, and a categorical priority of rationality (Shults 2003:225). Thus, Boethius provides a self that is primarily rational but also distinctly individual, thus opening "the door to the modern 'inner self' as the seat of unique personal identity" (Grenz 2001:67). It is the framing of the notion of person in such a way, Colin E. Gunton argues, that lies at the heart of the troubles that continue to plague the self in the modern West (Gunton 1997:92).

That is, the Boethian definition radicalizes both an essential unrelatedness and a fundamentally rational nature as the distinct characteristic of the individual self.

Thus, the project of inwardness that Augustine launched grows into the highly rationalized and individualized self that Boethius delivers. This then provides the basic building blocks of the self as a "stable, abiding reality that constitutes the individual human being" (Grenz 2001:67). It is this formulation of the internal and rational self, mediated through Boethius, that provides a link between the earlier neoplatonic views of Augustine and that of the Enlightenment self, particularly that provided by the Cartesian tradition.

It is Descartes who takes this individualized rational self and extends it into previously uncharted territory. That is, he gives the self of Augustinian interiority and Boethian rationalism a "radical twist" (C. Taylor 1989:143). This Descartes does by appropriating the Augustinian notion of cogito and then elevating human rationality to a new all-determinative level. The Cartesian self becomes a self of thinking substance. Human rationality becomes the supreme characteristic by which the self is truly a self. In the end, certain knowledge was the possession of this rational self, and this knowledge was fundamentally a personal knowledge, that is, knowledge that arose not from any outside source but from the personal knowing subject (Grenz 2001:70). What results from this Cartesian move is a notion of the self as primarily an autonomous, a-contextual, rational subject. So influential is this Cartesian elevation of the knowing of the self that Taylor can state, "The modern epistemological tradition from Descartes, and all that has flowed from it in modern culture, has made this standpoint fundamental" (C. Taylor 1989:131). It is perhaps correct to say that Descartes set the stage for the next three hundred years of philosophy and thinking about the human self (Grenz 2001:70).

Gunton draws attention to an enduring influence resulting from this Cartesian legacy (1997:84). With such a radicalized conflation of the human with the thinking mind, only loosely connected to the physical body, Descartes program leads to a strong dualism. Descartes' position configures the human person as essentially a non-spatial thinking mind inside a box of a body of matter. A result of this is the now classic problem of other minds. Defining a person in such a manner gives rise to the inevitable problem of how people are related to one another and provides a definition of the human self that does not require relationality as a constitutive element.

The Independent Self

It is specifically Kant, however, who provides the final philosophical coup de grâce for the movement of the lone individual into the center as focus of all knowing (Grenz 1996:80). Kant's thinking in particular downplays the role of community and firmly entrenches the radically isolated and discrete individual that would become the fundamental building block in the modern project of the self. This view of the self as an autonomous unit, no longer defined by the social environment and distinguishable from the way one acts in public, is one particularly characteristic of post-Enlightenment thinking (MacIntyre 1985:31). Such a self is not only a single self of rational essence, but also an autonomous self that can function alone without significant reference to the "other." It is only in this post-Kantian Enlightenment Western context that the individual gains complete ascendancy in value over that of community and relationship (Gergen 1971:239). Iris Murdoch comments that such an individual self

> . . . is with us still, free, independent, lonely, powerful, rational, responsible, brave, the hero of so many novels and books of moral philosophy. The *raison d'être* of this attractive but misleading creature is not far to seek. He is the offspring of the age of science, confidently rational and yet increasingly aware of his alienation from the material universe which his discoveries reveal. (1971:80)

The material world with which the Kantian self is increasingly at odds includes not only the inanimate world, but also more importantly for this study, that of relationships and other human persons.

The construction of the edifice of the modern Western self receives its final philosophical capstone from Kant (Grenz 2001:76). It is a self-autonomous individual, supremely free of all outside itself, whether human community, history, institutions, or moral strictures. Such a self is the logical outcome of the rationalizing and individualizing trajectories traceable to Augustine, Boethius, and Descartes. It is a self that "has acquired the attributes of the God of classical theology" (Kerr 1986:17). As Fergus Kerr notes, quoting philosopher Charles Taylor, such a self is "a novel variant of (the) very old aspiration to spiritual freedom" (1986:25). Such a quest is a profoundly spiritual one that attempts to transcend the world and others, thus operating as an a-contextual and a-relational entity. Ultimately, however, the roots of this "very old aspiration" lie not in the flow of Western philosophy or culture but in human rebellion in the Garden of Eden. The great irony is that this self that emerges from modern Western culture, a culture that the Christian tradition has shaped to a significant degree, "had already received a glorious incarnation nearly a century earlier in the world of Milton: his proper name is Lucifer" (Murdoch 1971:80). Viewed this way, the ultimate shape given the modern Western self is not simply a false one, but more profoundly and terribly, an idolatrous one.

The Subjective Self

One final component for the construction of the picture of the modern Western self as it relates to the issue of face comes from the influence of modern Western psychology. In a list that the authors claim is by no means exhaustive, Mischel and Morf provide sixty-six types of self-related notions that modern Western psychology has studied under the rubric of the self (2003:12). The self has proven as enigmatic and seemingly inexhaustible area of study in modern psychology, just as it has in philosophy and theology.

One specific notion regarding the self that has arisen out of the Western psychological tradition is the distinction between the so-called public and the private self. Such a distinction, which became an area of acute concern in the sixteenth century (Baumeister 1998:726–27), forms a critical step in the evolution of the modern Western self. This psychological conceptualization parallels the inner/outer dichotomy that has arisen in the Western theological and philosophical discussions of the self. Such an inner/outer dichotomy inevitably drives a wedge between the supposed essence and accidents of a person. From this standpoint, that which is interior holds position as the essence while the outer functions as less determinative phenomena not directly constitutive of the true self. What differs is how this modern psychological sense of the inner and outer self extends the notion of the inner essence into the various ways, more or less "authentic," by which we structure our revealing and projecting of a social, outer self into social space.

It is likely true that people from every culture have a sense of an internal entity, which dreams, thinks, and experiences separate from what others can perceive. That is, some understanding and some representation of the private, inner aspects of the self may well be universal (Markus and

Kitayama 1991:225). What marks the particular Western version as distinctive, however, is the categorical priority the internal assumes. Some general sense of an inner/outer distinction of the self may indeed be natural for most humans, but for many Westerners this inner self forms the center of identity and constitutes the core of who they conceive themselves to be (Mischel and Morf 2003:7).[5] The putative inner core or essence, variously revealed in daily life, constitutes for many in the modern West that which is most "real" or "true."

The influence of this notion is clear in everyday life. In a recent conversion over coffee, a friend made such a distinction instinctively when I asked him to offer his personal thoughts on the topic of face. This able-minded PhD student immediately objected that his problem with face was that it was fundamentally an external and social phenomenon and "not who I really am." Such draws upon this modern psychological distinction evident in, for example, William James's functionalist understanding of the human self. The self is composed of two dimensions: the "I" of internal self-consciousness and the "me" of objective social reality. This allows us to conceive of the person as duality—an objective and a subjective self. The outside world knows this social self while the other inner (and supposedly more "real") self remains hidden, internal only to the subjective actor.[6]

---

5. The particular content, structure, and significance of both the inner and outer self will differ in varying culture contexts. As Hazel Markus and Shinobu Kitayama note, in some cultures the individual as a discrete set of inner personal attributes is not the primary unit of consciousness. Instead, "the sense of belongingness to a social relation may become so strong that it makes better sense to think of the relationship as the functional unit of conscious reflection" (Markus and Kitayama 1991:226).

6. Lakoff and Johnson discuss what they term a "Folk Theory of Essences" of the self (1999:282–88). They note that in English we tend to speak of the self in at least three distinct ways. First is the "inner self." This is what we consider the "real" self, which is contained within an "outer self," the self of public behavior. The second is the "external real self," which is the nice self the world usually sees, yet within which lurks a darker, insidious other self who may emerge when our guard is down, for example, when we are tired, drunk, or stressed. This is evident in the oft-heard phrase, especially in apologies, "That wasn't really me." The third is the "true self" where the person as subject inhabits a self that is incompatible with its true essence and may experience tension because it does not live up to or consistently with this supposed inner "true self." Such is implicit in the notion of "finding my true self" when one brings behavior more in line with what is considered characteristic of this "true self." It is first notion of the "inner self" that produces the distinction between the true inner me and the exterior façade that I am discussing (Lakoff and Johnson 1999:288).

Despite a growing body of research that people hold divergent views about the self, the dominant view of Western psychology continues to perpetuate this strong inner/outer dichotomy. By doing so, such an approach posits the individual as an independent, self-contained, autonomous entity that comprises a unique configuration of internal attributes, behaving primarily as a consequence of these attributes (Markus and Kitayama 1991:224). The "real" me exists in these internal attributes, accessible only to the mind of the individual. The outer, social self then functions as a sort of external shell and social epiphenomena.

Hazel Markus and Shinobu Kitayama term this the "independent self," which stands in contrast to the "interdependent self" so common among non-Western cultures. Those with an independent construal of the self hold these inner attributes to be dominant in regulating behavior. For both the self and others who view the self, these inner states represent that which typifies who a person truly is. Thus, the independent self should be unique, express itself, realize its own internal goals, and be direct (i.e., to say what is on its mind). The independent self finds its basis for self-esteem in the ability to express itself and the validation of its internal attributes (Markus and Kitayama 1991:230). Such stands in stark contrast, for example, to the pervasive Japanese view of self-expression in which "the straightforward claim of the naked ego" (1991:303) is experienced as childish. Here, as opposed to a Western independent self, self-assertion is authentic, but rather a sign of immaturity and childishness (1991:229).

Summary

I do not intend to offer in this brief survey a detailed history of the modern sense of personhood. Neither do I claim that this cursory glance surfaces all the various sources that ultimately produce what we term the modern Western self.[7] What I have attempted is to draw attention to specific dimensions of the Western self that has given rise to the strong resistance to face often found in the modern West. Whether the interiorized essence of the person that runs its course from Augustine through modern Western psychology, or the rationalized self of Boethius and Descartes, or the radical and lone individual of Kant—all converge to produce a particular Western self that exists without necessary reference to relationality and social context.

7. For such a survey, see Grenz 2001:58–137. Also, for a comprehensive account of the development of the modern Western definition of selfhood, see C. Taylor 1999.

Such a dominant Western notion of the independent, rational, internal self inherently resists face. Face is a relational, public dimension of the self that seeks community acceptance and esteem. Indeed, it would seem proper, if one assumes the position of the Western self as autonomous, rational, and constituted by its essence and not its relations, that those in other cultures who invest great value in face may in fact not be fully formed or complete selves.

3

Sources of Prosopagnosia (Loss of Face):
The Misconstrual of Honor, Guilt, and Shame

THE PARTICULAR CONFIGURATION OF the self dominant in the modern West is a basic source of the prosopagnosia that hinders appreciation of face. A second primary source of confusion regarding face emerges from certain traditional anthropological conceptions related to so-called guilt cultures and shame cultures, or, in a more recent typology, justice cultures and honor cultures. Missiological reflection upon these notions has also taken these anthropological ideas as a point of departure. Yet, my contention is that many of these traditional notions regarding honor, shame, guilt, and justice are in fact mistaken. And, because many assume that face is a correlate of these so-called honor or shame cultures, they subsequently apply such misconceptions directly to the issue of face.[1]

> 1. One important preliminary point to make is to clarify the relationship between honor and shame. Though these concepts often co-occur, the conventional pairing of these two notions is actually a bit misleading. As Uni Wikan has discussed, honor and shame are not in fact binary opposites (Wikan 1984). They are not antipodal concepts, "the poles of one-and-the-same spectrum of social evaluation" (Kressel 1988:167). This is clear when one notices that shame is an affect. Honor, in contrast, is not. One feels shame. One does not feel honor, though one may indeed feel certain emotions that result from the appropriation of honor. In fact, what one normally feels when receiving honor is pride. One feels proud, a somewhat self-directed pleasure that derives from possession of or adherence to some type of excellence (G. Taylor 1985:20). Pride may take the form of a purely self-referential affect (a highly individualized, internal experience) or may involve relationship to wider social units (Goffman 1955:9–10; G. Taylor 1985:23ff.). Viewed this way, honor is a binary correlate to public shaming: shame, as an affect, lies in opposition to pride.

Shame and Guilt Cultures

It is only in the past twenty years or so that scholars have focused research explicitly upon theory development regarding shame and guilt (Gilbert and Andrews 1998:v–vii). Even so, the so-called experts frequently confuse the terms, carelessly conflating them and muddying the waters more than bringing clarity (Tangney and Dearing 2002:11). Traditionally, anthropologists have drawn a major distinction between shame cultures and guilt cultures. Indeed, it would be difficult to understate the level of influence this analytical distinction has had in the anthropological study of cultures. Though Mead was instrumental in establishing this distinction, Ruth Benedict popularized and established this cultural typology in *The Chrysanthemum and the Sword*, her work on Japanese culture. Her statement on the characteristics of shame and guilt cultures is now classic.

> True shame cultures rely on external sanctions for good behavior, not, as true guilt cultures do, as an internalized conviction of sin. Shame is a reaction to other people's criticism . . . it requires an audience. Guilt does not. (Benedict 1946:223)

Thus, the distinguishing mark of a shame culture is a dependence upon what others think. Conversely, it is not the perception of others that drives guilt culture but rather a person's own internal moral compass, the individual conscience.

Benedict's view corresponds to the developmental notions Erik Erikson proposed (Barrett 1995:27). Shame, in this view, is a developmental precursor to guilt. It exists prior to the development of internalized standards of positive and negative behavior. Shame tended to be viewed as a negative emotion one experienced when caught by someone. Guilt was the emotion accompanying misdeeds when these went against one's internalized convictions (1995:27). Again, Benedict is clear about this issue. "A society that inculcates absolute standards of morality and relies on men's developing a conscience is a guilt culture by definition" (Benedict 1946:222).

Although her distinction between shame and guilt cultures has been extremely influential, it is also correct to note that it has also been the target of considerable challenges.[2] The first mistaken notion regarding shame and guilt is that they differ in terms of the types of situations that cause

---

2. For those who reject this traditional distinction (though for differing reasons) see Barnett 1966, Creighton 1990, Lebra 1983, Lynd 1958, Rosaldo 1984, G. Taylor 1985.

these varying experiences. That is, the conventional notion of shame assumes an externalized experience, taking place vis-à-vis an observing audience. So, an external experience characterizes shame and an internal one constitutes guilt.

Related to this is the notion that internalized convictions form the basis of the guilt experience while shame is merely a response to social opinion. So, many conceive guilt as a function of a conscience, while shame results from preoccupation with public opinion. Recent research in emotional development and neurobiology, however, indicate that both guilt and shame involve the conscience.[3] Anthropologist Melford Spiro states categorically that the internalization of norms is necessary for both shame and guilt. That is,

> . . . a shame—no less than a guilt-oriented superego constitutes a conscience. By producing anxiety concerning anticipated punishment, both of them inform the individual that his anticipated act is wrong, and motivate him to refrain from transgression. (Spiro 1958:409)

Spiro thus rejects the traditional characterization of shame and guilt cultures based upon an idea of internal-versus-external orientation. Rather, he contends that both equally involve the internalization of values (1958:406ff.). Both shame and guilt rely upon the individual conscience and can exist as either an internal or an external experience. Contrary to traditional thinking, shame is both a public and private phenomenon (Lewis 1995:75).

Likewise, many often asserted that guilt and shame differed because each was a result of a different type of transgression. In reality, however, neither shame nor guilt differs in terms of the types of transgressions or failures involved. No specific type of acts exclusively leads to either shame or guilt (M. Lewis 1995:63) That is, neither guilt nor shame co-occur with discretely different types of behavior (Tangney and Dearing 2002:17). The types of behavior that produce both shame and guilt are essentially similar (2002:14). Therefore, current empirical researchers patently reject the traditional notions that the difference between shame and guilt rests in the context of the experience (e.g., a putative public/private difference) or the types of causes (e.g., particular shame-inducing acts versus guilt-inducing acts) (Tangney 2003:387).

---

3. "Both shame and guilt are included under the rubric of the conscience" (Tangney and Dearing 2002:150).

The putative distinctions that exist in much of the literature on guilt and shame clearly involve inadequate conceptualizations. Indeed, there are quite a number of similarities between the two experiences are considerable: (1) both fall into the category of "moral" emotions; (2) both are "self-conscious," self-referential emotions; (3) both are negatively valenced emotions; (4) both involve internal attributions of one sort or another; (5) both are typically experienced in interpersonal contexts; and (6) the negative events that give rise to both are highly similar (frequently involving moral failures or transgressions) (Tangney and Dearing 2002:25). Additionally, shame and guilt are similar since both are affects that "constrain behavior into channels that are socially approved of and/or culturally appropriate" (Greenwald and Harder 1998:227). Both serve to maintain social bonds, and thus enable healthy social functioning.

There are fundamental and inherent dimensions of contrast between shame and guilt, but not those that traditional anthropology or missiology often assumes. In a now classic study, Piers and Singer define guilt as what occurs whenever a boundary (set by the superego) is touched or transgressed (Piers and Singer 1953:11). Guilt anxiety, then, accompanies transgression. Shame, however, occurs when a person does not attain a goal (either presented or accepted by the ego ideal). Shame thus follows failure to live up to goals or ideals in whatever particular forms these might take.

Accordingly, the human reactions to shame and guilt tend to be quite different. "The psychological reaction associated with guilt concerns fear of punishment; the unconscious . . . threat implied in shame anxiety is abandonment" (Piers and Singer 1953:11). Shame is an affect related to indignity and alienation. When shamed, a person feels naked, defeated, or a lack of dignity and worth. There exists the acute fear of exposure and being defective (Kaufman 1974:569).

The following table helps to draw out some important distinctions between guilt and shame.

Shame is a global statement about the self. That is, the focus in shame is not so much on the deed or the failure, but rather on the resulting inadequacy that the self experiences, often made painfully real by the exposure of the inadequacy or failure. As these two dimensions (i.e., the cause and the self's subsequent evaluation of itself) fuse together the self becomes both subject and object. Herein lies the most fundamental distinction between shame and guilt. Shame is the complete closure of the self-object circle. One appropriates subjectively one's own actions—the person and

TABLE 1: CHARACTERISTICS OF GUILT AND SHAME

(Adapted from Tangney and Dearing 2002:20–25, and G. Taylor 1985:85–92)

Dimension	Guilt	Shame
Focus of evaluation	I *did* that *thing*. What I *did* was wrong.	*I* did that horrible thing. *I* am bad, defective.
Nature of problem	Discrete acts	Global inadequacy, falling short
Self as Agent	Required	Agency not required
Type of responsibility	Causal responsibility	Responsibility possible but not required
Type of solution	Solution involves retribution, repayment and/or punishment	Solution involves change of state of self
Experience	Feelings of self-condemnation, regret, remorse	Feelings as inadequate, failure, compromised state, unworthiness, shrinking, and powerlessness
Phenomenological reaction	Desire to confess, apologize, or repair	Impulse to hide, escape, or strike back
Focus of failure	Infraction or neglect of duties, responsibilities, and/or obligations; concern with wrong done	Failure; not measuring up; concern with the kind of person one is
Type of attribution	Localized/specific	Absolute/global
Possibly vicarious?	No	Yes
Relation with the self	Self disfigured by deed(s) but remains essentially the same; Think of self as doer of the deed; focus on deed or omission	Self viewed as a piece with what has been done (i.e., fits well with what I am)
Degree of distress	Generally less painful than shame	Generally more painful than guilt

its own deeds become profoundly intertwined. The self thus functions in a global way, that is, what one does is not abstracted and externalized but is appropriated as an inherent part of the self. With the experience of guilt, the self remains a subject alone. One makes the misdeed or failure external to one's self. In contrast to shame, the focus of the self in guilt is on the behavior that caused the interruption, namely, the specific act that remains external to the self. Helen Lynd expresses this idea well.

> Since shame involves the whole self, it cannot be easily removed. An action that brings guilt can be separated from the self. We can say, "I did that, but that action does not reflect the real me." Thus, guilt can be mitigated, nullified, expiated. Shame cannot. It is not an isolated act that can be attached from the self. . . . It is pervasive as anxiety is pervasive; its focus is not a separate act, but revelation of the whole self. The thing that has been exposed is what I am. (1958:50)

The command associated with guilt would be something like, "Stop. What you have done is wrong and violates the standard or rule." In contrast, the command interpreted from the perspective of shame would be, "Stop. What you have done is wrong. You are no good." As such, the shame command is more severe because it is more profoundly a statement about the self, not simply an action abstracted and isolated from the self.

An impressive amount of recent empirical studies seem to indicate, along with Michael Lewis as well as Piers and Singer, that the primary distinction between these two experiences is attribution and subsequent interpretive movements, an evaluation of the entire self versus focus upon specific behavior (Tangney and Dearing 2002:20–21).

> As it turns out, shame and guilt differ not so much in the content or structure of the situations that engender them, but rather in the manner in which people construe self-relevant negative events. For example, the key difference between shame and guilt does not center merely on a public-private dimension. In fact, there is little empirical support for the commonly held assumption that shame arises from public exposure of some failure or transgression whereas guilt arises from the more private pangs of one's internalized conscience. Rather, there is substantial evidence supporting Lewis's (1971) contention that the fundamental difference between shame and guilt centers on the role of the self. Shame involves global negative evaluations of the self (i.e., "Who *I* am"). Guilt involves a more articulated condemnation of a specific behavior (i.e., "What I *did*"). (2002:24)

Shame involves global attribution where the wrong committed is internalized and appropriated at the most fundamental evaluative level of the self. There may be attention given to the wrong committed but the primarily focus is upon the defective nature of the self. Shame viewed in this way reflects a more fundamental problem. The self is defective. Guilt occurs when individuals evaluate their behavior as failure and in turn reflect more upon the self's action. This involves specific attribution and focuses on the offense of the act without necessarily drawing explicit implications about the self (Lynd 1958:76). There may indeed be subsequent conclusions regarding specific features of the self (or perhaps even regarding the entire self) but these conclusions are not inherent to the experience of guilt nor are they required. In summary, guilt is more about the deed, specifically in its status as offense. Fundamentally, shame relates more to the doer and the inadequacy of the doer.

Self-blame and failing to meet standards are often correlates of shame but are not essential to the shame experience. Rather, Gilbert contends, shame is "an inner experience of the self as an unattractive social agent," an experience of "being in the social world as an undesired self, a self one does not wish to be" (1998:22). It is not so much distance from a desired ideal self that produces shame as much as the proximity of the individual to an "undesirable self" (1998:19). That is, the shame experience is linked closely to negative feelings that derive from being who we do not want to be. Shame is not so much a notion of "I failed to be beautiful" but rather "I am ugly." At its core, the shamed self is a self that is deficient and falls short of some good goal or a standard of excellence.

The experience of guilt always has an associated corrective action, something that the individual can do (but does not necessarily do) that can repair the failure. Rectifications of the failure in some way or taking measures to prevent it from happening again are two possible corrective paths. Certain forms of punishment are also frequently enjoined to absolve guilt. In contrast, one who is shamed attempts to hide and disappear. From the perspective of shame one does not merely view the thing one has done that is wrong but rather regards the very self as defective. In this way, shame points to a much deeper reality. It is not the action of a person that is wrong. Rather, the person itself is wrong. Because of this, when the self experiences shame, it recoils, feeling inferior and defective. If there is to be corrective action, it must occur at a more fundamental level. Since the effect is primarily upon the self, any proper corrective measure must involve a remaking or renovation of the self in some way.

It is important for any discussion of shame to differentiate between our beliefs about how others see us and how we view our own selves (Gilbert 1998:16). When others judge us negatively, we often experience external shame. Here is the realm of public scorn, stigma, humiliation, ridicule, contempt, and shaming. The focus in this type of shame experience is the world outside the actor, that is, a public view. It is a personal fear of negative public evaluation and loss of public honor or face that can lead to great amounts of personal anxiety (1998:17).

A related but distinctly different experience is that of internal shame. This is the negative subjective sense of a person who either accepts negative public judgment or embraces their own negative self-judgment. Here is the realm of feelings of inferiority and failure, where an actor views their self as bad, worthless, and defective (Gilbert 1998:17–18). Important for this discussion is that although internal and external shame can and often are correlates, this is not necessarily the case (1998:20). This means that there exists a critical difference between "being shamed" and "feeling ashamed" (1998:21).

To summarize, shame is not, as has often been assumed, an experience tied to external sanctions and public opinion. It is simply not true that all cases of feeling shame are cases of public exposure or require an external audience (G. Taylor 1985:58). The feeling of shame may be a purely private affair, experienced when the self fails to achieve a goal or desired state. It may also be associated with a more external component, that of public shaming. At its core, shame is about the defective, unattractive self.

> Perhaps self-blame, self-consciousness, failing to meet standards, and negative social comparisons, although common correlates of shame, are not central to it. Rather, it is an inner experience of self as an unattractive social agent, under pressure to limit possible damage to self via escape or appeasement, which captures shame most closely. It does not matter if one is rendered unattractive by one's own or other people's actions; what matters in (*sic*) the sense of personal unattractiveness—being in the social world as an undesired self, a self one does not wish to be. (Gilbert 1998:22)

Although shame is often viewed as a negative experience,[4] it is not exclusively so. It is axiomatic that severe and extreme shame experience, especially if prolonged, can lead to maladaptive psychological functioning (Greenwald and Harder 1998:225), yet there does exist a milder, positive function for shame. This is the function of shame that James W. Fowler terms the "custodian of personal worthiness" (Fowler 1996:105). Often, this is referred to as a sense of shame. Such shame restricts certain behaviors, helping build our character and image in eyes of others and self. It

---

4. Webb (2000:2) discusses how, especially in Western literature, shame was viewed as pathogenic, "an unhealthy response linked to damaged self-esteem."

helps to guard a sense of personal worthiness and the relationships that constitute membership in valued communities (1996:107). Shame also plays an essential and positive role in formation of conscience (1996:105). Such "discretionary shame" guides our decisions, our sense of self-worth, and membership in groups. This type of shame is in distinction to the more common notion of shame, "disgrace shame," the painful emotion felt when the self comes to see itself as defective and unworthy.

Shame is apparently a universal experience. "The context and nature of the standards and the expressions of shame may differ; however, the mechanism for eliciting shame remains intact" (Lewis 1995:212). Guilt, as research seems to indicate, also exists across all cultures. Though present universally, clearly shame and guilt experiences vary across cultures.

For example, comparative research suggests that for highly individualistic cultures, shame and guilt experiences are often rather similar, whereas in highly collectivist cultures the two experiences differ considerably (Wallbott and Scherer 1995:483). Takie Sugiyama Lebra (1983) reverses Benedict's shame orientation and actually subsumes Japanese shame under the rubric of guilt. Her study also points out several culturally specific traits regarding shame and guilt. She notes how both shame and guilt result from "processing stress into self-punishment" (1983:192). Lebra highlights the notion of stress rather than the typical norm violation because for Japanese norm violation does not appear to be a necessary condition for either shame or guilt (1983:193). For Japanese, shame typically occurs when a person visualizes others as an audience or spectators. She notes two types of Japanese shame—a deep, inner shame, and a surface-level shame that is more like a type of embarrassment. The Japanese seem very sensitive to this surface-level type of shame, which does not depend upon any norm or standard violation but can result simply from praise or focused attention (1983:194).

Lebra's study of Japanese shame and guilt challenges any attempt to label Japanese society as a "shame culture," for, as she points out, a "keen sense of guilt has been recognized to prevail among Japanese" (1983:192). Japanese guilt arises from the awareness of one's action or lack of action that injures another in some way (1983:203) or simply when another appears as a victim or suffers because of one's own actions (1983:193). Such "guilt-arousing" behavior might include "causing trouble," "causing worry," "being selfish," or having to be "looked after" (1983:205). Japanese guilt relates to a type of harm done to another person by the guilty party rather than a transgression of an abstract legal or moral code. It involves behavior closely relates to the concept of *on*, ("a favor or benevolence which makes it receiver morally indebted to its donor") (Lebra 1971:245). Japanese, then, often feel guilt with reference to their mother, whom they conceptualize as a creditor and sufferer (1971:245). When Japanese feel guilty, it is not because they have broken a sort of law of reciprocity but because they have acted wrongly against someone. Here, the Japanese norms or social "laws" seem personalized and focused on relationship rather than depending upon abstracted legal codes. Guilt occurs when the other appears as a victim or suffers because of one's own action (1983:193).

Granted, either shame or guilt may indeed predominate in certain cultural contexts (Brandes 1987:123), yet no single culture experiences either shame or guilt to the exclusion of the other experience. Rather, it is more correct to state that each culture has its own balance and its own integrative hierarchy of these two internal controls (Augsburger 1992:82). Since "the degree of internalization of the sanctions varies, no culture can be unequivocally called one or the other" (Peristiany and Pitt-Rivers 1992:6). Such an opposition then is a false one as far as cultures are concerned (1992:7). Since both shame and guilt seem to be ubiquitous, the strong dichotomy indicated by the conventional terms of "shame culture" and "guilt culture" is naïve and simplistic. To label a given culture in these ways is thus analytically unhelpful and potentially detrimental to empathetic understanding of other people and cultures.

Similarly, we would do well to exercise great caution when defining the meanings of these terms. Milton Barnett stresses the need for culturally specific, emic study of terms and concepts related to shame and guilt. "Similarities in concepts of shame and guilt, like those of time, space and color, have to be proved and not taken for granted" (Barnett 1966:281). Piers and Singer offer a similar caution:

> Psychological characterizations and comparisons of cultures ... in terms of shame and guilt ... are of low validity because they seek to isolate "pure" psychological categories ... their validity and usefulness will increase as they abandon this "psychologism" and develop instead characterizing constructs in which the emotional emphases of a culture are integrally related to cultural values, world view, overt behavior, and features of social organization. (1953:100)

The question of why these various experiences do tend to predominate in certain cultures is legitimate. An in-depth attempt to answer such goes well beyond the purview of this study. Some things, however, do seem clear and offer hints as to why the gravity to ascribe these as dominant cultural modes continues.

The increase in the dominance of guilt in Western cultures seems to parallel the development of the inner self. Such seems to have become a common conception for the first time in the sixteenth century (Baumeister 1987:165). Before the Middle Ages, Western cultures generally lacked significant levels of personal introspection (1987:164). With the emergence of this hidden, inner self, however, came a concomitant increase in personal introspection. Just as public honor was losing its ascendancy, this flourishing of introspection finally reached a pinnacle during the sixteenth century (1987:165). This, of course, is not to deny the existence of the guilt experience before this period. Yet viewing this gradual development of the Western for of an inner, introspective self may help explain the centrality that the guilt experience seems to occupy in many modern Western cultures.

This development is significant for as the self focuses increasingly on individual deeds through personal introspection, guilt emerges as the primary experience of the self. The rigors of penance, the self-examination characteristic of monastic life, and the soul-searching that followed in the dreaded path of the Black Death, all played a part in leading to the introspective, guilt-laden conscience of pre-Reformation Europe (Westerholm 1988:67). Subsequently, during the Reformation, guilt played an increasingly central role in personal conscience (Piers and Singer 1953:54). So then, the "introspective conscience of the West" becomes fundamental to the context within which Reformation and post-Reformation thinkers formulated their theology. Of course, the experience of personal guilt does not end with the Reformation but continues well into the twentieth century as a central concept in both Protestant (e.g., Reinhold Niebuhr) and Catholic (e.g., T. S. Elliot) thinking. Even among the non-religious (e.g., Freudians, and some existentialists) individual guilt continued to function as a central concept to explain the human predicament (Lynd 1961:17).

Spiro associates the development of guilt or shame as originating from certain types of early childhood discipline, specifically, differing child-rearing patterns. Those societies that train a child with only relatively few agents of socialization who administer punishments lead to individuals who internalize the values of the socializing agent but also "introject" the agent. The introject becomes the significant other for the person. It is the withdrawal of the introject's love that constitutes punishment, that is, feelings of guilt (Spiro 1958:408). In contrast are those cultures "in which the child is trained by a number of socializing agents, or in which the trainers discipline the child by claiming that other agents will punish him, do not produce individuals with 'guilt-oriented' superegos. For, though these individuals internalize the values of the socializing agents, they do not introject the agents themselves. Since the significant others continue to remain external, it is withdrawal of the love of others that constitutes the anticipated punishment. Because this punishment, when it comes, is experienced as shame, we may refer to this type of superego as 'shame-oriented'" (1958:408–9). If true, then differences in the predominance of shame or guilt in a particular culture would parallel the dominant type of child-rearing patterns.

Others (Barrett 1995) argue that a number of non-disciplinary factors create these tendencies. Lack of clarity about the source of the two experiences suggests much more study on the socialization of shame and guilt is necessary (1995:56–57). Alan Shore argues that shame originates in the disruption of expected attachment bonds. This triggers a sudden "contraction of the self" (Shore 1998:66). If prolonged or frequent, such experiences can result in shame-oriented individuals.

In the end, it is not altogether clear why shame or guilt appear more prevalent in certain cultures. Yet, what is clear is that the affect of shame "comes to play a central role in the regulation of all emotional expression and therefore all human interaction" (Shore 1998:72). Far from a developmentally inferior experience or a phenomenon of collectivist cultures, shame appears to be a universal and essential experience in all cultures. Accordingly, it is crucial in the study of shame and guilt to probe for the cultural nuances and contextually specific dimensions of these two experiences. Only then may we adequately understand the dynamics and function of the shame and guilt experiences.

Face, Honor, and Shame in Missiological Literature

Non-Western forms of honor, shame, and face have often baffled Western missionaries. Describing typical evangelical responses to so-called honor cultures or shame cultures, Roland Muller (2000) notes that

> . . . faced with such situations, many missionaries are exasperated. The culture that they are living in seems to have no sense of right and wrong. If people don't feel they have broken God's law, then there is no need for salvation or a savior. Christ's death on the cross

seems futile and meaningless. The western evangelist, locked into his legal model of salvation, seems powerless to adequately explain the gospel so that people will respond. (2000:35)

The missiological literature does not offer a considerably better picture. Though addressing the notion of shame to some extent, missiological publications have essentially overlooked the topic of honor and face. For example, the *Evangelical Dictionary of Missions* (Moreau 2000) contains no entry for either face or honor, though it does contain brief but generally helpful entries for shame and guilt. Likewise, the *Dictionary of Asian Christianity* (Sunquist 2001) contains no information regarding either honor or face, surprising since such appears to be such a fundamental experience in many Asian contexts. Such neglect is as inexplicable as it is alarming.

The work of Ruth Lienhard (2000; 2001) represents a recent and nuanced attempt to integrate the notion of honor and shame into missiological theory. Yet even though she addresses explicitly the issues of honor, guilt, and shame, the misconceptions discussed above persist. Lienhard too easily assumes the traditional distinctions between shame and guilt. For example, she offers the traditional definition of guilt as a legal-based notion.[5] The problem here is not her conclusion but that without serious justification, she too easily assumes Benedict's dichotomy. It is unfortunate she does not engage more seriously the differences between the two since these notions are not peripheral to her work but actually form a fundamental component of her analysis.[6]

What have missiologists written concerning shame? Missiologist and anthropologist Paul Hiebert offers what appears to be a common understanding among contemporary missiologists:

> Shame is a reaction to other people's criticism, an acute personal chagrin at our failure to live up to our obligations and the expectations others have of us. In true shame-oriented cultures, every person has a place and a duty in the society. One maintains self-respect, not by choosing what is good rather than what is evil, but by choosing what is expected of one. Personal desires are sunk in the collective expectation. (1985:212)

---

5. Guilt "is the result of not following the rules, of not keeping promises" (Lienhard 2001:134).

6. Though she acknowledges those who find fault with Benedict's distinction, she advances no evidence to substantiate her acceptance of the Benedict position.

Commenting on guilt, Hiebert goes on to note that

> ... guilt is a feeling that arises when we violate the absolute standards of morality within us, when we violate our conscience. A person may suffer from guilt although no one else knows of his or her misdeed; this feeling of guilt is relieved by confessing the misdeed and making restitution. True guilt cultures rely on an internalized conviction of sin as the enforcer of good behavior, not, as shame cultures do, on external sanctions. Guilt cultures emphasize punishment and forgiveness as ways of restoring the moral order; shame cultures stress self-denial and humility as ways of restoring the social order. (1985:213)

Referring specifically to the notions of shame and guilt cultures, missiologist David J. Hesselgrave writes that for "guilt cultures there is the fear of the consequences of disobeying the laws of God, society, or one's own conscience. In shame cultures there is the fear of being found out" (Hesselgrave 1984:213). According to Hesselgrave, those in a shame culture are so completely tied to the opinions of others that "there is no need for shame unless one is caught in his shameful behavior" (1991:611). Though both address the issue, Loewen (1970) and Hesselgrave (1984) are heavily dependent upon Benedict's inadequate definitions of shame as external (social opinion) and guilt as internal (conscience). Thailand missionary John R. Davis also echoes this notion when he writes that "people from guilt-oriented cultures have a deeper sense of personal wrongdoing, while people from shame-oriented cultures have a sense of corporate offense" (Davis 1993:52).

The definitions present in most contemporary missiological literature rest upon the unfortunate perpetuation of deficient notions regarding shame and guilt. Thus, the conventional notion of shame as other-directed and guilt as originating from an internal conscience continue to hold sway. Guilt is about absolute standards while shame depends upon varying social currents. As I have already demonstrated, such notions trade upon earlier misconceptions regarding differences between guilt and shame.

"Honor" and "Justice" Cultures

Recently, two missiologists have offered a new typology to differentiate cultures. Instead of shame cultures and guilt cultures, Lienhard and Klaus Müller (1996) make a distinction between honor cultures and justice cultures. Lienhard contends that such a division is more proper since shame and guilt are simply "expressions of the more underlying core values of *honor* and *justice*" (Lienhard 2001:132). She distinguishes between honor and justice cultures thusly: honor cultures emphasize a "conscience (that) is trained to concentrate on values," whereas in a justice-oriented culture, "conscience reacts to norms" (Lienhard 2001:134). This basic difference, she contends, leads to a difference of emphasizing relationships (honor/shame) over against sin (justice/guilt).

To her credit, what drives this distinction is that she has noticed something quite important about honor and shame. That is, they are not binary opposites. Yet, in trying to find a better correlative for honor/shame cultures, she opts uncritically for justice/guilt. Her distinction between honor societies and justice-oriented societies is, unfortunately, quite tenuous. Indeed, she offers this distinction as an assertion for which she does not provide any significant argumentation or justification. Lienhard apparently draws much of the conceptual framework of honor and justice cultures from the work of Müller. Like Lienhard, his writings constitute some of the few extended treatment of issues of shame and guilt in missions. Yet, like Lienhard, there are significant problems with the overall picture Müller paints of shame, honor, and guilt.

Müller is certainly right in contending that both guilt and shame are a function of the human conscience. Unfortunately, his treatment assumes much of Benedict's outdated notions of shame and guilt. Thus, shame results from a conscience that takes it cue from society while guilt results from abstract principles inculcated into the individual's conscience, regardless of social context (1996:8). Shame and "sin" in an honor society are only public (1996:3). Shame seems primarily external, consisting simply in the loss of public honor or prestige (1996:5). Guilt, in contrast, is the loss of the right (1996:5). Müller posits guilt, a personal knowledge of wrong that can occur without the presence of an outside observer, as characteristic of Western countries (1996:5). He also makes the unsupported and grossly reckless assertion that in most non-Western cultures people do not feel guilt after sin.[7]

Müller applies his notions issues of shame and guilt and honor and justice specifically to the nature of the gospel and missionary activity. It is in this application that his ideas become particularly problematic. For

---

7. "In den meisten nicht-westlichen Kulturen dagegen kommt bei einer "Sünde" kein Schuldgefühl auf" (Müller 1996:7).

example, in discussing the proclamation of the gospel in missionary contexts, Müller takes up Johan Bavinck's notion of elenctics.[8]

> Elenctics is the German expression for "elenchein," that in 2 Tim. 3:16 (for punishment) comes and means something like "to be guided by guilt." That is the goal of the proclamation of the gospel: that people should be convicted of their guilt before God in their very consciences, and should accept redemption from the saving work of Jesus Christ. (1996:3)[9]

Bavinck's notion of guilt-based elenctics, which Müller picks up, rests upon not only improper exegetical conclusions and faulty word study, but also relies on outdated notions of the nature of guilt and shame.[10]

Additional ideas are problematic. An honor society, Müller contends, has its source of authority in society itself and such is incompatible with a notion of a God who stands above societal standards.[11] The forgiveness

---

8. This understanding apparently originates from the work of Johan Bavinck, who writes that "The term 'elenctic' is derived from the Greek verb elengchein. In Homer the verb has the meaning of 'to bring to shame.' It is connected with the word elengchos that signifies shame. In later Attic Greek the significance of the term underwent a certain change so that the emphasis fell more upon the conviction of guilt, the demonstration of guilt. It is this latter significance that it has in the New Testament" (Bavinck 1960:221). Interestingly, the entry in the *Theological Dictionary of the New Testament* upon which Bavinck bases his assertion does not in fact suggest the association with guilt as Bavinck contends. Indeed, there appears no good reason to deny a strong sense of "to bring to shame" or "to convict with shame" as the term clearly has in earlier Greek. Hesselgrave also follows Bavinck's line of interpretation, contending that elengchein "refers to conviction of *guilt*" (Hesselgrave 1983:480, emphasis in original) and is not cultural but transcultural. Hesselgrave also assumes the guilt-shame distinction from Benedict and applies such to his missiology. So then, guilt "is most compatible with, if not derived from, the Judeo-Christian view of a holy and omniscient God as the Author of both the revealed Law and the human conscience" (1983:479). Likewise, shame is often an obstacle to true guilt since it is "often so preoccupied with the approval or disapproval of others that he cannot consider the requirements of God" (1983:480). Such presents us with a clear example of a missiologist misconstruing exegetical sources, which then is subsequently "canonized" and considered basic to later missiological writing.

9. "Elenktik (engl. elenctics) ist der deutsche Begriff für 'elengchein', das in 2.Tim.3,16 (für "Strafe") vorkommt und soviel bedeutet wie 'von Schuld überführen'. Das ist das Ziel der Evangeliumsverkündigung: Die Menschen sollen in ihrem Gewissen von ihrer Schuld vor Gott überführt werden und die Erlösung durch das Heilswerk Jesu Christi annehmen" (Müller 1996:3).

10. Bavinck's ideas also set the terms for the framework Hesselgrave uses in his discussion of guilt, shame, and cross-cultural notions of sin.

11. "Jedenfalls ist das nicht die Vorstellung von einem Gott, der Gesellschaft übergeordnet ist, nicht manipulierbar und unbestechlich" (Müller 1996:2–3).

of sins is based upon a guilt consciousness before God, not upon feelings of public shame.[12] His interpretation is flawed, however, by assuming that which is to be proved. That is, if sin equals "guilt," then of course the gospel must essentially be about guiltiness.[13]

In the end, Müller's approach seems predicated more upon a very modern penal substitutionary view of atonement than putatively biblical material. Additionally, he fails to differentiate properly between the two dimensions of the affect of shame (internal or subjective shame) and the social experience of being shamed (external or objective shame). The major flaw in his argument is that he juxtaposes the affect of guilt improperly with the social experiences related to public shaming and humiliation. His Western bias together with his lack of proper understanding of the differences between honor/justice and shame/guilt damages to a serious degree his overall treatment of the topic. The work of Müller and others who advocate similar ideas unfortunately continues to perpetuate the general misunderstandings that adversely affect missionary views of honor, shame, guilt, and face.

Summary

This brief survey of shame-guilt and justice-honor highlights the fundamental inadequacies of these conventional typologies and the conceptual notions upon which they stand. I would suggest part of the general misunderstanding relating to face in the Western world emerges from an improper understanding of the shame and guilt experiences as I have highlighted above. Those operating with these mistaken traditional notions subsume face under the rubric of honor or shame cultures, making face primarily a possession of these cultures and not of Western or putatively Christian cultures. Face then automatically partakes of the negative images those in the West often hold toward these non-Western culture types. Thus, many associate face with a lack of conscience, lack of principled living, lack of proper levels of personal guilt, and an overdependence upon the opinion of others. This, as I have attempted to demonstrate, is simply not the case.

Traditional post-Reformation Protestant theology often reinforces these mistaken readings of shame and guilt experiences. In particular, this

---

12. "Sündenvergebung geschieht aufgrund von Schuldbewußtsein vor Gott, nicht aufgrund eines Empfindens von Scham vor Menschen" (Müller 1996:9).

13. "Das Wort Gottes ist "schuld-orientiert", d.h. es zielt darauf, daß der Mensch gerecht wird vor Gott" (Müller 1996:9).

is so regarding the notions of sin, guilt, and atonement. Such Western theological formulations are dependent to a large degree on Greco-Roman legal theories. The emphasis on penal, retributive justice and legal transaction in atonement theory has resulted in a concomitant emphasis on the dimension of guilt in relation to sin and God's relationship with his creation. The concept of guilt has provided the essential matrix within which discussion of atonement has centered ever since the time of the Protestant Reformation.[14] In worship, Western churches frequently confess guilt over moral transgressions (i.e., the breaking of the law of God). Seldom, however, do these same churches make intentional use of concepts related to social honor or shame. Western atonement formulations speak often of the release of our guilt-ridden souls. Quite absent, however, are notions of shame. Indeed, much post-Reformation theology has subsumed the human feelings of unworthiness and shame within the larger rubric of guilt and subsequently defining the salvific work of Christ exclusively in terms of guilt (Kraus 1990:208). It is not surprising that this fundamental characteristic of Western culture has become a dominant bias in Western theologizing in general and missionary proclamation in particular (Karen 1992:40–70).[15]

To understand face properly, it is imperative to first gain a critical and more nuanced understanding of the proper differences between the traditional pairing of shame/guilt and justice/honor cultural types. This means to move beyond the simplistic and inadequate conceptualizations that often characterize Western thinking generally and missiological thinking in particular regarding face. Such a broadening of perspective will allow us to move beyond reckless face-oblivious and face-averse positions, opening up a new opportunity to probe how face, honor, shame, and guilt are present in human relationality.

---

14. Stendahl 1977:78–96. The ideas Stendahl presented in this chapter broke new ground, challenging the hegemony of faulty Western presuppositions that skewed interpretations of Paul and other New Testament writers.

15. In this article, Robert Karen discusses the serious neglect of issues of shame within the psychotherapeutic disciplines and a recent resurgence of attention to shame. Clearly, theology is not the only discipline affected by Western preoccupation with guilt. Although one could make a plausible argument that such should be a legitimate emphasis for those in the West, the lack of serious attention to the experience of shame (present in many forms) should be examined with greater scrutiny.

PART 2

Recovering Face

4

Face and Facework Theory

FACE CAN BE A quite elusive notion. Lu Hsün, commenting on this, queries, "But what is this thing called face? It is all very well if you don't stop to think, but the more you think the more confused you grow" (1960:129). Indeed, once we make face a discrete object of study it can seem quite mystifying. Inconsistent usage among researchers highlights an ambiguity present in much of the literature on face (Morisaki and Gudykunst 1994:47). This elusive and confusing nature, partly, it seems, emerges from the inherent complexity of face. Regarding such complexity, Ting-Toomey and Cocroft comment that face is an

> ... intoxicating metaphor that connects communication with social life. It is a multifaceted construct that takes on dimensions of identity issues, social cognitive issues, affective issues, and communication issues. It is a construct that captivates the interest of scholars from diverse disciplines. (1994:307)

Though pervasive in human life, face is often a confounding subject to study.

Usage of the specific term "face" in the vein I have been discussing is a recent addition to the Western linguistic lexicon, entering conventional parlance only in the last two hundred years (Ervin-Tripp, Nakamura, and Guo 1995:45). The specific referencing of face-related behavior as "face" is then not an indigenous lexical designation in most Western social contexts. Most commentators accept the conventional notion that the ancient

Chinese were the first to use the term "face" to designate the various phenomena assumed under the rubric of face and facework theory. Therefore, though we in the West actively engage in face-related activity, often such quite easily "slips under the radar" as our language tends not to designate such as "face."[1]

In an attempt to understand more completely this area of face, a multi-disciplinary research project involving scholars from various areas (e.g., anthropology, sociology, communication theory, social psychology, cross-cultural psychology, linguistics, conflict theory) has recently emerged (Tracy 1990:209).[2] This modern academic study of face moves beyond this traditional Chinese concept, yet forms "recognizable extensions" of it (1990:210). Additionally, self-presentation theory, a subdiscipline of social psychology investigating issues of social identity, parallels to a remarkable degree the same issues and concerns of face and facework theory.

The theoretical discussions of face in both face theory and self-presentation theory substantiate a fundamental point I am trying to make. That is, the typical ambivalence and aversion to face I have described results from basic Western cultural biases. The scholarly treatment of face and facework helps us understand the two sources (i.e., a modern Western self-construal and misunderstanding of honor, guilt, and shame) of prosopagnosia I have highlighted in the previous two chapters. In addition, the theoretical discussions regarding face provide concepts helpful for a fully understanding of this important dimension of human relationality.

In this chapter, I attempt to draw upon key discussions in face theory and self-presentation theory to demonstrate three points that are important for understanding the "about face" I am suggesting. These are that face: (1) is a ubiquitous human phenomenon present in all social contexts

---

1. In the modern Western world, we tend to collapse face and face-related behavior into other categories, such as politeness, image, identity, or various extensions of personal dignity and esteem. As Goffman notes in his seminal essay on face, even in modern Western culture, "the members of every social circle may be expected to have some knowledge of face-work and some experience in its use. In our society, this kind of capacity is sometimes called tact, *savoir-faire*, diplomacy, or social skill." Yet, all such activity is "modified, prescriptively or proscriptively, by considerations of face" (Goffman 1955:217).

2. The various applications of face and facework theory are quite broad and include such diverse topics as how aerobic workout instructors manage face wants among workout participants (Delin 1998), the rationalizations readers of popular-level romance fiction offer in defense of their reading practices (Brackett 2000), how to assist mediators to move parties through successful conflict negotiation (Van Ginkel 2004), and understanding the effect of self-construal and conflict styles in online learning environments (Walsh, Gregory, Lake, and Gunawardena 2003).

and not limited to any particular culture, (2) represents a complex relational dynamic that resists simple, mono-dimensional conceptualizations, and (3) differs considerably in varying cultural contexts.

Face as a Ubiquitous Phenomenon

Face is not simply a possession of certain (e.g., East Asian) cultures. What scholars refer to as face and facework appears to be present universally in every culture and functions as an important element of all human relationality (albeit an often overlooked one). Such a perspective deflates the mistaken notion of face and non-face cultures. Wherever there is human culture, there face also exists.

Face theory and self-presentation theory both postulate that people profoundly occupy themselves in every social interaction with the projection of symbolic information regarding the self. If these perspectives are accurate, then face is not some ancillary or optional feature of the human person. Face, by this account, emerges as a foundational dimension of human relationality, identity construction, personhood, and social life. Regarding this, Robyn Penman notes that

> . . . facework is one of the consistencies brought about by the organized setting of humans relating to others in a social existence. That it has endured, despite the exigencies of the human social condition, suggests the how basic such a mechanism is. By basic I am not suggesting it is unsophisticated, rather it is primary in that it provides a shared basis for a social order. We could not have a social order without something like the mechanism that I am labeling as facework. (Penman 1994:25)

Indeed, in some cultures, notably many from East Asia, the ratification of face and face-related needs lies at the very heart of communication (Scollon and Scollon 1994:139). Therefore, whether recognized explicitly or designated by a specific appellation, face, it seems, pervades all human relationality and culture.

The account of self-presentation Barry Schlenker provides is helpful here. Self-presentation involves the various behaviors and attitudes of people as they project and attempt to regulate the impressions they desire. The key assumption of self-presentation theory is that all human relationality involves being inescapably caught up in the constant sending and receiving of information about the self and other selves. The presentation of the self in social space, from such a perspective, involves "a range of activities that are united by the central idea that social behavior is a performance that symbolically communicates information about self to others" (Schlenker 2003:494). This encoding and decoding of self-relevant information is like a dramatic performance. The study of self-presentation involves examining how people, as agents, try to shape the attitudes and behaviors of audiences through the presentation of self-relevant information and how people, as targets, respond to the self-presentation activities of others (2003:492).

These various activities cannot be conceived of within the self-contained framework of the isolated individual. The factors that determine self-presentation are multiplex, including the self, the self's relations with others, the image or messages the self intends to project, and the social context within which the relations and the self-presentation occur. That is, self-presentation

> ... reflects the transaction between self and audience in a particular social context. It is not purely an expression of self, purely a role-played response to situational pressures, or purely conformity to the identity expectations of salient others. (Schlenker 2003:498)

What we find is that individuals always occupy themselves in goal-directed communication that ties together actor, audience, and social context. For the self, to be involved in any type of communication assumes this fundamental dynamic of self-presentation.

This is an especially important point to stress. Self-presentation is not something *some* of us do *some* of the time. The presentation in social space of symbolic information about the self is a dynamic process that is both enduring and ubiquitous. We are always encoding information about the self into our relationships. Thus, human relationality inevitably involves self-presentation. The only way we know one another is through the various ways we present our selves to one another. This is the case since none of us have internal access to other selves. We know one another only through a medium, a bridge of some kind. Such a presentation of the self is a necessary mediating structure for all our relationality and communication. In truth then, the self can only exist within the matrix of one's own and others' self-presentation. It is our existence as selves, as individuals who are unique and differentiated in certain respects from the other, that the phenomenon of self-presentation becomes a necessity. It is this desire to connect and communicate with others that these presentations allow us to constitute relationships. Simply put, to be a self is to be, inescapably, a self involved in self-presentation.

The notion of self-presentation from a modern Western perspective might appear inauthentic, contrived, or unnecessarily calculated. Such thinking, however, stems from the Western belief that the self is truly itself when allowed to engage in unfettered self-expression of the internal characteristics that constitute a putative true essence. This again draws upon the notion of the self as an internally contained entity that should be maximally free from the imposition of outside influence, whether social structure or other persons. Yet, pitting this notion of self-expression (authentic, spontaneous, originating from a true internal self) against self-presentation (inauthentic, labored, influenced by social pressures that originate from without) is wrongheaded and unnecessary. Though such reflects real differences in motive and strategies, it is not the case that one involves self-presentation and one does not. Self-presentation theorists point out the significant fact that both equally involve self-presentation (Schlenker 2003:494).

To understand how that which people label "natural" and "contrived" are both equally products of self-presentation, we must understand the twin notions from self-presentation theory of automaticity and controlled responses. Automaticity refers to "modulated units of action that eventually 'settle in' to become habits" (2003:495). The automatic mode may occur in individuals as the result of consistent practice, frequent rewards, or routinized and habitual activity. Such automatic self-presentation becomes the normal mode in social interaction unless something happens to threaten the actor's image of self or other. Such is termed automatic because in the actor's mind during this automatic mode, there is no explicit awareness of trying to control or manage an impression.

It is imperative to note, however, that the goal-directed activity of constructing and protecting a desired identity still occurs (2003:495). Though there is no focal or explicit awareness, these automatic scripts or programs running in the background continue to maintain specific identity goals and actively work to accomplish these goals (2003:495). Although such behavior is essentially automatic, it still involves the presentation of the self, albeit a habitually determined, tacit self-presentation.

This is analogous to the operating system of a computer. When using a word processor, I am aware of my fingers upon the keyboard and the various functions of the program that allow me to construct my paper. Yet, all the while, though not a point of focal attention, the operating system working tacitly in the background is just as critical and real to the proper functioning of my work as is my explicit awareness of the work done using my word processor.

Consider the example of two college professors. The first, in explicit self-awareness, prepares a lecture with great care and time, taking into account audience, delivery, and tone of voice. The second ignores all these and teaches in an automatic mode, simply being himself. The first delivers a high-quality, effective lecture while the second is careless and dull. Schlenker notes that the first professor

> . . . is packaging information in order to create a desired impact on the audience. Yet, just because it is "packaged," this superior performance would not be considered more superficial, inauthentic, deceptive, or self-centered than that of the bad lecturer. Indeed, the attention to the audience and careful packaging increase the likelihood that the good teacher's goal—communicating truthful, meaningful information to the class—will be accomplished. (2003:493)

Though the presentation of the first professor occurs with great intentionality and awareness such does not imply deception or a lack of authenticity. Likewise, that the other followed a more automatic mode of self-expression does not automatically indicate a superior presentation.

Self-presentation occurs even among friends and intimates, in long-standing friendships and marriages, and does not necessarily involve conscious attention and control. This, in contrast to much popular-level thinking in the West, means that face does not become less of an issue as relationships are more intimate.

> Even when people interact in comfortable settings with familiar friends, a desired self-presentation script—or self-program—contains instructions about important features of self that are relevant and how they are symbolically communicated through actions. (Schlenker 2003:495)

The key distinction is between automatic self-presentations and those that result from explicit control. The antithetical authentic-versus-inauthentic polarity that a modern Western model of the self might require is not essential to understand the presentation of self.

Self-presentation theory also asserts that any attempt to communicate an "accurate" or "truthful" impression of the self requires as much self-presentation skill as it does to convey one that is patently false (Schlenker

2003:493). The key difference lies in the motive behind the presentation. Both truthful and false motives can guide and presentation of the self, whether automatic or controlled. This again obviates any necessary distinction based upon a false polarization between unforced self-expression on the one hand and a strenuous self-presentation on the other.

The mark of a mature person, one who functions as a competent social actor, is not an unfettered penchant for complete self-expression over against self-presentation. Such thinking does often exist, particularly as a result of thinking of the self in a modern, Western mode of internal essence. Yet, in practice, that this is not the case is especially clear since we know that to act in pure self-expression can often be selfish, socially incompetent, hurtful to others, and damaging to our relationships. Parents often instruct their children that, upon receiving a gift, they should not tell the giver exactly what they think but rather express gratitude and thanks. Likewise, if we happen to be listening to a tiresome, boring person going on and on, it would be rather uncharitable to engage in unrestrained self-expression between the sentences in their narrative and make such comments as "Oh, you're killing me," "How unbelievably boring you are," or "When will you finish with this drivel?"

This does not mean that an exclusive orientation to others is more proper. An individual may lose personal integrity if the agendas of others take over the individual's presentation of self. Neither of these extremes, however, is actually a problem of self-presentation, but rather one relating to self- or other-orientation. Schlenker argues that maturity is the ability to modulate properly between inner (principles and personal preferences) and outer concerns (expectations and preferences of others).

> To be oriented exclusively toward outer concerns is to allow others to dictate one's life. Conversely, to be oriented exclusively toward inner concerns often amounts to being egocentric, eccentric, and unable to deal effectively with others. Balancing inner and outer concerns evidences more mature social functioning. (Schlenker 2003:506)

What we learn from an overview of self-presentation theory is that the self is not a discrete individual, who acts upon some putative inner core of inviolable personal conviction, supposedly unconcerned about the presence and opinion of others. Just the opposite—the other impinges on our selves in a quite inescapable manner. Who we think we are, how we view and value the other, the type of relationship that should ideally exist between us, and the context within which this evaluation happens all play a part in the presentation of the self. To remark "It's not who I am" is not a critique of self-presentation. Rather, such a sentiment indicates an awareness of (and, likely, a preference for) a specific type of self-presentation, that is, an automatic presentation over against one that is controlled. And, such manifestations of self-presentation are always partial (we cannot know everything about another person), modulated (sometimes automatic, sometimes consciously controlled), and contextual (always a function of our identity goals vis-à-vis others in a social context).

Both face theory and self-presentation theory suggest that the projection of self or face is a universal human activity. Face exists as an indispensable epiphenomenon of all social intercourse and simply defies the simplistic conception, often popular in Western folk concepts of face, that one may do face or not. Such a universal notion of face also resists the prevalent notion that some cultures do face while others do not. Penman makes this point with clarity.

> Facework is not something that we do some of the time, it is something that we unavoidably do all the time—it is the core of our social selves. That it is called face and facework is curious but not critical here. What is critical is that the mechanism the label stands seems to be as enduring as human social existence. In the very act of communicating with others we are inevitably commenting on the other and our relationship with them. And in that commenting we are maintaining or changing the identity of the other in relationship to us. (Penman 1994:21)

To try to dispose of face would be akin to trying to eliminate DNA from human life, or the notion of the self from human thought. To be human is to have face and "do" face, that is, engage in facework. "The mutual knowledge of members' public self-image or face, and the social necessity to orient oneself to it in interaction, are universal" (Brown and Levinson 1978:62). If such is true, then any notion that paints face as entirely illegitimate, misguided, or even evil is categorically wrong.

Face as a Complex and Multivalent Phenomenon

A second critical point the theoretical discussions of face entail is that face is not a unitary thing but a multivalent happening. Face is both complex and dynamic. This is true because face is fundamentally a phenomenon generated in interpersonal social space. As such, face is inherently a product of the human self involved in relationality.

Recent academic discussions point out the great complexity of face, moving the understanding of face beyond simplistic mono-dimensional conceptualizations. This multi-disciplinary project takes its academic point of departure from the seminal work of Erving Goffman. Goffman's major contribution to this discussion is the critical step of identifying a prevalent human social phenomenon and labeling this "face." By doing so, Goffman legitimated face and facework as a discrete subject for academic research. It is his 1955 work "On Face-Work: An Analysis of Ritual Elements in Social Interaction" that puts face on the academic map. Here, Goffman offers a dramaturgical approach to understanding the social function of face. That is, face is the social image each social "actor" projects onto the "stage" of the social world. Goffman defines face as

> ... the positive social value a person effectively claims for himself by the line others assume he has taken during a particular contact (and) an image of the self delineated in terms of approved social attributes-albeit an image that others may share, as when a person makes a good showing for his profession or religion by making a good showing of himself. (1955:213)

The incredible complexity inhering in face derives from the nature of face as a conjoint co-construction involving the social agent and others. William R. Cupach and Sandra Metts suggest that a Goffmanesque approach to face assumes that face is always a basic component for constituting any sense of self (1994:2). Indeed, face is a necessary function of the self and all may be said to "have" or "possess" face. Yet, because of its inherent complexity face is, ironically, never the exclusive property of the one who possesses it.

> While his social face can be his most personal possession and the center of his security and pleasure, it is only on loan to him from society; it will be withdrawn unless he conducts himself in a way that is worthy of it. (1955:215)

Goffman makes the important point that face is not something located in a person's body or a personality trait "but rather something that is diffusely located in the flow of events in the encounter and becomes manifest only when these events are read and interpreted for the appraisals expressed in them" (1955:214).

Because of this dynamic nature, Goffman conceives face not as a single, one-dimensional mode of human activity, but one that adjusts to meet the variable contexts within which people make their face claims (1955:215). It is in the constant interplay between the self and others within changing contexts that face comes about. Thus, face involves both social-relational and personal-identity components. Face occupies a major role in defining the very conception of self and personal identity every individual projects in all social situations.

Face theory assumes that in every interactive situation, people position themselves to have their face projections supported and maintained. Likewise, competent social functioning assumes the ability to support the face claims of others. This mutual face maintenance is so natural and pervasive in human activity that it functions as a "taken-for-granted principle of interaction" (Cupach and Metts 1994:4). Such face affirmation provides a foundation of mutual regard that is critical to human relationality. This most general level of face competence is the basis of interpersonal competence, personal identity confirmation, and mutual social respect (1994:15). These differing functions of face provide the essential mutual solidarity for all human relationality.

Positive Face and Negative Face

Though Goffman initiated the Western study of face, it was the work of Penelope Brown and John Levinson (1978) that provided a substantive theoretical framework for understanding face. Though they note their reliance on Goffman's work and the English folk notion of face associated with embarrassment and humiliation (1978:61), their sociolinguistic theory of politeness surpassed the more limited social-psychological focus of Goffman, emphasizing the critical importance of language and discourse for understanding face. Brown and Levinson also represent the first approach explicating face in major theoretical components.

According to their theory, face refers to the identity each person claims in interaction with others. That is, face is "the public self-image that every member wants to claim for himself" (1978:61). Like Goffman, Brown and Levinson assert that face is not something only certain individuals have. Rather, face is something that all competent adult members of society necessarily possess (1978:61). Face-related behavior is not something limited to specific situations or enacted only at certain times but forms an important point of attention in every social interaction (1978:61).

The value of the work of Brown and Levinson is their discussion of two distinct though closely related dimensions of face, which they term "desires" or "face-wants" (Brown and Levinson 1978:13). The first of these is "negative face." Such is a personal desire for autonomy and non-imposition, "the want of every 'competent adult member' that his actions be unimpeded by others" (1978:62). Much of what people normally consider formal politeness falls under the rubric of negative face.

The second face dimension is "positive face," which consists of the desire to be approved. This is the positive self-image that all people claim and the parallel "want of every member that his wants be desirable to at least some others" (Brown and Levinson 1978:62). This includes the "desire to be ratified, understood, approved of, liked or admired" (1978:62). Together, negative face and positive face comprise the basic impulses of human face "navigation." The centripetal or isolating impulse of negative face forms the basis for strategies of non-imposition, deference, avoidance, and forms of "negative" politeness. The centrifugal or exocentric force of positive face works in the opposite direction, seeking connection through positive affirmation and esteem. By oscillating between these valences of positive and negative face, individuals shape their various face configurations and face-related behavior to accomplish different social goals and negotiate potentially face-threatening acts. This leads us to facework, a notion in face theory critical for a fuller understanding of the complexity of face.

Facework

A phenomenon intimately associated with face is the concept of facework. Facework is essentially the enactment of face strategies, verbal and nonverbal moves, self-presentation acts, and impression management interaction (Ting-Toomey 1994:1). People generally exert considerable effort to gain face and, once possessed, to hold onto face. Yet, as a positive social commodity face can also be maintained, damaged, lost, recovered, and enhanced. As a product of human relationality, face is not inert. People must attend constantly to their face in all interactive contexts (Brown and Levinson 1978:61). The various strategic enactments designed to attend to and shape our malleable face we term facework.

Indirectness in speech is a frequent and recognizable type of facework, yet the array of facework options extends far beyond this single type. So, for example, facework options include apologies (accepting responsibility), accounts (statements made to explain away), avoidance (withdrawal or escape), aggression, and humor (Edelmann 1994:239–243). The notion of face is so basic to all social interaction that Goffman can state confidently that to study the dynamics of facework is "to study the traffic rules of social interaction" (Goffman 1955:216). Though not a conventional term, facework is neither peripheral to nor optional for social interaction. Face and facework form the basis of any social order. As Penman notes, "we could not have a social order without something like the mechanism that I am labeling . . . facework" (1994:25).

Face as a Culturally and Contextually Variable Phenomenon

Although face is present universally, it varies greatly across cultures. Particularly, the culturally specific patterns of self-construal play a critical role in the generation of face. This, in turn, enables us to understand more clearly similarities and dissimilarities between Western and non-Western experiences of face. An awareness of diverse culturally formed versions of face alerts us to a critical need to study the culturally specific shape of face. Specifically this means to investigate face as it is manifest in particular cultural and linguistic contexts. To understand face within a broader cultural matrix requires us to be especially attentive to social honor, a parallel concept that necessarily affects the specific contextual shape face will take.

Until recently, most of the substantive study of face came from within Western academic circles. Though there had been a limited number of scholarly treatments from a non-Western perspective, such were sporadic and only obliquely connected to each other.[3] Although they focus on discourse in the Western world, Brown and Levinson make the important connection between folk understandings of face and basic cultural notions such as social persona, social honor, shame, virtue, and redemption (Brown and Levinson 1978:13). They assume that specific cultures will differ in the various contents of face. That is, the exact limits of negative face and the basis on which positive face is construed will differ throughout cultures. In addition, cultural differences will lead to substantive variations in facework strategies. Though this was an admission in their work (and that of Goffman as well), their study of face occurred exclusively within a Western cultural context.

As the number of face studies from diverse cultural contexts grew, a fundamental division in the literature on face became increasingly apparent. This consisted of those studies approaching face from within a Western context and those studying face within a non-Western context.

---

3. These include studies regarding face from China (Cheng 1986; Ho 1976; Hu 1944; Hwang 1987; Lu 1960), Japan (Matsumoto 1988), and Thailand (Sanit 1975).

Yet, this divide in the literature on face went deeper than mere geography (Morisaki and Gudykunst 1994:52). It became increasingly clear that the academic notion of face developed within a thoroughly Western framework obscured the great cultural variation that existed among different types of face construal. It was not simply that face (defined by Goffman or Brown and Levinson) occurred in different cultural contexts but that *face itself* differed in other cultures.

The analytical study of face took a major step forward with the edited volume *The Challenge of Facework* (Ting-Toomey 1994). In this work, theorists and researchers from various disciplines sought to probe more deeply into the issues of face and facework. Particularly significant was the number of articles that sought to understand face within a cross-cultural framework. By advocating analytical categories for cross-cultural investigation into face, this work moved the study of face beyond the narrower range of previous studies that studied face within the parameters of the Western cultural context.

Stella Ting-Toomey (2004:218), the most influential and prolific contemporary face theorist, notes that face is about "identity respect" and "social self-worth." Like Goffman as well as Brown and Levinson, she highlights how face serves as "a precious identity resource in communication because it can be threatened, enhanced, undermined, and bargained over on both emotional and cognitive appraisal levels." Yet, her specific contribution is in providing a theoretical framework for understanding face and facework issues that emphasizes the culturally variable shape of face. This she does through her self-designated "Face Negotiation Theory."[4] A basic point in this face negotiation theory posits that people in every culture simultaneously seek to maintain and negotiate face in every social situation (Ting-Toomey 2004:219). The face orientation and needs of each individual depend upon factors that differ according to individuals, situations, and cultures. Such influence individual choices from a wide range of various facework strategies used in social interaction and, specifically, in conflict situations. Face dynamics, then, vary both in different social situations within any specific culture (interpersonal variation) and in culturally distinct forms (intercultural variation).

---

4. Her face-negotiation theory posits seven basic thematic clusters. These are face locus, face valence, face contents, facework strategies, face temporality, face conflict styles, and face tempo (Ting-Toomey 2004:225–31).

The Independent and Interdependent Self

A significant issue many studies of face consider when discussing these cross-cultural differences are two broad cultural types of face—independent face and interdependent face. These two face types, in turn, correspond with the construal of self in either individualist/independent or collectivist/interdependent modes.

Western conceptualization regarding the self often posits the individual as an independent, self-contained, autonomous entity. This self consists of a unique set of internal attributes, which in turn form the motivational force for the behavior of the self (Markus and Kitayama 1991:224). The "real" me exists in these internal attributes, accessible only to the mind of the individual. The outer, social self then functions as a type of external shell, a type of social epiphenomena that is a pragmatic requirement for social functioning but not basic to the essence of the self.

Markus and Kitayama term this common Western configuration of the self as the "independent self." Those with an independent construal of the self hold these inner attributes to be dominant in regulating behavior. For both the self and others who view the self, these inner states represent that which typifies who the person truly is. Thus, the independent self should be unique, express itself, realize its own internal goals, and be direct (i.e., to say what is on one's mind). The independent self finds its basis for self-esteem in the ability to express itself and find validation of its internal attributes (Markus and Kitayama 1991:230).

This independent self stands in stark contrast the interdependent self (Shweder 1984:14–15; Kitayama, Markus, and Matsumoto 1995:443). In contrast to an independent self-construal, some cultures do not conceive of a discrete set of inner personal attributes as the primary unit of individual consciousness. Instead, "the sense of belongingness to a social relation may become so strong that it makes better sense to think of the relationship as the functional unit of conscious reflection" (Markus and Kitayama 1991:226). Such is an embedded self, one interdependently connected to others in a web of social relations.

This interdependent self "may be more likely to use interpretation of the situation or expectations held by relevant others in determining their own performance or behavior. As a consequence, their success (and hence 'self-esteem') may depend primarily on the standards or criteria held by the relevant others or the perceived expectations of these others" (Kitayama, Markus, and Matsumoto 1995:444–45). So, for example, from the pervasive Japanese perspective, the independent self-expression involved in "the straightforward claim of the naked ego" (Markus and Kitayama 1991:303) is improper under most conditions. What would appear to a Western independent self as authentic self-assertion would be immature and childish from the perspective of a Japanese interdependent self-configuration (1991:229).

The construal of the self has important implications for the area of face. For those who operate with an independent notion of the self, such things as individual attributes, abilities, and personal competencies will define face. This type of independent face will likely place great emphasis on personal face competence. Additionally, those with independent face will also maintain greater concern for negative face.[5]

Those with an interdependent view of the self will focus upon rather different characteristics. Interdependent face will likely relate to proper role enactment. The face deference that results from such interdependent relations acts to sustain these relations while the greater relational distance inherent in a more independent self undergirds non-imposition (i.e., negative-face rights). Those who maintain this type of face concern will also tend to consider face vis-à-vis group approval and disapproval (Ting-Toomey and Cocroft 1994:327). Interdependent selves view face as a mechanism through which people negotiate reciprocity and social relationships (Morisaki and Gudykunst 1994:58). Similarly, those in contexts of high interdependence will also be more vulnerable to face consequences resulting from the actions of others.

A helpful example of interdependent face is that from the context of Japan. Japanese face resists the more Western, independent-face definition offered by Brown and Levinson. Specifically, for the Japanese, there appears to be little negative-face need to preserve individual self-territory (Matsumoto 1988:408). The right to non-imposition, as the negative-face

---

5. Societies that many consider as "less polite" correspond to positive politeness or positive face societies while those that have been thought of as "more polite" exhibit a negative politeness or negative face orientation (Sifianou 1992:43). This is because members of high-group societies (where the interdependent construal of self tends to predominate) often conceive of behavior as duty that does not require overt politeness (Sifianou 1992:42). Where the independent construal of self dominates, society often conceptualizes behavior as a matter of individual discretion rather than conforming to social norms and duty. This results in a greater need for negative face politeness since people recognize requests for specific behavior as imposition. In positive politeness contexts, individuals feel less need to apologize, ask permission, and give thanks since personal behavior does not carry the same level of imposition (Sifianou 1992:42).

concept requires, does not appear to be a salient feature of Japanese culture. Rather, the Japanese interdependent self, embedded in interpersonal relationships, produces a type of face highly considerate of deference, both as a way of constituting group solidarity and social hierarchy (1988:409). This is particularly evident by noting the honorific nature of Japanese language, which reflects the embeddedness of the self in the hierarchy of rank ordering and the relational obligations inherent in such a system (1988:414). Face in Japan tends to involve the proper role of the self in Japanese society rather than function as a vehicle for the personal self-expression, as may occur more in the independent-self context of the Western world. Japanese face "is intimately bound up with showing recognition of one's relative position in the communicative context and with the maintenance of the social ranking order" (1988:415). Japanese facework is less about self-definition than social acceptance and group harmony (1988:407).

Methodologically, this means that face analysis in such contexts must extend investigation from a lone individual to: (1) actions by the individual in response to others; (2) actions by others closely associated with the individual; (3) actions directed at the individual by those with whom the individual is interacting; (4) actions directed at the individual by people closely associated with those with whom the individual is interacting; and (5) actions directed at people closely associated with the individual by people with whom the individual in interacting directly or indirectly (Ho 1994:271).

Although each culture will generally prescribe an independent-self or interdependent-self construal, each person, it seems, actually has both an independent and an interdependent construal of self on which they rely (Morisaki and Gudykunst 1994:65). What is culturally variable is the particular face construal that people use in guiding their behavior in a given situation (1994:65). Such means that face research must not rest content with sweeping generalizations of entire cultures (e.g., Japanese face, American face, Thai face). Totalizing statements are naïve since such not only gloss over variations within cultures but also individual-level variations each person modulates through in their daily lives.

Types of Face

Moving beyond the dual notions of positive face and negative face, Lim illustrates the cultural complexity and variation of face through three types of face dimensions (Lim 1994:221). The first is what he calls "autonomy face." This includes values such as "independent," "in control of self," "self-sufficient," and "initiative." People who claim this aspect of face desire to be free from others' interference or control. This face claim is primarily about desire to be free from imposition and parallels the negative-face concept Brown and Levinson advance. Second is what Lim refers to as "fellowship face." This is the positive image people project so others will see them as worthy companions. Terms usually associated with this type of face include "likeable," "cooperative," "agreeable," and "affiliated." Fellowship face is a function of the desire to be included. Essentially, fellowship face is Brown and Levinson's positive face translated into a collective context. It is a group application of positive face. "Competence face" is the final dimension. This is the face projection concerned with accomplishment and reputation. Terms such as "experienced," "accomplished," "prosperous," and "distinguished" imply this competence-face dimension. A person concerned with this type of face desires acknowledgment of their abilities, in essence, public respect. This may exist in an individual mode or, alternately, translate into groupness. Thus, a single person may be concerned with his own competence face (positive individual face). Alternately, a person may demonstrate greatest concern for the competence face of a larger social entity, perhaps even deriving individual competence face from the competence face of the larger group.

This typology helps us understand an oft-noted difference between Western and Asian face. No individual enjoys, it seems, the experience of losing face. Yet, for example, many have observed that face-loss avoidance is not the primary concern driving American face. The driving force for much Western face is to seek approval, recognition, and success of the self *qua* individual. Those who are oriented to a high degree of both autonomy face and competence face (on an individual level) will tend to focus more upon distinguishing themselves in terms of an increase in individual face characteristics. Such will naturally decrease concern for social approval or the potential disruption of group harmony that individual face pursuit might cause due to the dynamics of both the autonomy face and individually oriented competence-face concerns. In contrast, many Asian societies focus on avoiding disapproval. In such an environment, face concerns will take on fellowship-face characteristics. Since there is a higher desire for social inclusion, the loss of esteem from significant others will be more painful. People will likely expend greater energy to avoid such. So, many from the Western world concern themselves more with the gaining of face while many Asians tend to seek to prevent face loss (Ho 1994:273).[6]

Personal Face and Social Face

There is for the human self an implicit face orientation in all social situations. This means, first, that there is the personal dimension of face that is the possession of all persons. Such "personal face" exists by virtue of an individual being a member of society and in relationship with others. This is a pervasive phenomenon that all participants in social space automatically generate. A second type of face, a "social face," inheres more to prestigious individuals who are well know or differentiate themselves from the common folk in some particular way. This is a valence of face closely associated with social distinction. The first, more personal type of face dimension, that is, "personal face," correlates with human personhood (i.e., all people by virtue of being a human possess this sort of face) and relationality (this dimension is generated by participation in relationships within social space). The second type, "social face," connects more closely with the notion of social status.[7]

These twin concepts of personal and social face reflect important dual distinctives of face. Personal face, potentially available to every person, is constituted partly by the seemingly universal desire to avoid shame (the desire to avoid relational rupture or loss of acceptance). What people loose in face depletion is social capital, the ability to function as a competent social actor. If one is not in a state of shame, then one functions as socially competent actor and, to that extent, possesses (personal) face. It is upon this base that one may, by various strategies, extend one's face into the realm of social face or simply rest content with personal face. While the rationale for and extent of seeking social face may vary, the motivational gravity to possess and maintain personal face is unquestionable.

This basic difference is clearly present in Chinese face. David Yau-Fai Ho notes that in Mandarin there are two face terms, *mien-tzu* and *lien*. Though similarities exist, these two types of Chinese face differ in

---

6. Indeed, the experience of face loss itself can differ widely across different cultural contexts. Japanese seem to feel face loss more often when they are not able to maintain in-group harmony. Americans, on the other hand, feel face loss when they experience personal failure (Morisaki and Gudykunst 1994:56).

7. I borrow the terms "personal face" and "social face" from face researcher Takuo Hayashi, though my usage differs from his (Hayashi 2004).

considerable ways. *Mien-tzu* is not fixed in amount but is variable. This type of face may vary considerably given differing social contexts. People may add to their *mien-tzu*, increasing it in greater levels. Alternately, one may decrease in *mien-tzu*. In contrast, *lien* is a universal type of face, the possession of which is simply by virtue of being human. Unlike *mien-tzu*, however, it is impossible to increase *lien*. It is static and does not vary in quantity. One may either gain or lose *mien-tzu*, but one may only lose *lien* (Ho 1976:869–70). Indeed, in the Chinese context, to lose *lien* is equivalent to demotion from the human family (Hu 1944:61). To have no *lien* is to cease being a legitimate person. Another important distinction to which Ho draws our attention is that of the fluidity versus fixedness of face. In comparing the Chinese notion of face to Western notions, Ho notes this important distinction. Western face, as Goffman notes, is dynamic, "diffusely located in the flow of events" (Goffman 1955:214). Such a notion of a fluid, diffuse type of face (i.e., Western face) contrasts sharply with the Chinese notion. For the Chinese, face generally attaches to persons (Ho 1994:274). This means that whereas Western face may be built upon the ever-changing achievements and permutations of the self in variable contexts, Chinese face seems to be defined "in terms of the more enduring, publicly perceived attributes that function to locate a person's position in his/her social network" (1994:274). If true, Western face appears more dynamic and elastic, attached to fluctuations in self and performance, while the Chinese conception is more fixed and static, leading to a face somewhat more difficult to alter. Perhaps it is correct to conceive certain non-Western types of face (e.g., Chinese) as oriented toward social face, embedded in the intricacies of the webs of social relations, whereas much Western face is predominantly a person-wise face phenomenon that parallels the notion of personal face. If true, such would help explain another key difference between the typical Western conception of face and those of many other cultures. For many Westerners, face functions in a transactional way. It is a utilitarian tool that personal desires guide. In contrast, face may hold significant moral implications. Thus, for many Chinese, face

> . . . is not simply an issue of social technique; it is also a measure of one's wisdom in dealing with the world. Protecting other's *mien-tzu* implies that interactants take their relational responsibilities seriously, and is a sign of respect both for oneself and for the other. Since damaging the other's *mien-tzu* may mean the end of a given relationship, it is incumbent on each social actor

> to protect each other's *mien-tzu* by all available means. (Chang and Holt 1994:112)

Attention to face in social contexts is constitutive of effective interpersonal relationship. The presence of sincere emotional concern for another will inevitably lead to respect for the other's face. To lack concern for another's face is characteristic of a "bad" person. Lack of proper concern for face may damage relationships even if no conflict exists. Proper facework is therefore an essential component for effective social life in Chinese society (Chang and Holt 1994:123). Understanding the moral dimension of Chinese face mitigates against a conception of face as simply a surface phenomenon or preoccupation for mere formal politeness.

> If we simply attempt to describe *mien-tzu* alone, without reference to other cultural concepts, we run the risk of losing the essence of *mien-tzu's* cultural meaning, leading in turn to the misjudgment that Chinese tend to overemphasize external formality at the expense of personal autonomy. Indeed, equating *mien-tzu* with formality utterly fails to capture the richness and delicacy of Chinese interactional episodes, which always manifest subtle awareness of other parties' *mien-tz.u* (1994:123)

An adequate understanding of face in the Chinese context, then, may potentially yield rich knowledge of Chinese cultural life (1994:124). What is true of Chinese culture is likely true of all cultural contexts. That is, face represents powerful culturally shaped moral currents.

Because of this, face is a potentially fruitful avenue to enhance cultural understanding. Studying face can provide rich insight regarding not only social intercourse but also the culturally salient values of a particular society (Ho 1976:874). This is because face always reflects positive social values. Thus, "since any positive social value can be an element of face, face is as complex as the value system of a society" (Lim 1994:210). Such makes the study of face particularly important for those wishing to understand the basic cultural values in a given cultural context.

Face, Identity, and the Self

The type of self that face theory (and the parallel area of self-presentation theory) assumes is, in many respects, similar to the relational social self of modern social psychology. Tracy makes the important observation that the notion of face allows us to move beyond the unsolvable conundrum of a true self versus a strategic self (Tracy 1990:215). Face moves us beyond essence to social situations where people make and respond to identity claims. When considering the function of face, a dynamic interplay between two basic conceptual poles is evident, that is, identity and relationship (Penman 1994:17). At every level of communication, we are invariably commenting on the other as well as our relationship with them. By doing this, we are maintaining or changing the identity of the other in relationship to ourselves (1994:21). Face is a function of the projection of any type of identity claim. I cannot know you in a direct, immediate way. I cannot enter your mind and so am dependent upon what you reveal to me. Since this is the case, relationship must always come by some structure of mediation. Thus, instead of direct access to some independent self, what I know of you is essentially a projection of self (i.e., your face) and my validation or rejection of that projection. In this sense, who you believe yourself to be and the identity that the world grants depends upon one's face. Face then occupies a central role in the creation of human identity (1994:20–21). This is so because it involves the projection of self-image and impression management, which has as an ultimate goal the shaping and instilling a particular favorable image in the minds of others (Hwang 1987:960).[8]

Face also functions to protect personal identity. Both pride and fear play a constructive role in forming social honor and face. I want others to think well of me (despite what I may actually be like). Sometimes I may wish others think better of me than is truly warranted. Likewise, I may not want others to know my true state, for example, my weaknesses, sins, or socially frowned upon opinions. I fear potential exposure of these and the embarrassment such would produce. Face can protect me by creating a specific social identity that may intentionally "mask" certain less socially approved traits. Relational issues are foundational to issues of face. Again, any attempt to project face requires a social response from others. Therefore, to gain the type of face response most desire, there is a continual need for positive relationships with those from whom people seek face validation. Relational reciprocity then, becomes an essential part of the dynamics of face. As Ho notes, face is about both extending face to others as well as safeguarding one's own face (Ho 1976:882).[9]

8. It is conceivable, however, that someone might have a particular interest in projecting a negative image, for example, a person whose continued reliance upon the assistance of others required their projection of an image of helplessness or inadequacy of some kind.

9. Kwang-Kuo Hwang (1987) argues against the Western assumption in literature

As a basic part of relationship, face functions as a central factor in any attempt to alter or influence the behavior of another. Such attempts are potentially face-threatening so people often take great care to balance what it is they are seeking with the support of their interaction partner's face (Wilson and Kunkel 2000:195). Furthermore, any attempt "to alter another person's behavior inherently is face-threatening; consequently, individuals use politeness to balance their competing desires to be clear about what they want and to support their interaction partner's face" (2000:195). Face and facework, in this regard, are means of manipulating a given relationship or situation. Facework is a reflection of one's relational intentions and action goals. As such, it is proper to conceive face as a type of power and facework as various attempts to preserve and use such face-related power (Hwang 1987:961). Besides being a force that influences the behavior of others, face also functions to limit one's own social action. Concern for face can generate pressure to conform. In contexts where concern for others' face is high it is a powerful mechanism that drives other-directed behavior as people act in ways that demonstrate a high level of sensitivity to how others perceive one's actions and the effect they have on others (Ho 1994:272). Face plays a significant role at every level of social interaction. It functions as a structuring mechanism for social interaction by guiding the formation of both social identity and relationships (Goffman 1955:226).

Face, Social Honor, and Claim-Right

Also critical for a proper understanding of face is the close link between face and the broader notion of social honor. As Ting-Toomey notes (2004:220), culturally specific honor codes are always closely associated with face and facework behavior. The concept of face highlights, in a very specific way, the communicative and relational dimensions of social honor. A particularly critical issue for a proper understanding of face is that of face as a type of claim-right.

This notion of honor as a claim-right is a key feature of anthropologist Frank Stewart's brilliant analysis of social honor. Indeed, it is honor

---

on interpersonal behavior that people act as isolated individuals making decisions based upon self-interest. In particular, he applies the Chinese notion of *bao* (relational reciprocity) to the study of face, highlighting how reciprocity undergirds the hierarchically ordered Chinese social world. He concludes that it is impossible to understand Chinese face without reference to this basic pattern of relations.

as a claim-right that illuminates how systems of honor (and dishonor) actually work. Stewart suggests that at its core, honor is a right. More specifically, honor is the possession of, or claim to possess, a right to certain types of behavior toward myself. It is "a right that something be done by another" (Stewart 1994:21). The bearer of this right, for whatever specific reasons, possesses characteristics that entitle him to the right to respect (1994:21). What actually constitutes the basis of this right can vary widely (e.g., social standing, moral virtue, physical characteristics, wealth). The world, however, has the obligation to offer a certain type of respectful behavior to the bearer of the right.

If true, this explains why both personal insult (assault on internal honor) and the withdrawal of respect from society (failure to support external honor) are problematic. I believe that, because I am a certain type of person or because I have done such and such, I am worthy of respect. Society owes such to me. This is inherent in the well-known definition of honor from anthropologist Julian Pitt-Rivers—honor is one's "estimation of his own worth, his claim to pride, but it also the acknowledgment of that claim, his excellence recognized by society, his right to pride" (Pitt-Rivers 1977:1). Again, honor "implies not merely an habitual preference for a given mode of conduct, but the entitlement to a certain treatment in return" (1977:1). Not to receive such honor produces frustration. The various experiences associated with the concept of honor then depend to a large degree upon this dynamic of being a claim-right. I believe that because I am such-and-such type of person, I am *worthy* of respect. Society in effect *owes* such to me. I am thus *entitled* to a specific treatment in return. The notion of claim-right is the "trigger" that activates any honor system.

Like social honor, face also functions because of this claim-right. To possess face involves a "debt" that should be "paid" by proper behavior. That is, I "earned" or "deserve" face because I "associate" or "conform" to norms, status role expectations, or other behavior that a given culture specifies as face-productive. The particular face logic will differ from culture to culture. Yet, the notion of claim-right will always answer the questions, "By virtue of what is this person due face?" and "To what sorts of behavior does this type of face entitle a person?" From such a perspective, we may gloss the loss of face as "losing the right to a certain type of respect." Viewing face as a claim-right also allows us to understand face attachment. Though we all possess face and engage in facework, not everyone invests face and face-related behavior with the same degree of significance.

Some, convinced of their absolute right to the type of face-deferent behavior deemed appropriate for their type of face, will be resolute in their vigorous defense of their face. They will also likely be equally vigorous in the demand that others act in accordance with the proper face-deferential behavior. When people do not appropriately serve the face claim-rights of others, or are denied the proper face claim-right respect and behavior due them, conflict will often result. This is so because such individuals hold to a high level of face attachment. The attitude of such a person would be something like, "I am rightfully entitled to treatment in accordance with my level of face and I will demand that such behavior be rendered!"

Alternately, there is the individual who wears their face and concomitant claim-rights more loosely. This very different approach works with a relativized perspective on face claim-rights. Such an individual may very well recognize the validity of these face claim-rights and the general appropriateness of the requisite face-deferential behavior others should render. Despite this awareness, however, these people hold such claims as relative and may allow other considerations (the needs of others, pragmatic concerns, a desire to avoid conflict) to limit, possibly even eliminate, any attempts to demand or expect the appropriate deferential behavior from others. Such, ultimately, is the result of a low level of face attachment. The attitude that typifies this type of person would be, "Face is fine if you can get it, but I'm not going to demand it or work hard to enforce appropriate face-related behavior." Similarly, face attachment may vary in the different dimensions of face. Thus, a person may be profoundly attached to their claim-right involved with personal face yet remain unconcerned with their social face. Or, an individual may hold a high level of attachment to their negative-face wants yet not attach particular significant at all to their positive face. The level of face attachment for an individual or even entire culture may also differ variously among competence face, autonomy face, and fellowship face.

Summary

The concept of face has been the victim of loose conceptualizations and imprecise definitions.[10] Ting-Toomey, reflecting on this, notes that

---

10. Such is evident in the varying definitions of face that scholars have rendered. Thus, Goffman identifies face as "the positive social value a person effectively claims for himself by the line others assume he has taken during a particular contact" (1955:213). The sociolinguist politeness approach Brown and Levinson offer designates face as "the

... the conceptualizations, the linkages, and the operationalizations of face or facework in conjunction with other face-related concepts remain vague and fuzzy. How face is being conceptualized and evoked is not specified in some studies, and the corresponding relationships between face and facework process often are not articulated. Further, the cultural, relational, contextual, or communication parameters of face and face behavior have not been clearly identified. (1994:2)

Rather than offer a specific definition of face or a comprehensive theory, I have provided a discussion of basic dimensions of face that is particularly important for a more adequate and Christian account toward which this project works.

First, face is a universal phenomenon. Any account of face, then, must reject an understanding that posits face as something inherently wrong or only a possession of certain cultures. The ubiquity of face is not a cause for lament but provides the opportunity to develop healthier and more adequate understanding of face and facework.

Second, face is clearly a dynamic and complex reality. This is partly attributable to the ways face relates directly to the self. It is a projection of the human self and only exists as an extension of or correlate to our selves, whether conceived of as more independent or more interdependent. Yet, face does not reside within a solitary individual. It is an inherently social notion and differs considerably from self-esteem, self-concept, self-image, ego, and pride, since the self can claim all these irrespective of another's perspective (Lim 1994:210). One may not speak of face as some personal possession, something lodged within the self (though a person may indeed hold to some ideal of the face they possess or claim). Face is a meaningful notion only in relation to others within a social matrix of some kind (Ho 1976:882). Being a social reality, face is inherently relational. As Ting-Toomey notes, face "entails the presentation of a civilized front to another individual within the webs of interconnected relationships in a particular

---

public self-image that every member wants to claim for himself (herself)" (1978:66). Face, contends Ting-Toomey, "involves the claimed sense of self-respect or self-dignity in an interactive situation" (1994:3). Cupach and Metts define face as the "conception of self that each person displays in particular interactions with others," which is essentially an "identity that he or she wants to assume and wants others to accept" (1994:3). Tracy designates face as the "socially situated identities people claim or attribute to others" (1990:210). Ho offers a definition more relational in scope: "In terms of two interacting parties, face is the reciprocated compliance, respect, and/or deference that each party expects from, and extends to, the other party" (1976:883).

culture" (Ting-Toomey 1994:1). Though a projection of the social agent, the fact that others also play an active and essential part in the construction of face makes face dynamics a considerably variable reality. Such reflects, as Arundale notes, the conjoint co-constructing roles of both self and other in the production of face (2004).

Finally, face is a culturally variable phenomenon. Specific cultural contexts profoundly shape the various configurations face takes. The distinguishing of different types of face (e.g., autonomy face, competence face, fellowship face, social face, personal face) provides a way of viewing face as universal yet culturally distinct. The culturally specific norms of social honor will dictate much of the specific shape face will take. Specifically, face involves a claim-right. When people project their face, it is an implicit claim for validation, though the "value placed upon (face) and the means for attaining it vary considerably" (Hu 1944:45). The individual claims face from society. Society then has the option of granting or rejecting this claim. Thus, face always involves the dynamic interplay of application (by the social agent) and ratification or rejection (by others). What we term "face" is only a single moment extracted from the dynamic ebb and flow of this application-and-response dialectic. The culturally specific shape of face, and the varying face "logic" that activates face in its cultural contexts, requires any accounts of face to be culturally specific and linguistically nuanced. We should refrain from prematurely applying general models to face research. It is only after understanding the distinct characteristics and culturally specific shape of face that face researchers can effectively address the critical face questions.[11] These distinctions, as face theory and self-presentation theory suggest, provide critical conceptual notions for moving awareness of face beyond negative stereotypes and typical Western misunderstandings. Additionally, viewing face as a universal, culturally variable phenomenon related to the human self in relationship provides a critical link to the theological perspectives I develop in Part 3.

---

11. Such questions would include, though are not limited to, the following: What is the role of culture in framing the specific notions of face and facework strategies? What does a given context require to produce face? How can we uncover culturally relevant, situated domains of face? How can we prevent our own cultural biases from eclipsing our own interpretation and theorizing about face and facework? (Ting-Toomey and Cocroft 1994:325–26).

5

Theoretical Reflections on Thai Face

ANTHROPOLOGY CAN BE A trendy enterprise. Traditionally, Western academic culture has been the context in which scholars have carried out formal Thai anthropological studies. As such, it comes as no surprise that while the subject of study has been Thai culture, the Western academic community has set the agenda. Thus, one can read scholarly debates on the problem of Thai religious consistency (i.e., how Buddhism, Brahmanism, and Thai animism interrelate), how to explain apparent individualistic behavior in a supposed collectivistic culture, and to what extent notions of power underwrite Thai society. These studies, as helpful as they may indeed be, raise the more basic question of whether they are addressing fundamental issues or are simply mirroring the particular Western scholarly tastes and trends.

Despite this general neglect, several have offered substantive treatments of Thai face. In this section, I summarize those scholars whose discussions are essential for understanding the study of Thai face.

Thai Face as "Social Cosmetic"

Phillips (1965) offers the first extended treatment on issues relating to Thai face. In his study on Thai peasant personality, Philips developed the notion of the "social cosmetic," shorthand for the Thai preoccupation with issues of gaining or preserving face (i.e., honor) and avoidance of losing face (i.e., shame).[1] He terms this cosmetic as a mode of politeness that represents a Thai's sense of civilized social interaction, aimed at maintaining social equilibrium (1965:66).

Phillips lists the positive strategies that accompany this social cosmetic, for example, choosing topics of conversation of interest or entertaining to others; flattering others to make them feel good; being silent, attentive, and eager when others are speaking; not challenging the veracity of a speaker's statement; expressing disagreement or alternative views carefully and indirectly; laughter and smiling, particularly if the topic is uncomfortable one; and preoccupation with small talk (Phillips 1965:71–72). In essence, what he provides is a listing of preferred Thai facework strategies.

He notes that as a function of this social cosmetic, Thai conversation emphasizes formality and respect.

> The actual topic of conversation or non-verbal ritual that links the participating individuals together may be either meaningful or inconsequential, but that is essentially irrelevant when compared to the fact that the respect the participants feel for each other is being communicated. In essence, much of the villagers' interaction is based on certain formal, rather than substantive, considerations, the net effect of which is to minimize the impact that they might have upon each other but to maximize each person's sense of psychic independence and integrity. (Phillips 1965:66–67)

Likewise, avoidance of shameful topics in conversation is

> . . . one of the most pronounced facets of village social life. To a Westerner accustomed to outspokenness, the types of situations that villagers define as embarrassing and the lengths to which they will go to avoid them sometimes appear to border on the sadomasochistic. (1965:69)

Phillips is representative of a religious approach to Thai face. That is, he contends that ultimate motivation for face and facework is accumulation of Buddhist merit, that is, the meritorious value that accrues to those who act in accordance with the social cosmetic (Phillips 1965:76). To act appropriately is "both a manifestation and validation of the self that one is a fine, proper, and upstanding person; that to treat others well is to perform one's role as a civilized, meritorious person" (1965:76). Assuming the

---

1. Although not specifically referencing the notion of face, he does quote Goffman's idea of face as somewhat parallel to his notion of social cosmetic (Phillips 1965:66).

norm of an idealized "meritorious person," Phillips concludes that the use of such social cosmetic strategies fulfillls this basic religious impulse.

Thai Face as "Facade"

Another approach is that taken by Mulder (1985; 1997; 2000). He writes of "presentation" (essentially a synonym for face), which is a kind of projected ego that society is always judging. Mulder distinguishes his discussion of face by a starkly negative evaluation, highlighting what he sees as the detrimental effects such has on Thai society.

He notes how for Thais this presentation of the self functions as a person's chief claim to status and forms the core of their social identity (Mulder 1985:66). This presentation of self through the vehicle of face comes to define a person's value and identity. Indeed, face is for many Thais so intimately connected to personal identity that for face to be detached or suffer loss may lead to a total collapse of personal identity (Mulder 2000:54). According to Mulder, such face presentation defines the social persona of each Thai person more in terms of conformity and power than of knowledge, integrity, or morality. It is the world of make-believe in which many people invest a great deal of emotion. When others attack that image, people's feelings of identity may collapse (2000:54).

Given such attachment to face, many Thais invest significant emotional and social resources. This importance also leads to a style of interpersonal relationality that is often extremely face-sensitive.

> Interaction between presentations, or "faces," should be smooth and fluid, and there is great security in kindness as a means to keep interaction so. Presentation, however, is much more than the enactment of non-committed kindness and unequal mutuality. It is an item in which is heavily invested and the investment is both an investment in smooth interaction and an investment in the personal show of being "big," of having prestige and being a social somebody. (Mulder 1985:68)

Because of such significant emotional and social investment, there exists a pervasive fear of "selling face," which functions to keep people in line, act morally, and enhance social conformity (Mulder 2000:63). "Everybody knows that all are extremely vulnerable to affronts against their 'face' and that revenge for a perceived insult, however unintended, may have extremely unpleasant consequences" (2000:88).

He does not limit his discussion to the individual, however, but engages broader social and political issues. For example, he describes a preoccupation with honor and face among Thai police. Such an attachment to image, Mulder notes, leads to a police force concerned to work against the image of Thailand in the world's eye as a haven of prostitutes and lawless power brokers, but does nothing to work against the actual wrongs of prostitution and criminality. This attachment to the facade of face, Mulder contends, perpetuates a system where those who bristle when Thailand loses face on a national scale (e.g., international news media pointing out Thailand's drug and prostitution business) are the very same individuals actively involved in the prostitution or drug trade.

Similarly, Mulder notes the financial motivation that results in the production of a positive national face. He provides an extended discussion on what he terms "image anxiety" in Thai politics and the national public media (Mulder 1997:183–241).[2] Such "image anxiety" leads Thais to ignore substantive issues and instead uphold a certain face for political or economic reasons (1997:201). Extreme versions of this, Mulder claims, result in the treatment of people as "irrelevant nationals under the sway of personalities and parochial interests that either manipulate or simply ignore them" (1997:201). In this way, Thai politics can often degenerate into a crass extended exercise in face manipulation oriented around power and personal aggrandizement. So, lack of appropriate government transparency, rampant vote buying during elections, and plagiarism in thesis writing among government officials all ultimately result from this kind of face anxiety (1997:216).

Thai Face as the "Ego Self"

Sanit Samarkan (1975) published the first significant piece on the salience of face for Thai culture. To date, it remains the single substantive treatment of face in the Thai language. In it, he defines Thai face as essentially a projection of the self, the representation of the Thai ego (1975:500). His research is valuable as it sets the definition of face as the "ego self," a definition utilized in much subsequent Thai research.[3]

---

2. His work also contains a serious and lengthy critique of the Thai government, which created a "National Identity Office of the Prime Minister," responsible to portray images appropriate to the goals and ideology of present Thai government interests (Mulder 1997:283–306).

3. This forms the basic understanding of face in the subsequent research of Suntaree Komin (1991; 1998) and Margaret Ukosakul (1999).

Sanit notes that the Thai language uses the term "face" as a metaphor more frequently than any other body part (Sanit 1975:497). He notes also that those who show positive regard for face are those that society holds in high esteem and in a personal way, find personal satisfaction when they act in accordance to the values of society. "A person who demonstrates very positive behavior related to face invariably is a person that society praises and in a personal way may be said to have succeeded and be happy" (1975:500–501; my translation).

His commentary on various Thai facework strategies, though brief, offers insight into the motivation and function of Thai face. Thus, the face behavior that is most correct or consistent with Thai culture is that of "upholding face," which includes "saving face," knowing how to "love face," and knowing how to "redeem face" (Sanit 1975:503). The Thai language designates those who desire others to admire them, or to see themselves as people of importance as people who "want to gain face" (1975:501). Sanit rightly points out the Thai distaste for anything that leads to loss or destruction of face. All such behavior is unacceptable to the Thai and most will go to great lengths in order to protect or keep from losing their own or others' face and endeavor to regain face if lost (1975:505). Face for most Thais is extremely important and one must labor to save or maintain face regardless of the cost. He concludes that Thai face practices are generally positive and right. Yet, he laments the increasing tendency for many to use material goods to enhance their own face. Instead, Sanit contends, the Thai people should exalt moral goodness and law-abiding lives as constitutive of their face (1975:505).

The research of Thai social psychologist Suntaree Komin offers an analysis of Thai personality and culture that assigns a preeminent position to face (1991; 1998). She argues against those who would posit religious explanations for Thai culture and, particular, those who would understand face and face-related behavior within a framework of Buddhism and merit accumulation.[4] Instead, Suntaree offers a sociocultural approach. Relying on an extensive nationwide survey, Suntaree provides statistical

4. For example, both Klausner (1993) and Mole (1973) argue that conflict avoidance and other Thai face behavior should be understood as result of Buddhist principles. In perhaps the most extensive treatment of this sort, Philips (1965) argues for its salience and prevalence as a Thai social modality under the rubric of "social cosmetic." He explains the motivation for this primarily in terms of its "meritorious" value, that is, the accumulation of Buddhist merit (Phillips 1965:76). Holding to the norms of an idealized "good person" created by Buddhist notions, he concludes that the use of such social cosmetic strategies fulfills this basic religious impulse.

and empirical evidence that would seem to place face and face concerns at the very core of the Thai psyche.

She offers a composite of ten cultural values most salient for Thai people. Among these ten most basic cultural values, she places the issue of Thai face as primary. Preserving one another's ego (face) is, according to Suntaree, the most fundamental rule of all Thai social interaction (1991:135). Indeed, so central is the preeminent concern for face maintenance that eight of the remaining nine most basic cultural values all function, she contends, to uphold and maintain Thai face.

Face, according to Suntaree, is essentially the ego self and is closely associated with pride, honor, and dignity (1998:222). For the Thai, face is not only central but also very sensitive. Thais "cannot tolerate any violation of the 'ego' self" (1991:134). Despite a cool and calm front, Thais can exhibit strong emotional reactions, particularly if the self or anybody close to the self (e.g., a father or mother) becomes the object of insult (1991:133).

This ego orientation which constitutes face lies behind much of the everyday patterns of Thai social behavior (Suntaree 1991:148) and undergirds many basic Thai cultural values, for example, *kreng chai* (polite social deference), criticism and conflict avoidance, indirectness in speech, and a joyful, carefree, smiling persona. Such Thai cultural characteristics are essentially "defense mechanisms to maintain the 'cosmetic' cover of mutual respect and acceptance while leaving the ego untouched. For the Thai, whenever the self-esteem is violated, strong emotional conflicts result, and once such violation of the self occurs, it often remains irreconcilable" (Suntaree 1998:224). All this is due to the high level of importance most Thais attach to face. In essence, Suntaree offers a view of Thai social life that results from protecting and enhancing self face and other face. That is, "preserving one another's 'ego' is the basic rule of all Thai interactions" (Suntaree 1991:135).

Thai Face as the "Container of Honor"

Margaret Ukosakul offers the most extensive treatment of Thai face (Ukosakul 1999). Working from the theoretical perspective of cognitive linguistics, Ukosakul provides a most useful and illuminating explicit treatment of the metaphorical nature of Thai face. Her use of cognitive linguistics seeks to demonstrate the interrelationship between metaphorical uses of "face" and reality (i.e., lived out experience). "In particular, for the Thai, the word naa 'face' is used as a metonym for the person" (1999:vii).

This follows the definition of face offered by Suntaree and Sanit as "ego" or "ego self" (1999:7) and is closely associated with one's self-esteem, dignity, pride, and honor (1999:132).

By describing the conceptual organization underlying the idioms that characterize the Thai concept of face, Ukosakul demonstrates the significance of face in Thai culture. The large number of contemporary face metaphors in the Thai language highlights the cultural salience that face, honor, and shame play in Thai culture (Ukosakul 1999:130). In particular, she suggests five specific metaphorical dimensions of Thai face: (1) face as the person, (2) face as personality, (3) face as personal honor, (4) face as countenance, and (5) face as emotions (e.g., anger, happiness and sadness, fear, and shame).

Ukosakul's Prototype Model of Thai Shame

An intriguing feature of her analysis is the construction of a prototypical scenario of shame—a "coherent conceptual organization underlying the idioms that characterize the Thai concept of shame" (Ukosakul 1999:115). At the heart of this prototypical scenario is a container schema, that is, that face is like a container with honor constituting the internal contents. When there is damage to the container (face) then the contents (honor) also suffer damage. Thus, if there is an offending event, the damage to face results in the loss of honor. As she explains, "The container is the face. The content is honor. The physical damage to the container is emotional damage to the face. The restoration of the container is restoration of the face" (1999:129). She postulates this as consisting of five distinct stages: Stage 1—Offending Events; Stage 2—Loss of Honor; Stage 3—Behavioral Reaction; Stage 4—Recovering Honor; Stage 5—Preservation of Honor.

Thai Face as "Social Capital"

Aside from Ukosakul, Leela Bilmes (2001) offers the only other significant treatment of Thai face that interacts with the broader discussions of face and facework theory. She offers a sociolinguistic approach that examines the various ways face relates to Thai lexical forms and conventions. Her major goal is to examine Brown and Levinson's politeness theory against the Thai case. Yet, an ancillary goal, indeed an important one, is to explicate the concept of face in Thai culture. For her data she relies on discourse gained from Thai television talk shows and so, in contrast to Ukosakul, her methodology makes explicit use of actual discourse.

She highlights Thai linguistic features that relate directly to the issues of face. Thus, she discusses pronominal references and person-referring expressions (e.g., nicknames, status terms, kinship terms, and non-usage of pronominal reference), status or politeness particles, discourse particles that modify illocutionary force, and various other forms of Thai linguistic politeness. She also highlights the use of indirectness in Thai discourse. Particularly helpful is her analysis of Thai language usage and positive politeness (or positive face). She notes how Thais show interest in the addressee, flatter, compliment, and "entertain" in interactive situations. Her conclusion is that Thais demonstrate a strong orientation toward positive face and fellowship face, rather than autonomy face or negative face. "Social unity, to a much greater degree than individual rights or autonomy, is of paramount importance to Thais" (Bilmes 2001:188).

She advances strong reservations regarding the adequacy of Brown and Levinson's politeness theory to explain the dynamics of Thai face (Bilmes 2001:217–219). In contrast to the non-impositional negative politeness of Brown and Levinson, Bilmes contends that face and facework in Thai discourse generally function to preserve group harmony. Negative politeness is evident among Thais, yet "its aim is not, as Brown and Levinson predict, to preserve the hearer's autonomy and rights to property. Instead, the overarching goal of the polite behavior . . . is to keep the peace among the members of the main social unit, the group" (2001:202). Thai facework is oriented not toward preservation of the individual's social "space" but designed to foster group solidarity, personal inclusion, and smooth relationality. So, negative politeness as conceived by Brown and Levinson is inadequate to describe Thai facework and politeness phenomenon (2001:222). In contrast to much Western face theory, and that of Brown and Levinson in particular, Bilmes draws attention to the critically important affiliative and social nature of Thai face.

Additionally, she notes how face is more of a constant in Thai life (Bilmes 2001:212) and functions as precious social capital (2001:213) in contrast to the more Goffmanesque notion of face as situationally defined and predicated on the strategic goals of the individual actor.

A Critical Appraisal of Approaches to Thai Face

Having surveyed the significant treatments of face in Thai culture, I am now in a position to offer appraisal of these various accounts. These brief critiques will set the stage for the subsequent analysis of Thai face I offer in the following chapter.

"Social Cosmetic" and "Facade"

More than any other commentator on Thai face, Mulder consistently draws attention to the dark side of face, that is, how face, image, and honor function as a subterfuge for continuing unrighteous and even illegal activity. Yet, for all his social commentary, his understanding of face seems to work more from a commitment to a Western, supposedly non-face culture.

Speaking of face, Mulder notes that a posture of "self, of presenting one's social mask, is far from what a westerner, familiar as he is with popular psychology, would call personality" (1997:306). In social situations that involve peers or intimates, "people do not need to maintain the facade of presentation, but speak their mind (though not their psyche), and enjoy the pleasure of direct access . . . it is the occasion to sublimate frustrations and to relax" (Mulder 2000:65). Mulder paints a picture of a frustrated essentialized self behind the facade of self-presentation or face yearning for greater self-expression. He suggests a realm of "direct access" which can supposedly bypass face. Face is a mask that hides "the latent whirlpool of emotions and drives." He admires, in almost heroic terms, the Thai who flaunts these face constraints, refusing to fit in with social expectations and surroundings. Such "try to stand on their own feet, and seem indifferent to the socially inspired self-identity with which most people have to content themselves" (2000:91).

Clearly, Mulder does not offer neutral ethnographic description. Indeed, his treatment borders on ethnocentric polemics. An apparent commitment to Western presuppositions about the self and social relations biases profoundly his commentary on Thai face. Essentially, his critique rails against the fellowship-face dimension of Thai face. His strong cultural bias toward an individually oriented autonomy face and competence face prevents Mulder from understanding the fuller, and indeed positive, dynamics in Thai face. Additionally, Mulder is guilty of a problem that besets much Western discussion of face. That is, he views face as a facade that could—and, in fact, should—be disposed of in favor of a more direct and "truthful" mode of sociality. If face theory and self-presentation theory are correct, however, we simply cannot escape face as Mulder suggests.

Mulder also seems to hold a decisive attachment to the modern Western independent self. His only support for a claim-right for honor or face seems to lie in the autonomy-face expressions characteristic of this Western individualistic social mode. Though he effectively highlights what qualifies as the dark side of face, his overall treatment is severely limited by his almost exclusive glossing of face as a negative and a deceptive facade. His evaluation of Thai face does not reflect an understanding of the critical theoretical frameworks that would enable a more nuanced, and consequently less biased, interpretation.

Though not beset by the same level of negative Western bias, Phillips also falls prey to certain Western conceptions. His notion of face as a social cosmetic fails to provide an adequate understanding of face. This is the case because, so labeled, "social cosmetic" is not the universally present and socially necessary experience face actually represents. A cosmetic is something one applies as another layer to an already existing face. It is a decorative, second-order phenomenon. Yet, as face theorists and self-presentation theorists demonstrate, face is not something we can choose to either put on or leave off. Face represents a first-order social happening; though existing in varying modes, it nevertheless remains a necessary component of human relationality.

Phillips emphasizes the negative-face dimensions inherent in Thai sociality. Thus, he notes "formal" rather than "substantive" relationality, which aims to minimize imposition and provide personal independence (Phillips 1965:66–67). Likewise, his interpretation posits a basic face orientation toward preventing face loss and avoidance of imposition. Though true enough, his interpretation seems one-sided and misses the substantive bonding force face clearly presents for most Thais.

Additionally, the notion of social cosmetic reveals a rather individualistic and Western evaluation of face as an external social veneer concealing truth and authentic expression. He understands face as a surface-level phenomenon applied to the more basic human self. The essentialized, internal self of the modern West seems to lurk in the background of his evaluation. Both he and Mulder view face primarily as a projection of the individual self rather than, as the face theorists contend, something co-created in the flow of social interaction. Finally, Phillip's notion of the putative meritorious function of face is clearly inadequate to explain face, as it is both too individualistic and bypasses the clear sociocultural and identity-boundary functions of face.

"The Ego Self"

The evaluations of face Sanit and Suntaree provide are critical for three reasons. First, they are both Thai researchers and so evaluate face as cultural insiders. Indeed, the work of Sanit represents not only the first academic attempt to explicate the notion of Thai face but remains the only substantive treatment published in Thai. Unfortunately, he bases his analysis mostly on personal experiences and anecdotes. However accurate his conclusions, his weak research data and lack of rigorous methodology are problematic.

Both Sanit and Suntaree recognize the critical importance of face for most Thais. Their research argues persuasively that face is at the core of Thai personality and is responsible for much of Thai culture. By doing so, they make a strong case for understanding face and its function in social terms, and not as a product of Buddhist impulses. Though both Sanit and Suntaree discuss negative dimensions of Thai face, they recognize and evaluate the positive social function as well. In this, they appear to avoid the strong Western bias of Mulder and Phillips.

Yet, some question does remain about the way this "ego self" relates to face. Suntaree seems to equivocate here. She adheres to face as the "ego self" or "ego representation." Thus, "the 'face' is identical with 'ego' and is very sensitive" (Suntaree 1991:135). Yet, she can also use the concept of the "true self" to frame her discussion. In writing about the facework strategies involved in the Thai "social cosmetic," Suntaree notes that "while there may be some who internalize such traits and develop 'affiliative' personalities, for many others, the 'dependent' behavior only serves as a means, as social ritual independent of the true self" (1998:223). Such confusion may represent her reliance on typologies of the self from Western social psychology rather than the more recent and cross-culturally helpful notions of independent self and interdependent self.

"Container of Honor" and "Social Capital"

The work of Ukosakul has much to commend. Her cognitive linguistic approach focuses on actual linguistic conventions and represents a much more rigorous approach than many others who rely upon the "anthropological privilege" of anecdotal commentary. The sheer number of the face idioms she discusses[5] lends strong support of her overall contention that

---

5. She discusses twenty-eight idioms for "The Face Stands for the Person," twenty-two idioms for "The Face Stands for One's Personality," thirty-five idioms for "The Face Stands for One's Honor," sixteen idioms for "The Face Stands for One's Countenance,"

face (and the parallel experiences of honor and shame) is central to Thai society (Ukosakul 1999:130).

Her work, however, also exhibits several weaknesses.[6] First, she highlights two critical dimensions of face-related experience, that is, honor and shame. Yet, by tying her examination of face to the notions of honor and shame she unnecessarily restricts her study. Though clearly salient components of the face "game," the experiences connected with face encompass a broader range of cultural phenomena than honor and shame.

One problem is that her notion of honor essentially collapses the closely related yet clearly distinct notions of reputation, dignity, fame, prestige, self-esteem, and respect. Though all these are unquestionably types of social honor and are variously related to face, it is highly questionable whether in fact these terms can be so easily conflated.

Another limitation involves her use of cognitive linguistic methodology. Although she does consult individual Thais (she interviewed seven people—Ukosakul 1999:3) to elicit metaphors and other face-related information, the majority of her data comes from literary sources (e.g., dictionaries, thesauruses, and other non-personal sources of linguistic information). This approach is problematic because it does not actually rest upon a foundation of insider information and discourse. Indeed, this is the same type of criticism some have leveled against the cognitive linguistic approach of Lakoff (Quinn and Strauss 1996:159). Since Ukosakul explicitly follows Lakoff in her approach, it is no surprise that her research reflects the same limitations.

She does little work in the area of establishing the basic parameters of face itself, that is, the particular constitutive elements of face and the various ways face may be given or lost. Indeed, in her analysis, it seems that she places an undo stress on issues relating to loss of face and glosses over the equally critical issue of positive face gain and maintenance. Her prototypical scenario of shame (Ukosakul 1999:115–131) privileges the experience of shame rather than face or honor. This is unfortunate since shame is a byproduct of the loss of face. Possession of face is actually the proper center of the Thai face experience. Such would form a more proper center for a prototypical scenario. This fundamental importance of face

---

and sixty-six idioms for "The Face Stands for One's Expression of Emotions" (Ukosakul 1999:136–226).

6. Much of my critique here relies upon an interpretation of Thai face that I propose in the next chapter.

possession suggests that there should be an additional stage, which her model assumes but does not make explicit. That is, the entire prototypical scenario moves between the twin poles of face possession and face recovery (which is once again gaining the state of face possession).

Her prototypical scenario of shame (face loss) relies on a container schema, contending that the face is like a container with honor constituting the contents within. When there is damage to the container (face) then the contents (honor) also suffer damage. Thus, if there is an offending event, the damage to face results in the loss of honor. This use of the container schema, however, is problematic. Viewing face as a container with honor as its contents ignores the reciprocal co-constituting relationship that exists between the two notions. Face does not exist prior to or independently of honor. The honor-face link does not appear to be one of linear causality but rather one of co-constitution. This relationship is clearly more complicated than the overly simplistic conceptualization Ukosakul advances.

Her contention that all Thai linguistic terms that describe honor involve either the term *nâ* (face) or *kìat* (honor) is incorrect (Ukosakul 1999:67). Likewise, her contention that all shame-inducing events must be of a public nature (1999:118) reflects an outdated and incorrect understanding of the shame experience. Lastly, it is unfortunate that her work demonstrates an overreliance on poor sources (e.g., Noble 1975, Chaiyan 1994) to substantiate major parts of her argument. So, for example, it would have been better to elicit the stages of her prototypical scenario from actual emic information rather than use the questionable framework from a popular-level source such as Noble.

Bilmes is surely correct in her suspicion of the adequacy of the politeness theory of Brown and Levinson to explicate Thai face. Her examination of the function of negative politeness or negative face in the Thai language provides solid grounds for viewing the function of Thai face in relation to group harmony. Clearly, face functions as a form of useable social capital.

Although the validity of some of her study is limited by the large number of sweeping generalizations and apriorism in her argumentation, Bilmes's work remains valuable for it is a critical evaluation of Thai face within the larger framework of face and facework theory and its reliance on face-laden discourse of actual Thai speakers.

Together, Ukosakul and Bilmes remind us the necessity to study actual discourse in specific linguistic contexts. Their careful attention to what Thai people actually say about face (whether in conventionalized idiomatic usage per Ukosakul or that of Thai television talk shows per Bilmes) is a reminder of Herzfeld's directive of "ethnographic particularism" (Herzfeld 1980:349). They also illustrate multifaceted dimensions of face and face-related behavior.

Summary

The critical issue of Thai face has not often received proper scholarly attention. Although there are examples to the contrary, most do not interact with the broader academic discussions involving face and facework. Yet, the research various scholars offer legitimates face not simply as a proper area of study but as a central issue for understanding Thai culture.

Having surveyed important theoretical concepts from face theory and self-presentation theory, and interacted with academic discussions of Thai face, I am now in a better position to make a preliminary assessment of Thai face. As Bilmes has shown, an application of Western face theory (e.g., Brown and Levinson) proves inadequate in the Thai context. Though the contributions of these scholars highlights important aspects of Thai face, there remains a need for a fuller descriptions of the mechanics of Thai facework and a more adequate definition of face in Thai culture. Such a treatment must acknowledge how face is ubiquitous and central, multivalent and complex, and culturally specific in its shape. It is toward this goal that the next chapter proceeds.

6

A Description of Thai Face

FACE IS PREGNANT WITH cultural meaning. That is, face in the Thai context functions as a nexus for important cultural values and patterns. This chapter attempts to probe this meaning more deeply and to explain more fully the "key" in which Thai face is played. To do this, I will examine interview data to understand salient dynamics of Thai face and facework.

As I noted earlier, many face and facework theorists now argue the need for self-critical and reflexive awareness of various shortcomings of existing studies. Two issues stand out—a critical need for more detailed studies, and analyses that are culturally specific. This project, following such an agenda, attempts to pay particular attention to the culturally specific contours and shape of face as it exists in the Thai cultural context. By doing so, I plan to develop a middle-range, domain- and linguistically-specific, emic framework for understanding Thai face. Such, I believe, resists Herzfeld's notion of using honor terminology as glosses for extremely general and varying dimensions of such experiences. This description of Thai face also aspires to provide the linguistically nuanced, culturally and domain specific study for which many have recently called (Chang and Holt 1994, Ting-Toomey and Cocroft 1994, Tracy and Baratz 1994).

Based upon such an approach, I will contend that an adequate cultural model of Thai face involves the following characteristics: face is a *possession* connected to the *self* that arises from *acceptance* and *distinction*, and it is *visible*, *valuable*, and *variable*. Such a generalized cultural model likely serves as a map (albeit, a tacit map most Thais are not aware of in any explicit fashion) for much Thai social interaction, providing cues and directions for navigating social space and also functioning as an interpretive heuristic through which many Thais naturally view others' actions and motives.[1] I will also identify an eight-stage prototypical Thai face scenario, which is an important component of this cultural model.

Methodology

Since this book represents an effort to develop data-rich, emic understandings of Thai face, the research methods I employed both served the goals of exploratory research as well as research designed to develop a relatively broad framework. It was not a testing of preliminary hypotheses. Also, I did not attempt to address any specific theoretical issues nor apply specific theory to a context. This book represents an attempt—albeit a preliminary one—to build from the ground-up a more robust understanding of what some Thai people think regarding the issue of face. Instead of formal and discrete stages, this work represents what Grounded Theory advocates, that is, data collection, data analysis, and theory building in a dynamic, iterative dialectic that does not follow a logico-deductive process. "The grounded theory method stresses discovery and theory development rather than logical deductive reasoning which relies on prior theoretical frameworks" (Charmaz 1994:96). This work, then, does not rely heavily on theoretical literature since practitioners of grounded theory contend that the data itself should shape the ideas and analysis (1994:96). During coding, grounded theorists carefully examine the statements and actions of respondents looking for patterns, inconsistencies, contradictions, and intended and unintended consequences (1994:98). Once themes and patterns emerge, the researcher works with these, trying to understand how they interact and ultimately seeking to produce theories or models.

---

1. For example, a missionary who was working with a group of Thai church leaders noted how these Thais viewed the American "war on terror." Soon after the 2001 attack on the World Trade Center a Thai newspaper published a photo of American president George Bush at ground zero posing with what the Thai leaders and the missionary concluded was a somewhat macho look. One of the leaders remarked, "Complete broken face," referring to Bush's (and America's) wounded honor from the attacks. The others leaders concurred and what followed was a discussion on how Bush was acting to save the broken face of the American people. This interpretation was surprising to the missionary who would have anticipated other concerns (e.g., the need for justice, compassion, national safety) to be part of the way they conceived of Bush's rationale for war. Yet, for this group of Thai Christian leaders, face-related concerns, correct or not, were the natural impulse for viewing the situation.

There are many things that Thais do not explicitly reference as "face" that fall within the rubric of that which face theorists term face. These are legitimate areas to research and probe. Yet, a sort of "naturally occurring" place to begin studying such a vast topic is to focus upon face notions that are encoded linguistically into the Thai language. Such explicit and conventionalized face terminology remained the center of my study.

Happily, the Thai language contains a rich lexicon of such explicit face and face-related terms. Thais linguistically encode in their language much of the face "game," which, though present in other cultural contexts, is in them not as explicit and conventionalized in everyday language. An approach that focuses specifically on how native actors linguistically encode face notions seems a useful entry point for providing a fuller description of Thai face. So, an initial task was to form a sufficiently helpful taxonomy of face terms.

To do this I relied upon two phases of research. The first phase consisted of five informal interviews among local Thai Christians I conducted while in Pasadena, California. All were native speakers of the Thai language. My intent was simply to gain a fuller taxonomic map of face. I utilized free-listing (Bernard 2002:282–85) and frame elicitation (2002:285–87), two approaches particularly helpful in constructing folk taxonomies (2002:505). Initially, taxonomic analysis provided a helpful starting point, functioning as a heuristic device for further investigation. Componential analysis further guided my research, helping to formulate basic sub-hypotheses. Domain analysis, taxonomic analysis, and componential analysis (Spradley 1979:107ff.) yielded a clearer understanding of the conceptual domain of Thai face. This research led to basic understandings of Thai face and was critical for constructing an initial set of interview questions I used in the second stage of research.

The second stage involved informal interviews that I conducted among Thais in Chiang Mai, Thailand, during a one-month period from mid-January through mid-February 2004. I continued exploratory probing with seventeen semi-structured interviews seeking to extend ideas derived from non-structured interviews among Thais in Los Angeles. Specifically, I worked to extend the initial research interests from this earlier stage and to surface new face-related terminology, categories, and notions. I reached theoretical saturation at twenty-nine different facework strategies when I could no longer detect new categories or new relationships between categories.[2] To view the complete listing of these terms, see Appendix C.

2. One interesting facet of this process was discovering several different face-related

I took this information and, in dialogue with my Thai research assistant, constructed a structured interview guide. I then trained two Thai assistants in the use of the guide and the theoretical concerns that guided its particular shape. Together we conducted sixty-seven interviews, ranging in length from forty-five minutes to two hours. I conducted all interviews in the Thai language. The demographic breakdown for all respondents appears in Appendix A. For data analysis, I used the qualitative research program NVivo to evaluate responses.

Ideally, my interviews would have probed each one of the twenty-nine facework strategies. In reality, however, there simply was not enough time to do such a thorough examination of this rather extensive semantic domain. Perhaps if my focus were exclusively the meaning of these various strategies, I could have accomplished a more comprehensive study for all these terms. Yet, there were so many interesting and important dimensions to face that I also wished to understand. Therefore, in a practical compromise, I decided to focus specific questions on only a few of these particular strategies.

The rationale for choosing these specific terms was simple. As the interviews progressed it became increasingly clear that only a limited number of the entire range of facework strategies occurred with any regularity for most people. So, it was unlikely to be profitable to try to investigate every single facework term or saying. Several terms seemed to rise above the rest in terms of their overall significance for understanding the face game. Thus, I designed questions that addressed the following: *mi nâ* ("possess face"), *rák-sa nâ* ("save face"), *kû nâ* ("redeem face"), *sia nâ* ("lose face"), *khai nâ* ("sell face"), *dâi nâ* ("gain face"), and the related three strategies of *sà-noe nâ* ("promote face"), *ao nâ* ("take face"), and *yàk dâi nâ* ("want to get face").[3] In the end, I chose to focus on these particular terms, as they seemed to provide a clearer basic understanding of face and, particularly, the relational dimension of face and facework. Each term undoubtedly represents interesting and profitable areas for further study. Further study might examine all the various facework strategies available for frequency, salience, and greater definitional precision.

---

terms Ukosakul's work on Thai face utilized, terms that apparently were no longer part of contemporary Thai usage. The implication is that the lexicon of face terminology is likely never static and should not be assumed without soliciting terms from contemporary usage embedded in actual discourse.

3. For romanization of Thai characters, I follow the 1954 guidelines from the Thai Royal Institute.

Facework Strategies

I categorized all twenty-nine of the facework terms into a small number of basic themes. It is possibly to group these straightforwardly into the following categories: face possession, face depletion, face gain, face recovery, and face maintenance. These themes, then, form the outline of the ensuing discussion.

Face Possession

The phrase "possess face–possess eyes" is likely the most common way of referring to face possession. As I will discuss below, this tag has a rather specific meaning related to having a distinguishable amount of social face. This is to be distinguished from the more general phrase "possess face." Here, I will differentiate between these two by using the phrase "face-person" to designate one who "possesses face–possesses eyes" and the phrase "possess face" as a direct rendering of the Thai phrase "to possess face." This is not simply a linguistic convention but represents a significant distinction, which I will discuss presently.

An initial question I asked, aimed at developing a composite profile of someone who possessed face, was "Who is it that possesses face–possesses eyes?" The most typical responses identified such individuals as the prime minister of Thailand, the king, sports and entertainment stars, teachers, business people, those in "high society," and the wealthy. That is, for most people a face-person seemed to represent someone who was noticeably visible, of high status, and relatively well known.

I aimed to probe more deeply to understand the specific characteristics that such people exhibit, so I also asked, "What characteristics do you think face-people have?" Of the 132 responses, I coded the following themes:

TABLE 2: CHARACTERISTICS OF "FACE-PEOPLE"

Recognition	35
Status	30
Personal characteristics	20
Honor	17
Outstanding	15
Moral	8
Accepted by society	7

This falls into line with the general notion of a face-person, that is, an individual who is recognized, holds some level of status and honor, is distinguished or outstanding in some particular fashion. With such a definition, only certain and relatively distinct people can be properly termed face-people, for example, those with status or certain culturally affirmed traits that produce recognition. In this mode, face seems to represent an outward, visible, distinct level of societal status and recognition.

At one level, such a definition of a face-person seems self-evident. The human face is something that is seen and continuously on display. It is also something unique, as all people's faces are their own and belong to no other. However, this notion of face-person does not fully capture all the significant dimensions of Thai face. Though people do talk about face as the notion of what a face-person represents, there is more to possessing face. This appears to be true simply by probing everyday usage of face terms. That is, though few possess face as a face-person does, everyone can suffer all sorts of face loss. How is it that if only certain people possess face (i.e., face-people) others who are not face-people have face to lose? How can one suffer the loss of what one does not have?

To probe this conundrum I asked, "Do you think that everyone possesses face? Please explain." Interestingly, of the very same respondents that provided the profile of a face-person mentioned above, thirty-nine responded that everyone possessed face, while fifteen said that only some did. Clearly, it seemed, there was a dimension to face possession that marked a substantial difference for many between the notions of face-person and simple face possession. That a different dimension or valence of face was implicit here is also supported in another way. When answering questions regarding the types of people who are face people and the descriptive characteristics such people exhibit, no respondent offered a response hinting that face might be something every person could possess. In other words, there seemed to be such a clear difference between the notion of face-person (*these* sorts of people, *these* sorts of characteristics) and this other dimension of possessing face that no one thought to offer any disclaimer such as, "Well, such-and-such are face-people, but of course, everyone possesses face." It took other questions to tease out such a difference.

Typical of those who answered that only some people possessed face were the following responses: "Not every person. Mostly it's people with status [that] have people respect [them], people accept [them]" (B1:4); "Not every person because I think possessing face-possessing eyes is being know in high society, not the average person" (B15:1–3).[4] For these, it seems, the two phrases "possess face" and "possess face–possess eyes" were essentially synonymous or conflated.

Then there was the significantly higher percentage (72 percent) who responded that everyone possessed face. "All possess [face] because society has made it that way. The joining together of humans—there has got to be the giving of honor. [This] makes every person want to have a part of that society" (B13:1–2). "[All] possess [face] because every person has dignity, has a society. No one accepts their own less acceptable points. It all depends on how much we strive for it [face]" (B9:3–4). An important clue to understanding this apparent tension between the different dimensions of face is found in a trend that emerged among these responses. Fourteen of the thirty-nine who responded that all people possess face explicitly mention "society" as a causal factor. For these, it appears, face was a "universal" possession because living in society inevitably created face. At a basic level, then, being in relationship in social contexts apparently creates face.

To the question, "Do you agree with the statement, 'Every person is a face-person'?" seventeen respondents agreed while nine disagreed. Those that disagreed answered along the lines of face-people being socially outstanding and well known. That is, most who took issue with the question responded that being a face-person was about distinction. Not all are "known" and thus not all are face-people. Although many that agreed did not comment extensively on their rationale, some highlighted why it was they could associate the notion of face-person with everyone. Six responded with the rationale that all people, despite their standing or reputation, are part of society and are in relationship. In their own limited group, people still possessed face and in fact were face-people. "Every person is a face-person. [They] have space to show themselves" (M17: 4–5). That is, all people exist in social space and reveal themselves in that space. In society, all are known at some level by some people; thus, this relationality produces a face-person.

I asked in my interviews for respondents to reflect on these twin notions with the question, "What do you think about the statements 'All

---

4. From this point on, I will use a specific designation for my coded interview data. The letter and the first number represent the interviewee (e.g., B15 and M2 designate specific people I interviewed) and the number following the colon (e.g., B15:48) is the paragraph number in the text of that particular transcribed interview. All quoted material is a result of my own translation from transcribed interviews.

possess face' and 'All are face-people'?" The following provide perspectives on this distinction.

> [These] are not the same. "Every person possesses face" means having face because of our deeds and those outside will watch us, so that others will be the ones who tell whether we possess face or don't possess face in society. "Every person is a face-person" means every person thinks that they possess face-eyes, but every person that thinks they possess face does not mean that they themselves always possess face in society. (B6:7–8)

> "Every person possesses face" is something already natural, and if it is "Every person is a face-person" then that probably comes from ability which that person may have done something useful for society, might have a prominent reputation or be a business person, a movie star, or an older actor. (B4:8)

> Every person possesses face for sure, but not every person is a face-person. Possessing face means every person having a level of emotion that is; they do not want anyone to look down on them. The difference is whether they possess face great or small . . . possessing face is a cause that leads to being a face-person, which is a result of it. But, both of these two are states that are able to indicate differences of importance in society. Possessing face happens to everyone, but being a face person is only for certain groups and everyone all around knows [them]. (M3:7–8)

There was considerable variation of in the responses as to who actually possesses face and what constitutes a face-person. Some seemed to use the phrases interchangeably with little precision. The responses of others indicated that for them a distinction did in fact exist. Data expressed in these responses leads me to posit that two fundamental dimensions of Thai face exist. First, there seems to be a personal dimension that is the possession of nearly all people who live in society. This personal face exists by virtue of any person being a member of society and in relationship with others. It seems to be a pervasive phenomenon that all participants in the field of social space automatically generate. A second type of face inheres more to prestigious individuals who are well known or differentiate themselves from the common folk in some particular way. This is the valence of face that is closely associated with the face-person. The first correlates with personhood (i.e., all people by virtue of being a human possess this sort of face) and relationality (this dimension is generated by participation in relationships within social space). The second connects more closely with the notion of social status. This stereotypical face person is distinguished in outstanding ways from the average person.

For the sake of clarity, I would like to designate the first, more personal face dimension as "personal face." The second, status-like dimension I will term "social face." For some these are distinct and for others, apparently, they are conflated to a considerable degree. Depending on the usage, these two notions (i.e., "possess face" and "face-person") may occasionally represent essentially the same idea. When such conflation occurs, they both seem to point to the more status-oriented dimension of face possession. Occasionally, however, speakers clearly distinguish between the two, referring to distinct though related dimensions of face, that is, personal face and social face.

Though this is obviously not a precise distinction, nonetheless this notion of a social type of face (face-person) that is distinct and exists at a higher level on the reputation hierarchy, over against a more ubiquitous personal-level face that all people (in theory) possess, seems to be a pervasive feature in the interview data. Such is clearly a real difference though not a neat and tidy distinction.

Face Depletion

A sizable amount of face terms in Thai relate to the issue of face depletion. In fact, in my data collection ten of the twenty-nine terms I surfaced indicate damage of some sort to a person's face.[5] These, in turn, can be divided further into two types of face depletion—those that depend upon the action of the self and those that are the result of what another does to the self. Those face-depleting terms that depend upon the action of another, that is, where some person does injury to one's face, tend to be those that are more aggressive and violent (thus, "cut off face," "strike face," "snap off face," "hammer face," "impugn face," "face breaks," and "tear off face" all fall into this category).

Responses to one question asking how respondents would feel and what they would do if a friend caused them to lose face, indicate that at the very least, causing others to lose face can negatively affect relationships and even result in their dissolution. A well-known US slogan states, "Friends don't let friends drive drunk." In Thailand, perhaps, good friends do not do things that endanger another's face or impugn a friend's honor.

---

5. In no particular order, these terms are *sia nâ* "lose face," *khai nâ* "sell face," *tàt nâ* "cut off face," *ti nâ* "strike face," *hàk nâ* "snap off face," *tòk nâ* "hammer face," *yam nâ* "impugn face," *nâ tàek* "face breaks," and *chìk nâ* "tear off face."

Here, I narrowed the question to focus upon what is likely the most generic and prevalent type of face depletion, that is, to lose face. What causes face loss? The bald withdrawal of public approval is present but seems secondary. First, and most heavily coded, responses about face loss indicated that failure is the essence of personal face depletion. Failure here may represent, it seems, almost any conceivable type of failure. Indeed, respondents noted many different types of failures, including falling in front of others (physical failure), speaking wrongly (speaking failure), and forgetting to zip up one's pants (appearance failure). More heavily coded themes include failure to live up to a promise, general undifferentiated failure, and personal incompetence. The two most prevalent responses were the failure to realize one's goals or attempts to achieve, and moral failure of some kind (e.g., breaking the law, committing adultery, lying, or simply generic "doing bad things" or "doing evil"). The types of failures interviewees mentioned ran from minor errors to egregious moral offenses. What seems to be the common thread is acting in a certain way that is out of line, something incongruous with normal expectations of what one should do or how one should act. The level of severity varied widely.

A second factor was that of audience awareness. Specifically, this appeared as negative reactions from others including criticism, speaking negatively, others not accepting, rejection, and gossip. This again highlights what is a given throughout—face loss is inevitably something that occurs in public and is dependent upon the awareness and the reaction of others. Taken together, these two major themes form the essential ingredients for what constitutes a face-depleting scenario. That is, the joining of the failure of the actor (some type of demonstration that the self is not a competent social actor) together with the negative evaluation of an audience is what generates face depletion. Together, these form the basis for all situations that qualify as loss of face.

To lose face is undeniably something people do not desire. One respondent stated the obvious—"There is no human who wants to lose face" (B15:48). Thais, as a rule, do not like to lose face and want to avoid all face depleting situations. Why is it that people attempt to avoid losing face? Of the one hundred coded responses (see Appendix C), twenty-eight simply noted that what motivates people to avoid face loss is the reaction of others —either negative attitudes or negative talk. Nearly as many responded that face loss either "feels bad" or involves "shame." Surely, the opinions of others, that is, what they say and what they think of us, ultimately have an effect on people because people invest considerable importance in their identity goals. People try to project certain identities and desire to be perceived in ways consistent with those identities. When face is lost, so too is the approval and positive sentiment from others. If these others are significant to the self, then this loss of approval and acceptance becomes injury. "[Nobody] wants to lose face. It lowers their personal value, makes others view us as having less value" (B6:51–52). Thus, affective concerns seem to be the primary motivation for avoiding the loss of face. Utilitarian concerns are present but seemingly less important.

Other comments regarding face depletion provided a deeper understanding of the nature of face. That is, what does the face people lose consist of? One respondent, when asked the question of whether everyone possessed face, answered, "Yes, everyone because when people are going to do something they think first because they don't want to lose face and that shame makes them feel face loss. [This] demonstrates that everyone possesses face" (B7:3–4). This respondent presents as evidence of face possession the fact that people think about and try to avoid face loss. If a person takes care to not lose something, by implication they in fact possess that thing.

Such a contention also points to a characteristic inherent in the very language of face depletion and relates to the discussion of face possession above. That is, possessing face is in part avoiding a state of face loss. This is true because every person, regardless of social standing or face position, may potentially lose his or her face. Yet, if a person who has no face can lose face, then what is that thing they lose? Obviously, it is not the accumulation of positive social face they fear to lose, since they do not have it. What they do have, however, is the state of not experiencing face loss. What this suggests is that the dimension of personal face is partly about avoiding face loss. Though a person may not possess significant social face, continually functioning in a way that avoids face-depleting situations ensures that they maintain a positive personal face.

This prompted another question: "If a person loses face, is their face completely gone? If you think some remains, what characteristics does this remaining face have? How is it different from the face that has been lost?" Only two respondents answered that someone's face is completely gone when they lose face. Several mentioned that it ultimately depends on the matter. Clearly there was a distinction, though not precise, between big issues and small ones. "It all depends on whether it is a little deal or a big deal. If it is a really big deal, then there may be none left" (B14:27–28).

These responses indicated that, in theory, the cause of face loss might be so great that one's face is completely gone. Most, it seems, were content with the notion that face loss did not signal the extermination of one's face.

Seven people responded by conceptualizing face loss as composed of parts. For example, "It's not all gone. Possessing face has many times and many parts. But, the people who see us, who know us-they might be attached to the old face that has been lost. But face has many parts. Lose one [part] another one is added on in its place" (M18:31–32). Another responded, "It's not all gone. It depends on the situation because the face that is lost is only one part, not the whole thing" (M11:30–31).

This analysis of face depletion suggests that face does not cohere like a singular object that is either present in full or completely gone. Instead of being an issue of all or nothing, face loss seems more akin to degrees and components. Face loss is a gradated affair. Face loss occurs when personal failure meets the withdrawal of audience approval. Avoiding a state of face loss is the equivalent to possessing personal face.

Face Gain

The Thai facework strategy of gaining face provides us with additional insights into the nature of face. Part of this insight comes from the simple fact that face gain, in itself, is not a proper goal. Though it is a positive notion as such, gaining face is simply a bridge that links two states—the state of not possessing face (or possessing a lesser degree of face) and the state of possessing face (or possessing more face). Gaining face is what provides the link between these two.

One dimension of the face game apparent in the notion of gaining face is that of the source of face. Where does face come from? How is face generated? Two questions provided data for understanding the sources of face gain. These were, "What events make people gain face?" and "What positive ways are there of gaining face? What negative ways are there of gaining face?"

What was interesting here was the strong current of moral notions that were clear in the data from these two questions. If we return to the image of the stereotypical face—person as primarily one who is known, who is outstanding, and who is accepted—such is not necessarily constituted by inherent moral qualities, though of course such might be present accidentally. Among the responses, however, a strong tendency appeared that associated a moral dimension to the ideal notions of face gain. As one can see from Appendix D, fifty-nine of the eighty-one total responses under the theme "Performance" contain an obvious moral dimension. More specifically, these moral characteristics appeared in the form of benevolent help or service.

Additionally, the theme of proper motivation appeared. Those who mentioned such noted that a basic altruism should accompany face gain. People should not expect anything in return for the good they do. Their motivation should not be in the gain or recognition. The point here is simple. Though face is about being known and recognized by others, it is not always a purely surface-level, prideful face-seeking project. If the responses regarding the sources of face are any indication, face is something that people can invest with considerable moral value. This is especially the case, it seems, when people consider what it is that ideally gives people face.

"Promote Face," "Take Face," and "Want to Get Face"

During my interviews, I became aware of a distinct domain within the various facework terms of which I had not been previously aware. Repeatedly, I heard respondents mention the three specific terms "promote face," "take face," and "want to gain face" together and associate them closely. These terms represent the only facework terms in the Thai language that involve both face gain and active effort on the part of the self in that gain. That is, these three terms alone constitute strategies for active face gain on the part of an agent. The other terms that involve face gain are either passive (gain face) or the result of the action of another (give face). As such, these three terms form a small yet distinct domain. What is most striking about this group, however, is not that they are active face-gaining strategies. Each of the terms, whether mentioned together or separately, engendered strongly negative reactions. Not a single reference to these three terms was positive. Every coded example painted such as negative, and interviewees frequently used the extremely derogatory word, *sùeak* (เสือก), perhaps best glossed as "damned brown-noser," to refer to such a person. Clearly, this was not a positive category.

A story that illustrates such involves the dean of a Thai university. The dean, a very "big face" man, was at a party when the host, on the stage with a microphone, announced that the dean would now like to come up and sing a song. This was met on the part of the dean with red-faced belligerence. Upon seeing this, the MC began to apologize profusely and with great deference. The dean eventually came up and sang the song. Why did he view as an affront what many would consider an act of deference and honor? Likely it was because, from his perception, the host clearly had wronged him by presenting him as a person who was seeking opportunity to promote his face.

I construed two major themes from data regarding why people conceived these three terms so negatively. The first of these concerns motivation. Specifically, many respondents noted that those using such strategies had improper motivation. Face gain, apparently, is inappropriate if it is perceived to be insincere, that is, motivated by the gain of face itself. Such a critique is present in the following account given in the context of discussing the meaning of proper face gain.

> To gain face, for example, make lots of merit by looking at intention. If it happens [they] truly intend to make merit but people who make a lot of merit or is a person who that really likes to make merit—it is not taking face, in order that others see that they are a well-off person (even though they might not have anything), they want others to see that they are a person with a meritorious heart. (M19:11–14)

Here the contrast is between a person who invests in the merit-making itself (and presumably unconcerned about face issues) and another who is taking face, that is, in order to impress or be seen as someone interested in merit. This concern for active self-presentation, a sort of face aggrandizement, seems to rub against basic Thai attitudes regarding face and morality. In response to why people do not like those who promote face, one responded simply, "They are not good people—they should be humble" (M26:38–39). This implies that others view promoting face as arrogant, contravening the key Thai values of personal modesty and humility. Another responded, "Why do you have to go and show off for others to see and know about? A good person doesn't have to promote themselves at all" (B1:33–34). Another associated the motivation of honesty with proper face gain, while at the same time paralleling dishonesty with having an explicit desire to gain face. "[They] must be honest. If [they] are not good then they will be looked down upon. Well, really, [such is] wanting to get face" (M6:12–14).

Another characteristic that emerged as a theme was competition. Seemingly, a major cause of distaste for these facework strategies was that, by doing so, people were "sticking out" over against others. Several mentioned jealousy as well; no one wanted others to stand out in contrast to them as this would provoke feelings of jealousy and envy. The fact that these strategies are about face gain implies that prior to enacting them, actors do not possess significant face or function on a peer level with others. This may explain the strength of these negative feelings. That is, if people aggressively exceed in face stature those with whom they were relatively equal, feelings of jealousy are understandable. It would be interesting to know more fully the scope within which people thought such activity inappropriate.

The inappropriateness of promoting face, taking face, and wanting to get face lends further support to the notion that proper face gain must not be a gross or aggressive jockeying. Ideally, people should receive face passively. It should come to those who are not motivated by the face gain itself but exhibit humility and be invested in the significance of the activity that potentially leads to face gain.

Face Recovery

In Thai, two basic terms refer to the regaining of face once it has been lost. These are "redeem face" and "fix face." An additional way to designate face recovery is the generic term "gain face," which, when applied after face depletion, indicates a type of face recovery. The dynamics of face recovery were particularly interesting to me, and I designed several questions to probe this area.

First, I asked about the reasons people engage in redeeming face. The question, though focusing on face redemption, provides more than simple information regarding the dynamics of face recovery. It also reveals much about the nature of face. To ask why Thais attempt to redeem their own and others' face is to ask why they try to regain a state of face possession. It is to probe why people see face loss as undesirable as well as why the possession of face constitutes an attractive goal. Once again, the possession of face appears as the critical element for informing facework strategies.

The most heavily coded responses to this question fell into the following categories: "so others will view us correctly/positively," "social capital/utility," "face is a desirable good," "dignity and honor," and "acceptance." That people should view others rightly derived from the basic sense of being in a state of face loss as one where people look upon others disparagingly. So, people want to redeem face because they "don't want others to look on us negatively all the time and want them to view us in a new way" (B9:72), and "because it is making others come back and accept us again-it improves our image" (M18:72). To redeem face is to regain social capital—"it's like credit so that the next time people will trust us, it makes it possible that we can rely on others" (B10:75). Face is simply a good we want to regain—"we gain a good thing back, our face" (C5:75). It is about social honor—"in order to gain face—we will call our honor and dignity back" (C9:71).

Redeeming face is not only something people do for themselves. It is also a strategy people often enact on behalf of others. For whom do people do this? Answers stayed within the parameters of significant others, that is, family, close friends, and other loved ones. Most did not mention redeeming face for someone they did not know well. What was the rationale for doing this for others? Again, the responses were relatively uniform. People redeem face for those to whom they are emotionally attached or those whom they consider significant.

If another redeems a person's face, how does that person feel? Responses fell into a relatively consistent pattern that the following tripartite composite reaction encapsulates: it "feels good"; we are "thankful" that they "helped" us. First, thirty-two respondents conceptualized another helping us redeem our face as "feeling good." Clearly, people viewed someone helping another regain face as a decidedly positive thing. Relational indebtedness and feelings of gratitude are also present in the responses, as twenty mentioned that they would feel thankful and grateful. This points to how face and, in particular, restorative facework done for others can be a powerful tool for relational cohesion. Finally, assisting in redeeming face for another is considered a good way of helping another. Other less heavily coded responses also included being indebted to the other person's moral merit, feeling deeply touched, recognizing their generosity, and that such indicates a desire for relationship. Again, all this is not necessarily about the dynamics of redeeming, per se, but rather point to the way people conceive of the importance of face and the relational dimension inherent if another would invest in such a benevolent activity.

Face Maintenance

In Thai, the term *rák-sa* is slightly ambiguous as it can mean both "to heal" (i.e., to help bring about a renewed state of healthy face possession after one has suffered face harm) and "to keep/maintain" (as in to keep something in a state of healthiness). The question I posed in the interviews, "Is it important to save/maintain face after we have redeemed face?" was broad enough to encompass both senses.

Twenty-eight of thirty who responded felt it was indeed important to do so. Only two diverged in opinion, stating they did not think it important. So, *that* it is important to most is certainly clear. The responses as to *why* keeping face is important also points to a central theme mentioned above. In good tautological fashion, the most coded response as to why keeping face was important was, simply, that it was important. Respondents either stated this outright or, as was often the case, their response implied that face was an inherent good, a given. The large number of positive responses to the initial question of importance, together with the rationale that the importance of face is self-evident, point to a fundamental salience for face. There exists, it seems, a tremendous and pervasive desire to maintain face and avoid face loss. To maintain or keep face once it is regained

> . . . is more important than redeeming face because we have to maintain our credit. If we keep on losing face, we then lose our credit. It's like a car engine that you keep on fixing, which is not good, to keep on redeeming face. (M4:82-82)

Once face is regained, maintenance is critical to effective social functioning.

Non-Players

An interesting category that merits special attention emerged in these interviews. This is the person who self-consciously attempts to withdraw from the face game as most Thais currently practice it. I refer to such people as "non-players." In addition, although small compared to the total number of interviewees, this group represented attitudes that are important to examine briefly. This group of respondents expressed their non-playing approach in different ways. Some used the language of interest ("not interested in face") or consideration ("don't think much about face"). Five respondents lexicalized this perspective in quasi-Buddhist terms[6] (i.e., that one should "not attach to face") as in the following response: "Face is a food supplement from society—it makes us happy but we shouldn't attach much [to it]" (M4:87).

In the data I coded for this theme, two primary considerations seem to stand out. First, the basic critique and source of dissatisfaction with the face game as currently played was the perceived effort of people to add

---

6. This phrase (in Thai, *yúet tit*) is often used in Thai Buddhism to represent the notion of attachment and clinging to the world.

to their face, to increase positive social face. The responses of these non-players implied an aversion toward exerting effort required to gain face and the concomitant expectations that adhered to becoming a "big-face person." Such is expressed by the following: "To say it [face] is important, well, yes, but myself, I would rather be a person who doesn't have face and I don't have to worry to maintain it too" (M26:84–84). The face game, for some it seems, simply involves too much effort.

Second, there also seemed an implicit attempt to disestablish the face-loss standards within a group. Thus, those things in society that might constitute a lack of face or face loss might be relativized, bringing no face harm. Representative of this perspective is the following response to the question of how people in a group might react or feel when they lose face: "People in [my] group—no one thinks about the issue of face, so there is not a reaction or any feeling" (M19:19–20).

One respondent expressed an additional rationale for this non-player critique. In response to a question asking why people attempt to avoid face loss, the answer was, "Because they are not confident in themselves—they take others as their standard" (M17:43–44). This statement encapsulates well a basic concern that appeared in several of the non-player discussions of face. That is, what they were dissatisfied with was the fact that face was something dictated by the sentiment of others. Those concerned with the face game are, as one interviewee put it, people who are "low in individualism."

These non-players, however, are likely not as completely immune from the face game as they might suppose. If the face theorists are correct, anyone who denies interest in playing the face game is actually playing it at that very moment as they give deference to the one to whom they are speaking and seek to communicate a non-face face. Indeed, the only way to completely withdraw from the face game is to terminate one's role as a social actor in social space. This, not surprisingly, was something that none of the non-players in my interviews suggested. Further probing would likely reveal that despite their protestations of different dimensions of the Thai face game, these non-players are likely significantly involved in playing the face game at numerous levels.[7]

7. An interesting anecdote regarding the viability of a non-player perspective comes from a conversation I had with Dr. Suntaree Komin, prominent Thai social psychologist and author. When asking her about such non-players, she laughed and noted with a scoffing tone that one could likely "push" their faces and find out how much in fact their face truly meant to them. She noted that nearly all Thais would become defensive, deeply

In terms of the overall data, this perspective was clearly a minority one. I believe it remains significant, however, because such represents an internal critique that highlights a tension many feel and some (i.e., the non-players) use explicitly to justify a very different approach to social face. Also unclear is the extent to which an autonomy-face orientation motivates such non-players. As some suggested, the difficulty in playing the social-face game was difficult and thus formed part of their decision to withdraw. To what extent these individuals simply wanted to be left alone is a matter for further study. Still, it is altogether likely that many others would agree with the essence of the non-player face critique though not completely adopting the same non-player attitude or strategies.

The Function of Face

What does face *do* for people? What are the consequences of possessing face? Questions regarding the utility and function of face yielded interesting answers. What struck me most was an unexpected dual emphasis on the positive as well as the negative consequences of possessing face. As I worked through the interviews face appeared quite like a double-edged sword that could cut both ways or like the polarity of a magnet that can both repel and attract.

Many noted negative consequences. Significant among these were the forty responses coded for the category of personal infringement. Such included an increase in having to be watchful and careful of oneself, not being able to act freely as one would like, and an increase in the watchful eyes of others. Thirty-three responses were coded for the theme of negative relational consequences. Having face can, it seems, not only bring people together but also push them apart. It can create a situation where people are apt to use others for their own benefit and possibly cause relationships to be shallow.

There are positive consequences, however. As is clear from the coded themes (see Appendix E), the overwhelming benefit to possessing face is the relational benefit. In particular, what stands out is the value of receiving respect and honor. This again highlights the critical importance to many Thais of social honor and the power of face to generate respect. This relational value is manifested in such as wanting to have a relationship with

---

hurt, and angered by such face affronts. If true, such would indicate a withdrawal from the face "game" at one level but not a total abandonment or complete abdication.

others, respecting and fearing others, trusting others, accepting others—all these point to the profoundly relational nature of face.

An additional dimension to this relational aspect of face is its associative properties. Among the responses to the question asking how others act or feel when one gains face, seven specifically mentioned that others in the group gain face as well. This is expressed well in the following statement: "They will announce to others so that they would know what caused us to gain face because they want others to know about our good thing, our ability—they will gain face too because they are in our group" (M3:17–21). Likewise, in response to a question of how those in one's own group would react if another gained face, one interviewee stated, "We'd all join in gaining face and then make it known to others that in our group there is a person who possesses face" (M14:24). If possessing face is a valuable goal to which people aspire, and face can adhere to oneself if one possesses appropriate relational proximity to one who already possesses face or has recently gained face, then this associative property of face likely acts as a sort of social glue. More than this, face seems to function as a nexus that generates a bi-directional flow of relationship. As an individual gains face, others are drawn by this current toward the one possessing face. As these others associate themselves with the owner of greater face, face accrues to those in joining in relationship. Thus, face and relationality combine to form a causal nexus of centripetal and centrifugal forces.

In exploring this area of face and relationality, other significant dynamics emerged. Based on responses to questions about face and relationships, it appears that those who enjoy a significant level of relationship should avoid anything that might endanger the face of another or impugn another's honor. Should this occur, though, those who cause it will inevitably feel bad about what they did and about the effect it might have on others. In other words, good friends do not do things that endanger the face of others. And, if they do, they will likely feel terrible about it. A good example of this is the following statement: "feel bad because, you know, we're friends. They probably didn't want for us to lose face. They probably will not dare to even look at our face" (M21:51–52).

Clearly, not every relational rupture directly involves face or honor-related issues. It is equally obvious, however, that making others lose face, honor, or dignity causes relational friction and will likely result in relational estrangement. It appears that many Thais conceive personal wrongs or injurious actions toward the self as having some negative effect on face, honor, and dignity. Similarly, losing face (and honor or dignity) may have the effect of causing others to distance themselves from us.

This is evident in responses to the question of how we would feel if another friend did something that caused us to lose face. Respondents answered that such a friend, upon causing us to lose face, would feel profoundly terrible. Coded most densely were the feelings of guilt, sadness, and shame. Likewise, many felt that they would develop a strongly negative attitude toward such a person. For example, some would "really feel rotten toward that friend. I won't trust them. If there's an issue then I won't talk with them" (B1:44–45). "I feel disappointed because they have become a person I cannot trust and they did not maintain my face" (B15:51–51). Others said they would "feel as though they have no mutual respect [for us]" (B3:59–60) and be "angry and I won't trust them. I maybe won't dare to face them too because its like they do not respect our rights" (B8:58–60). In response to the question of what they would do in such a face-loss scenario, slightly more than half responded that they would not redress the issue, while the rest stated they would redress in some fashion. Though these differences likely reflect personal conflict styles as well as importance of the relationship, all responses referenced such a face-loss scenario as a negative experience that would cause a considerable degree of personal anxiety, whether they redressed or not.

While examining the data from these responses, it became clear that responses coded along two fundamental categories, that is, those of friends who side with us and those who delight in our face loss, possibly intending us some type of harm. Those in the first group will inevitably feel bad about what they did and the effect it has on us. They will likely seek to remedy the relational friction/rupture in some way (e.g., ask forgiveness, accept what they've done, or explain themselves). For the second, the operative notion seems to be that of personal delight in our misfortune, which indicates their intention to injure us in some way.

Causing one's friends to lose face is something good friends do not do and something those who wish ill on others try to accomplish. Causing others to lose face is considered relationally injurious and a considerable wrong. It is reason for the one responsible to feel guilty, sad, ashamed, or a host of other negative emotions at being the cause of face injury to another. People who maintain a positive relationship with another will feel bad (sad, empathy, pity) if the other loses face even if they were not the cause. They will try to comfort, encourage, and continue to relate with us and possibly try to help us redeem or fix our injured face.

The Relationship of Face with Social Honor

Thai face is the centerpiece of this chapter yet the broader area of social honor in Thai culture is a necessary part of the study. This is not a digression, as respondents frequently mentioned the link between face and two other prevalent forms of social honor in Thai culture. The exact nature of this connection remains, however, largely enigmatic. Even after much thought and substantial interviewing, this relationship between the three primary forms of social honor remains one of the "puzzling puzzles" of Thai face. This is a puzzle that begs a solution, since a connection offers to yield a more thorough understanding of what properly constitutes Thai face. The relationship between these terms seems complex and, admittedly difficult to describe fully. Yet, important clues to understanding the nature of face exist precisely in a fuller description of this relationship. The following section is an attempt to make some headway into understanding something about this important connection.

The three terms I mention here are *nâ*, *kìat*, and *sàk si*. The word *nâ* is a straightforward one, as it is literally "face" and represents both the physical human face as well as the metaphorical expression this study is addressing. Most gloss the second term, *kìat*, as "honor." The final term, *sàk si*, is often glossed as "dignity." For the purposes of this presentation this is a suitable translation. I will adopt these conventional translations for this paper, while suggesting that the culturally specific boundaries of meaning do not necessarily match those of the English terms "honor" and "dignity."

That the relationship between these three terms should be investigated is borne out by the close connection among them. That such a connection would exist is not a surprise. Ting-Toomey mentions this tendency of overlap in meaning between face and social honor. "Codes of honor and respect are tied closely to the everyday linguistic and nonverbal facework practice in each distinctive cultural community" (Ting-Toomey 2004:220). Once we admit this close connection, however, the precise relationship between the terms becomes murky. The 1995 *Thai Royal Institute Dictionary* (*Phót-chà-na-núkrom chà-bàp râtchá-ban-thít-yótthan*), regarded by most as the standard Thai language dictionary, defines the metaphorical use of face simply as "honor and dignity"[8] (1995:865).

---

8. Following the literal definitions of a body part, the dictionary notes succinctly, *kìat láe sàk si* ("เกียรติและศักดิ์ศรี").

Though these are closely connected, to equate them as if they were coterminous is simplistic and naïve.

The lack of proper understanding of this relationship is not limited to cultural outsiders. The general imprecision that many exhibit in speaking about these terms confirms that for many (most?) Thais the relationship between face, honor, and dignity is real but unclear. For example, sometimes people simply conflate the terms. Thus, one person responded that "as for every person possesses face-that means possesses dignity" (M1:7). When a friend makes a person loose face, it can also be characterized in terms of honor—"I'm fed up with that friend . . . because it is as thought they didn't give me honor" (B1:44–45).

One attempt to further this description was a simple question that asked about the characteristics of a face-person, a person of honor, and a person of dignity. I coded the results into detailed attributes. Then, I assembled these attributes into broader themes. The following chart takes these themes and lays them side-by-side for the terms face, honor, and dignity. The numbers represent the total number of attributes coded that fall within the specific thematic category. Those enlarged and darkened represent the term that has the largest number of attributes coded that fall within that particular category. An "x" signifies that this theme did not code for that term.

TABLE 3: CHARACTERISTICS OF FACE, HONOR, AND DIGNITY

	Face	Honor	Dignity
Acceptance	7	10	–
Distinction	15	1	–
Honor	17	32	–
Impractical	–	–	7
Morality	8	51	13
Personal characteristics	20	39	3
Recognition	35	11	–
Resolute	–	–	19
Self	–	3	79
Status	30	24	3
Valuable	–	–	7
Will not be insulted	–	3	13

The differences and similarities are quite stark on many points. As mentioned earlier, the prominent themes for a face-person include being recognized, holding some level of status and honor, and being distinguished or outstanding in some particular fashion. The full breakdown for characteristics of a face-person appears in Appendix F. In contrast, a person of honor does not seem to exhibit the strong tendencies toward distinction and the responses contain only a moderate mention of recognition. What does distinguish honor over against face is the pervasive moral sense for honor that emerged in the interviews. The characteristics of a person of honor covered a wide range of attributes, which centered on positive personal morality (e.g., not prideful, faithful) and appropriate treatment of other people (e.g., helps others, respects others, does not look down on others). The full breakdown of these themes is in Appendix G. This moral component coded fifty-one times whereas both face and dignity contained only minimal references to moral attributes. Also, a person with honor coded highest in "honor" (i.e., respect given to and received from others). This is not surprising since by definition a person of honor is one to whom honor is given and respect accrues. Overall, the following characterization captures much of the responses about honor and what a person of honor is.

> A person of honor is a person who has received acceptance and praise from society from some thing that they have done which has produced benefit for the community or something that society expects and is in harmony with the cultural standards of society. (M28:8)

Dignity also exhibited distinctive themes. To see the complete listing of attributes of a person of dignity see Appendix H. Interestingly, however, those themes in which dignity coded highest were attributes almost completely absent from either honor or face. Five such distinctive themes emerged in the data for dignity.

First, and most exceptional, was the profound emphasis on the role of the self. In contrast to honor (only three mentions of the self) and face (not one mention), seventy-nine times the notion of self (self-awareness, self-definition, self-pride, the real self, self-reliant, self-confidence) appeared. Clearly, this represents a major point of difference between dignity over against honor and face. Noting the category of honor also highlights this lack of relation to a broader social context. Both face and honor contain frequent references to respect and honor from others. Dignity, in contrast, contains no coded reference to honor.

Also unique to dignity were the themes "resolute" and "value." Most responses that mentioned "resolute" carried the idea of refusing to give in to others, to accept help from others, or to define another person's dignity. Though it is clear from the data that both face and honor are generally important to most Thais, dignity was the only term that contained specific references to being something valuable.

Strangely, dignity also coded another unique notion, that of being "impractical." The Thai phrase used to reference this was *kin mâi dâi* ("cannot eat it"). What these respondents seemed to mean was that dignity was something possessed solely by the individual and had no practical use outside of the level of self-definition and value. Therefore, though dignity is potentially valuable to an individual, it is also, in contrast to both face and honor, not something that carries utilitarian value. Finally, there were several references to a person of dignity resisting others who might look down on or insult another. Thus, a person of dignity is one that seems particularly invested in demanding the proper kind of treatment from others based on the fact of their dignity.

In order to test out the term of greatest salience, I presented a simple choice to each interviewee. If they had to choose between the three, which would they select? Only six respondents chose face and none offered a detailed rationale for this choice. Twenty-two chose honor. The basic rationale given paralleled those attributes that are characteristic of honor, that is, people desired the acceptance inherent in having honor or attached importance to the idea of a moral dimension that was a part of honor. Some mentioned that since every person had dignity, honor was more desirable. Others felt that dignity, though important, was simply not as practical as honor. Thirty respondents chose dignity. The rationale respondents provided for this choice, not surprisingly, related to dignity as a function of the self. Simply stated, for them, dignity was either from their self, directly related to their self, or the sole possession of the self. This was in contrast to face and honor, both of which come from society. There was also a secondary theme that dignity was desirable because even if one were not rich or famous one could find pride and satisfaction in being a person of dignity.

These three forms of social honor are undeniably distinct. In the Thai language, however, one interesting parallel is that all three can be "redeemed." Therefore, I decided to probe at the intended use of these terms by looking at the meaning of redeeming face, honor, and dignity. When asked if redeeming face, honor, and dignity were the same or different, forty responded that these were different and twenty felt them to be the same. Those who responded they were the same, however, emphasized dynamics over substance. For most respondents, the similarity noted involved the actual enactment of redeeming strategies, that is, of doing something to make an undesirable situation better.

> All three things are the same, that is, it is necessary to make the situation better and it might be interconnected. Having honor leads to having face. Redeeming dignity is the same as redeeming honor back as well. (B8:43–44)

Another mentioned that the difference is simply one of level.

> They are different specifically in the ways we redeem. For example, to redeem face we can do anything we want but redeeming dignity and honor, the technique is more difficult and [one] must only do things that are good. (M18:37–38)

Similarly, "They are the same exactly that we must be the one who goes and does it. But the difficulty in redeeming, that is different" (M27:36–37).

Those who responded that redeeming face, honor, and dignity were different mentioned this notion of levels of difficulty most frequently. That is, the essential difference was between levels of magnitude of cause (whether the incident was "small" or "large") and the differing level of difficulty in redeeming. Respondents felt that redeeming face could happen when the source of loss was relatively small or less significant. Alternately, if one had needed to redeem honor or dignity, this implied a loss of serious magnitude. Although resisting a discernable measure, there was a clear weighting among the three notions in terms of difficulty. Plainly, respondents referenced face as the least difficult to redeem. Again, this was because face, though possibly involving issues of greater weight, could also be lost in situations that involved matters of little consequence. Following face was honor, which though more difficult, still ranked less so than dignity. "Dignity, [when] lost it is completely lost. It is difficult to redeem" (B16:35–36). In fact, several mentioned that there were events so serious that redemption was virtually impossible, making dignity unrecoverable. As an example of this, three respondents mentioned a woman who had been raped. Presumably, this is so damaging to a victim's womanhood it leads to a state with no apparent remedy, a total and irrecoverable loss of dignity.

In another question aimed at exploring the interrelationship of these three notions, I asked if the loss of face had a negative impact on one's honor or dignity. Eight respondents of thirty-four answered that there was no necessary negative impact. Face loss, it seemed, was simply assumed to be less serious and therefore a discrete experience and unrelated to personal honor or dignity. The other respondents answered that, yes, the loss of face could negatively affect one's honor or dignity. The qualifier was that it ultimately depended on the severity of the matter. The more serious the source of face loss, the more likely it would impact honor and dignity. Thus one respondent, speaking of male dignity, noted, "men have dignity that must be maintained. When they lose face . . . [dignity] is lost too" (B21:49). Again, speaking particularly of male face and dignity, one respondent noted that these were essentially coterminous. "Men consider being a face-person just like dignity" (B23:45).

As I stated at the beginning of this section, these three forms of social honor are certainly interrelated, yet the precise nature of this connection is complex and obscure. That face encompasses a greater range of events (ranging from trivial to more weighty matters) allows that face loss might be a less severe experience and thus unrelated to the seemingly weightier issues of honor and dignity.

Honor appeared to relate more specifically to issues of a moral nature. Dignity appeared to correlate more with the self, possibly more along the lines of inviolable personal self-honor. Dignity is not something we get or gain. It is something we are. Thus, people automatically possess dignity if they possess membership in a class or group. For example, all people, by virtue of being human, possess human dignity. Likewise, all men possess male dignity, all Thais possess Thai dignity, and all women possess female dignity. This does not increase or decrease as does face or honor. It remains stable as long as one continues in proper relation to the group that engenders dignity. To say that someone is a "person who has no dignity" is an insult of the greatest severity. It is tantamount to saying that such a person is in fact not a person at all.

A Cultural Model of Thai Face

A schema is a flexible interpretive mental state that represents a distinct and strongly connected pattern of cognitive organization (D'Andrade 1995:142). A schema also exists exclusively within the minds of individuals. In contrast, a cultural model is a "cognitive schema that is intersubjectively shared by a social group" (Quinn and Strauss 1996:112). Such cultural models

> ... draw on a variety of types of idealized events, actors and other physical entities in these events, and relations among these, all of which are available to our understanding of ordinary experience: the typical, the stereotypical, the salient in memory, the mythic, the ideal successful, the ideal happy, and so on. (Holland and Quinn 1987:31)

This moves the notion of schema out of the individual mind and into the broader arena of shared social space. Such are important cognitive structures not only because they provide descriptive cultural knowledge but also because cultural models have motivational force. That is, within cultural models are embedded goals.[9]

The critical issue for this study is that language, as it appears in discourse, reflects underlying cultural models (Quinn and Strauss 1996:153).[10] Since discourse is the most basic of all symbolic cultural forms, it functions as the repository par excellence for understanding how people think, particularly as language represents the basic schema and cultural models present in a certain cultural context.

The ways language encodes various cultural models is particularly evident in the use of metaphorical language. This is so because schemas guide the selection of metaphor use in discourse (Quinn and Strauss 1996:144). Thus, by understanding the metaphors of a given language, one gains a key to understand the basic schema and cultural models in the context of that language.[11]

---

9. These cultural goals form an important bridge between culture and action. Yet, for this study, there is reason to refrain from extended discussion of the motivational force of a face model. This is that the deeper, more difficult to discern level of motivation can only be properly understood after the cultural model itself is clearly understood (D'Andrade and Strauss 1992:230). So, as these authors recommend, I will refrain from focusing on the motivational dimension of the cultural model for face and be content with the more modest task of describing the model. I will refer to motivation only obliquely as it relates to the general description.

10. As Roy G. D'Andrade and Claudia Strauss rightly contend, "talk, we believe, is the external matrix of all deeply internalized cultural schemas" (1992:230). This forms the basis for the priority cognitive anthropology places on the study of actual discourse.

11. "The most fundamental values in a culture will be coherent with the metaphorical structure of the most fundamental concepts in the culture" (Lakoff and Johnson 2003:22). The classic example of this is Quinn's study of the cultural model of American marriage. After examining extensive discourse on marriage gained from interviews,

I collected metaphors from three sources. First, I asked respondents what they thought face was like. This resulted in a number of images as they thought about and compared face with other areas of their normal experience. Second, in the process of reading and coding other questions, I highlighted the occasional use of metaphor in talking about face. These first two sources produce highly idiosyncratic metaphoric images, many of which are rich and suggestive. The conventionalized linguistic metaphors of facework, which I have discussed above, are also important sources of metaphoric description. That is, these facework terms are essentially conventionalized metaphors that highlight certain dimensions of meaning for face. Drawing metaphors from all three sources, I then categorized them (these categories can be viewed in Appendix I). From these categories, I then developed the following larger meta-themes:

- Possession
- Acceptance
- Self
- Valuable
- Variable
- Distinction
- Visible

What follows is a discussion of these notions, which I believe constitute a basic cultural model of Thai face. That is, this small number of basic classes of metaphors provides the framework for a widely shared Thai understanding of face schemas.

Possession

The single most prevalent metaphor within the interviews related to possession. It is quite simply the hub of the face game. This seems to be true not only because the most basic way of speaking of face involves the verb "to have/possess" but also because so many of the various metaphors used

---

Quinn concluded that a widely shared cultural model of American marriage could be represented by a small number of frequently recurring classes of metaphors. These she classed together into the following cultural model: American marriage is characterized by sharedness, lastingness, mutual benefit, compatibility, difficulty, effort, success or failure, and risk (D'Andrade 1995:169).

to describe face were also things people possess (e.g., money, power, jewelry, resources, tool, a diamond). It is also something that most, if not all, want to possess. Some will go to greater lengths than others to get positive social face. Yet, no sane person wants to lose face, especially personal face, and will go to great lengths to prevent face loss. That it is such a desirable possession makes the state of face possession the goal of and grounds for all facework.

It is also a specific type of possession, for face is itself ultimately a product of society. It is something given to us—a loan, as it were—from those around us, though indeed a gift that is revocable by the same suppliers. Thus, in the Thai language, face is something one can "give," "loose," and "preserve." Additionally, as the terms "promote face," "take face," and "want to get face" demonstrate, the ideal type of face gain should be passive. One should not jockey or play an aggressive part in gaining face. In this sense, face seems to be like a gift, a present given to oneself by others.

Acceptance

Face is about acceptance. Such is apparent in the notion of a "mask so they like us" or the frequently referenced "be accepted." In the Thai context, this notion speaks particularly of positive standing or membership in a social group. The way others think about us and whether they accept us is a key element motivating facework. Additionally, the frequently referenced notion of face as "honor" is also about acceptance. Society honors and respects those that it approves. Thus, for face to be like honor is also to imply acceptance.

Self

Although face clearly relates to the approval and acceptance that comes from social groups, it also concerns the self. Many metaphors fit within this rubric. These include the notion of confidence—"having" or "increasing" one's self-confidence. Some conceive face as boosting or increasing a sense of self or self-esteem—"something that enhances the self." Additionally, face can reflect and expresses the self, captured in the images of face being "like advertising space for the self," "a window," and a "reflection of our selfhood."

One reason that the various metaphors of face depletion appear in painful, even violent terms, is very probably this connection to the self.

This is likely, it seems, because just as damage to one's physical face hurts (because it is a part of us) so too injury to our metaphorical face is painful. It is, by extension, also a part of us. To lose something connected to us or to have a body part injured is inevitably painful. Such occurs because of the intimate relationship face maintains with the Thai notion of self.

Valuable

Face is useful. It has utilitarian value as a kind of resource or social capital. Many images convey this idea—"monetary resource," "a passport that helps us to make contact, ask for help, or coordinate work more conveniently," "gold you can sell," "credit," "a key to open the way, a shortcut for us." All these stress that face *does* something for its owner. It is not inert nor does it simply function in a conceptual manner. Face is valuable, "like a valuable resource all around us," "like money we must maintain so that it won't be gone." Several respondents referred to face as "like power" or "having power."

Variable

Several metaphors confirm that an essential characteristic of face is its nature as something quite variable. This is implicit in many of the conventional Thai facework terms. All notions of face depletion (e.g., loose, sell), face injury (e.g., break, cut-off, strike, snap off, hammer, tear off), and face gain (e.g., give, gain, take, promote, want to get, redeem, fix) involve alternating levels of face. For all that face may be, it is certainly not a constant. It can increase or decrease in varying levels, though Thais do not seem to ever quantify it in any absolute sense. Thus, one may have greater or lesser face, or may gain more face or lose some face.

Such variability is clear in the following quote:

> It's like white clothing. If there is face loss then there is black that stains the cloth. But it's not as if it will be black forever. We can still see white in the cloth and if we keep on doing good then it becomes white again. In the opposite way, if we just keep on losing face then the black will come on, the cloth will be dirty and there won't be anything good left. No one will want to look. (M4:31–33)

Because face is variable, it requires care and effort "like a tree that if we care for it well, it will thrive and grow." Why does face require effort and care?

Several images pointed to face as something impermanent, "like something that does not endure" or "like leaves that have fallen off."

This variability also manifested itself in another theme, that is, that face is something ambiguous and dangerous. It is dangerous because face is potentially addictive, "like drugs because we can become attached to it . . . we lose our selfhood because we chase along after face, pay attention to face." Face can be a perilous enterprise, "like a person riding the back of a tiger. Whenever [you] get down the tiger might make you lose face" (M14:25–26). It is a "double-edged sword." Face can be like "a weapon in our hand—it can hurt us or it can make us better." These and other such images all gain their force from the basic reality that face changes. One can have it one moment and loose it in the next. Face can, in a sense, come back and bite its owner.

This indeterminate and potentially dangerous sense of face is generated by the ever-present reality of the mutability of face. Specifically, the potential pain implied by these images of danger is likely the result of the real pain experienced in face loss. This includes all Thai facework terms involving face depletion and is present in statements that compare face to be "like a balloon that when we gain face, it inflates more and more and floats—[if] it floats really high then [it might] break. The higher it goes, the more it hurts when it comes down." Thus, whether shame or the forfeiture of relationship, approval, or utility, the loss of face can lead to painful damage and is often characterized as dangerous.

Distinction

Face is also about distinction. Several specific categories of images from the interviews fit into this theme. One was the oft-occurring notion that face was about positive difference. For example, some noted face was "being better than others," "like lifting your level up higher," "being higher," or "being number one." Many referenced face as like having social status. Others noted that face was like "the good" or "goodness." Both terms imply advantage and distinction. Yet, the single most prominent form of distinction respondents mentioned was that of social honor. Many simply stated that face was like "honor" or like "dignity." Others mentioned "words of praise" and "admiration."

Visible

Those that I interviewed frequently mentioned images that pointed to face as something that is external. Face, as would be expected, is something conceived of as visible. It is "like a crown on the head or a gold medal around the neck," a "picture on a TV screen," and "a poster that is put up all around." It is something that people can see.

Face was not something that people simply viewed but as also mentioned as something that is attractive. People looked at or viewed this beauty. That is, face as something beautiful relates the self's attempt to look good so that others will have a positive view. Face, respondents thought, was "like gold that you want to be beautiful," "like having a very beautiful thing that others want to look at, admire, and touch." It was like "putting on a new outfit. If it is expensive then people admire it and see that we look good and have class. But in the opposite way, if we dress sloppily people will look at us." Closely related to face as beautiful is a sense of it being inviting.

There was also a negative side to face as a visible reality. Many referenced face as something that obscures and covers. Thus, face is a "mask that obscures the ugly things inside" and "clothing that covers us." Because of this, some also thought of face as "deceptive," that is, representing things that were "unfaithful." Face was also conceived of as false, a "falsehood."

In summary, as I have said, a cultural model of Thai face would include the following basic categories: face is a *possession* connected to the *self* that arises from *acceptance* and *distinction*; it is *visible*, *valuable*, and *variable*. These fundamental notions about face constitute a widely shared Thai cultural model of face.

A Face Prototype Scenario

In the classical theory of categorization, all members of a category exhibit the defining characteristics of that category. Thus, all members have equal status as category members. Eleanor Rosch, in developing the notion of prototype theory, points to asymmetry among category members and category structure. She presents the idea of the "best example," which has special cognitive status. That is, certain members of any category are held by people as particularly representative of that category. These "most representative members" of a category she termed "prototypical" members (Lakoff 1987:41). Instead of the classical notion of categorization (i.e., some entity is either in or out without any differentiation), prototype categories are graded, with fuzzy boundaries and central members. There are some categories that are logically bounded but these are assumed to have prototypical members as well—better examples of the category than others (1987:56). These prototypes act as cognitive reference points of various sorts and form the basis for inferences (1987:45).

The difference between a prototype and a schema is that whereas a schema is an "organized framework of objects and relations which has yet to be filled in with concrete detail," a prototype contains an already specified set of details and expectations (D'Andrade 1995:124). The filling in of a schema creates a prototype. In this way, we can view prototypes as highly typical instantiations of schema (1995:124).

Prototype theory views meaning, specifically lexical meaning, as determined by an ideal or prototypical example. Rather than the clear-cut category boundaries of previous conceptions, this "fuzzy boundaries" approach allows us to define the best example and then to expect real-world examples to more or less fit this example, rather than perfectly or not at all. Thus, meaning becomes a matter of more or less rather than either/or.

Beyond studying the various metaphors and notions that adhere to a prototype model, one may also assume, for certain experiences, a rhythm and movement that adds a temporal dimension to the prototype. Lakoff terms such a prototype augmented with a dimension of temporality, a "prototypical scenario" (1987:397). Such a prototypical scenario is what I wish to explore next. Quinn, mentioned in note 11 above regarding her classic study of a cultural model of American marriage, also develops such a construct, that is, a prototypical sequence of events related to marriage. People use such prototypical scenarios, she contends, as mediating structures that guide reasoning and action related to marriage (Quinn and Strauss 1996:164).

From my interview data, and information the various commentators on Thai face offer, I contend that there exists an eight-stage prototypical scenario involving Thai face. This is represented in the following figure.

A Description of Thai Face   151

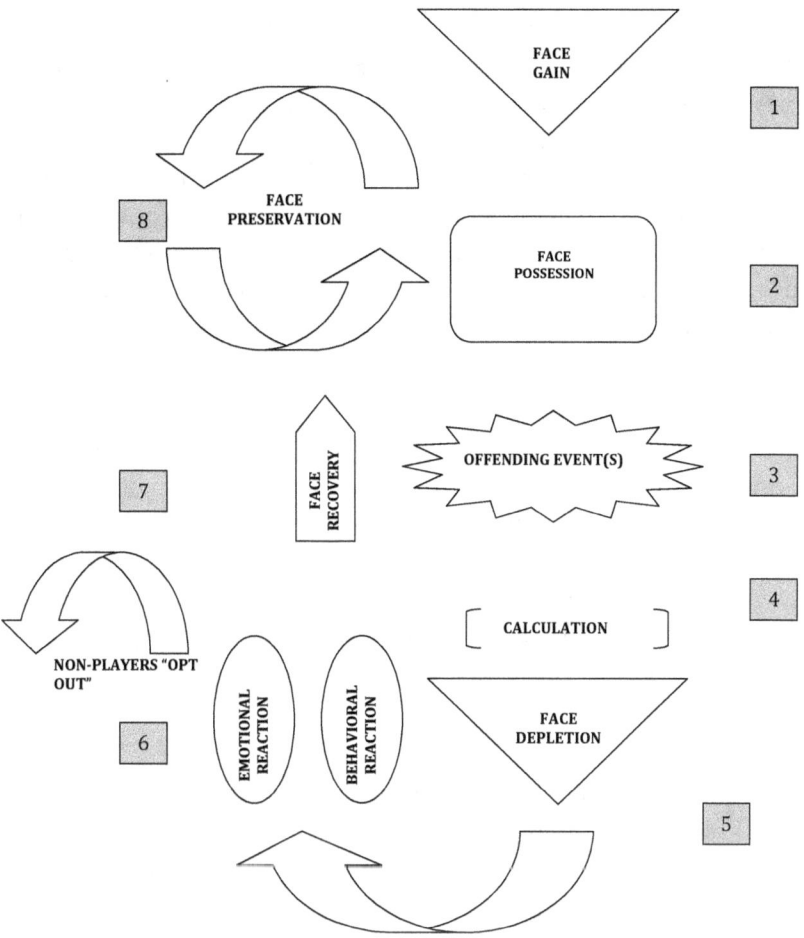

Figure 1: Prototype Face Scenario

Stage 1: Face Gain

At some point, the face experience begins with face gain, whether of a more personal type or of a social kind. As I have noted above, face may accrue based on a wide variety of sources. Indeed, these can range from methods most Thais judge as positive and legitimate to those clearly negative and illegitimate. The gaining of face is the necessary first step to the next stage.

Stage 2: Face Possession

This is in fact the primary goal of Thai facework. To possess face, whether personal face (i.e., living as a competent social actor not involved in states of shame) or social face (having social distinction and aggregated social honor), is primary to Thai face experience. Every single Thai facework term involves a movement away from this state (e.g., face depletion), progress toward this state (e.g., face gain, face recovery), or activity designed to preserve this state (e.g., face maintenance). Face possession constitutes the heart of the Thai face experience.

Stage 3: Offending Event(s)

Such occurrences may be either self-induced or caused by other social actors. Offending events also differ in severity, which brings about a concomitant level of potential face depletion. Thus, trivial infractions of social propriety (e.g., stumbling in public) create potential for minor levels of embarrassment ("broken face"), while egregious social sins can bring about greater levels of face depletion (and possibly depletion of honor or dignity as well).

Stage 4: Calculation

Between the moment of the offending event(s) and the determination of face depletion, a complex process of calculation must occur. This may take scarcely a moment though it could potentially take place over a lengthy period of time. This calculation would involve an assessment of the nature of the offending event, take into account public evaluation, and also include the relative level of the actor's face attachment. The actor must weight all these considerations and determine whether in fact they will consider the event face depleting or not, and if so, to what extent depletion has occurred. If calculation leads to a conclusion that the experience was not a face-depleting event, the actor continues to exist in the face-possession stage since their original level of face was not affected in any material fashion. It is here the issue of face attachment may become a critical factor.

Stage 5: Face Depletion

Face depletion is the negative assessment of the effects of offending events. It also appears as a variable experience. That is, face loss is not absolute in kind but varies from lesser to greater. Depletion may occur at both the personal- and social-face level. Conceivably, people may experience one type of loss without the other, though in all likelihood they tend to co-occur. This parallels the notion of subjective and objective shame. One may feel there to be some type of face loss even though observers do not evaluate the situation similarly. Likewise, social revocation of face and respect may occur without the individual accepting others' evaluative move. This would be akin to a social stigma or loss of social face where the individual actor remains unaffected psychologically. Such lack of personal psychological investment highlights how face depletion is a multivalent phenomenon that resists simple and one-dimensional reduction.

Similarly, some offending events result in face loss, others face loss plus the loss of honor, while others may constitute loss of face, honor, and dignity. An incident of face depletion may involve the loss of one, two, or all three of these respect-laden notions. Accordingly, this stage is fundamentally a loss of respect since respect (i.e., public recognition and acceptance based on some sort of distinction) is a necessary component of face, honor, and dignity.

Important to remember is that depletion involves not only a wide range of social gravity (relatively minor to considerable levels of loss) but also the evaluative posture, the face calculation, of both actor and observer(s). Such complexity makes this stage impossible to operationalize since all these variables delimit any particular case of face depletion. Because face functions as an important type of social capital, face loss involves the potential for relational loss and various types of social utility. Psychological investment and face attachment makes this stage particularly problematic.

Stage 6: Reaction(s)

Upon face depletion, there is an inevitable reaction that may occur at two levels, that is, an affective reaction and a behavioral reaction. These of course may be connected, though they are not so necessarily. One may indeed experience strong affective reactions (e.g., shame, anger, guilt) to face loss but refrain from any observable outward behavioral reaction. Likewise, a person may enact a specific type of visible reaction though not experience an analogous type of emotional reactions (e.g., one who expresses visible anger at an apparent snub though internally is not truly concerned with such).

These reactions may involve the use of strategies to redress the issue of face. It may also involve disengagement and avoidance. The potential variation of face-related reactions is enormous. We must understand such reactions, however, within the radically relational dimension of Thai face. Although it is true that affective and behavior reactions may occur in private, such is not just that of a solitary figure losing and enacting various facework strategies on their own. Indeed, interview data suggested that relational concerns are immanent at every stage and in every facework strategy.

Also important to note is that it is at this stage those whom I label "non-players" disengage. That is, due to a low level of face attachment (whether characteristically so or only dictated by the immediate circumstances) these individuals choose to not react.

Stage 7: Face Recovery

Five respondents in my interviews preferred to remain indifferent at this stage, simply allowing the issue to remain unaddressed. For some, simply forgetting or hoping others forget functions as key for redress. Presumably, if the issue is one of minor severity and others eventually forget, then one settles back into a state of face possession, that is, once again being a competent social actor. For most, however, face depletion is a deeply troubling situation that requires attention that is more active. The prospect of face recovery brings to many feelings of joy as they accomplish something important for themselves. Again, it is critical to keep in mind that this is not simply an issue of working to regain a personal possession, that is, ideational honor or personal face. In fact, the category of social utility coded as heavily as any single category among reasons for redeeming face. Thus, relationships, others' trust and acceptance, are clearly primary motivation for recovering face as honor, dignity, and respect. Ukosakul also collapses the two notions of "redeem face" and "fix face," which represent two different levels of strategies and further point to the variation of difficulty and seriousness of different types of face depletion.

Face recovery strategies may be either active or passive. Individuals may exert considerable causal effort in attempting to regain previous levels of face possession. Others may enact strategies on behalf of the individual who has lost face. Of course, as my interview data suggests, there are clear boundaries that constrain acceptable and illegitimate types of face-recovery strategies. If, in the process of attempting to regain face, others discovery false motives or illegitimate types of face-gain strategies, the attempt to recover face is deemed false and face recovery is unsuccessful. Indeed, such may result in increased face loss.

Stage 8: Face Preservation

Interviewees categorically noted that this stage was extremely important. This is especially so because the cumulative effect of long-term face loss can apparently result in rather serious, perhaps even permanent, face damage. The maintenance and preservation of face is "very important, because if we lose face a second time, this will make redeeming face harder than the first time and will cause a greater loss of faith [in us] than at first" (B17:86). People consider abnormal those who fail to "maintain their own face," possibly even rejecting such people as social pariahs. People consider respect for and appropriate effort to maintain one's own face not only a trait of ordinary people but also a requirement for normal social functioning.

The Logic of Thai Face

A face logic undergirds much of Thai culture. Indeed, since prototypical scenarios act as mediating cognitive structures that guide human action, the logic of Thai face is implicit in the prototypical face scenario just discussed. The strong drive to possess and maintain face, and the concomitant desire for acceptance and esteem, circumscribe this cultural logic. This face logic is relational and personalistic. Face, for many, represents a prominent goal. People want to gain, possess, and maintain face. At one level, this results from the positive affective value face holds for so many. Beyond this, face is highly valuable because of its usefulness. Because of the relative importance it holds for effective social functioning, face, for many Thais, represents a salient aspect of daily interaction. As Bilmes has noted, face represents a type of extremely valuable social capital. This makes face depletion highly problematic and undesirable. Yet, though face can be lost, it is also recoverable. That the state of lost face or shame is something reparable (fixed, redeemed, or regained) is clear. The mechanics of face recovery, however, were not a specific focus of my interview data. These dynamics remain an important issue for further study.

Besides being a significant goal, face for many also serves as a prominent means of relationality. Face represents a personalistic logic that functions within a relational framework, involving acceptance by broader social networks. Consideration for one's own face as well as the face needs of others produces a considerable array of facework options. Many of these strategies are encoded linguistically into conventional idiomatic Thai. These various strategies provide a road map that guides much of Thai social traffic. In particular, the approved forms of face gain and the strong cultural gravity to care for the faces of others.

As a pervasive relational phenomenon, face in Thai culture appears to function as a sort of social glue. As Bilmes noted by highlighting the inadequacy of face in the work of Brown and Levinson, Thai face is not simply a projection of a lone self. Face is involved in creating relationships, relational indebtedness, and exerting benign pressure to maintain social harmony by minimizing the potential face depletion so immanent in interpersonal conflicts. This represents the socially cohesive properties of face. As a goal and means of relationality, Thai face is social capital par excellence.

The complex social reality of face resists a reduction to formal, procedural, or legalistic terms. That is, the grammar by which Thai face functions is relational, personalistic, and often ad hoc. This logic, in part, is the force that drives the prototypical face scenario and also relates significantly to the broader issues of social honor. The interview data demonstrate that such face logic connects, in complex ways, with respect, honor, and dignity. Yet, to a large degree, the exact nature of this relationship remains unclear.

Thai face also contains a moral valence. Ideally, those who possess face should gain it based on positive cultural values. Specifically, this includes the notions of altruism (i.e., not interested primarily in the face gain itself) and benevolence (i.e., helping others). This type of disinterested "virtue of service" seems to provide an ideal moral framework for the notion of Thai face.

Of course, for Thais, face can be "wrong." My data indicates that most Thais hold strongly negative views toward activity that involves promoting face, taking face, or wanting to get face, as well as any excessive preoccupation of gaining social face (particularly "buying" face or gaining face through improper means). Active personal face gain is a censured form of Thai facework. This is so because the motive is for the "fruit" of face and not authentic concern for the appropriate face sources. Such represents a built-in critique of the Thai face game present in Thai culture and highlights one dimension of the moral nature of Thai face.

Summary

This study of Thai face variously confirms, corrects, and extends previous treatments of Thai face. As Suntaree, Sanit, and Ukosakul contend, respondents too note that face is clearly central to Thai personality and culture. It does not merely represent an interesting peripheral issue but forms a core component of all Thai forms of sociality.

My data leads me to understand the primary sources of face as acceptance and distinction. Together with Ukosakul and Suntaree, this highlights the critical importance of social honor for understanding face. Yet, in contrast with the rather one-directional approach of Ukosakul—that face is the container that holds honor (Ukosakul 1999:129)—the data belies any simplistic relationship between honor and face. Although stopping short of a definitive proposal, my study highlights the complicated yet clearly basic relationship of mutual constitution and interaction involved between face, honor, and dignity.

My cultural model also highlights face as an eminently useful form of social capital. As Bilmes notes, face bonds individuals with cohesive and centripetal social force. It plays a critical role in the production and maintenance of social harmony. In this way, Thai face is a function of the interdependent self mode, so dominant in Thai culture. While the insights Bilmes offers are helpful, my research provides greater depth and detail to this critical social utility dimension of Thai face.

This study corrects several points of inadequacy in previous treatments of Thai face. In contrast to Sanit, Mulder, Suntaree, (and to a less serious but still significant degree Ukosakul), my explication of Thai face relies on actual discourse. Thus, my study has the advantage of understanding face from an emic and discourse-rich perspective.

The cultural model of Thai face and the prototype scenario I present resists one-dimensional discussions of face. Clearly, face represents a complex and dynamic dialectic resulting from the Thai self acting in social situations. The implication is for subsequent studies of face to demonstrate a proper level of nuance as it examines Thai face. To collapse the various face dimensions (i.e., positive face, negative face, fellowship face, competence face, and autonomy face) under the single rubric of face is perhaps convenient but ultimately obfuscates important distinctions.

Also, much of the literature on Thai face continues to operate with Western categories of the self. This is clearly the case with Mulder and Phillips. Even Suntaree, as I have mentioned earlier, seems guilty of this.

Her uneven use of the terms "face," "ego self," and "ego orientation" is problematic and may represent her reliance on Western social-psychological typologies of the self. Her analysis would be much more valid if she had interacted with the notions of the interdependent self and the differing valences of face. The data seems quite consistent with an understanding of face in terms of the interdependent self.

I have also noted the built-in critique of face that the category of non-players provides. Mulder, as I have highlighted, focuses his analysis on this dark side of face. His discussion proceeds from a Western perspective, viewing face as negative, unhealthy, and ultimately undesirable. Yet, my analysis demonstrates that even non-players continue to be involved in the face game at varying levels. In particular, this points to the importance of face attachment as a critical issue for understanding Thai face. Attention to the issue of face attachment vis-à-vis a more nuanced notion of face could provide a potentially helpful way of modulating face concerns without a complete (and ultimately impossible) rejection of Thai face.

What I offer here also extends the discussion of Thai face into new areas. The cultural model I present specifies with more depth important characteristics of Thai face while also revealing dimensions not previously discussed. Face is an intersection—a node if you will—where basic cultural values meet with these practices. This account of Thai face demonstrates in specific ways how cultural forces shape face in specific contexts. For the Thai context, such cultural values include patron-client structures, personal merit and relational indebtedness, and collectivism. Face, particularly in its Thai form, represents a complex matrix where sociocultural notions and practices intersect. To say that face is a product of self and society is to move in a positive direction. To go further, we must understand that face is a complex and dynamic social phenomenon created by the intersection of identity goals projected into social space by the self and the response of society to the projection of these goals. The specific cultural values of any given context ground and influence profoundly these projections and responses. Thus, if one understands face in a given cultural context, then one has likely gone a long way in understanding much about said culture.

Far from the univocal conceptualization present in much popular-level thinking and even scholarship (e.g., Mulder), this study specifies many dimensions of complexity in Thai face. Face is multivalent. This complexity, in part, reflects the dual poles of a more inherent dimension, personal face, over against a variable dimension, social face. I have attempted to highlight an apparent distinction between personal face and its counterpart social face. Personal face, potentially available to every person, is constituted partly by the seemingly universal desire to avoid shame (the desire to avoid relational rupture or loss of acceptance) and by the status of any individual as a person. What people loose in face depletion is social capital, the ability to function as a competent social actor. If one is not in a state of shame, then one functions as socially competent actor and, to that extent, possesses (personal) face. It is upon this base that one may, by various strategies, extend one's face into the realm of social face or simply rest content with personal face. Though the rationale for and extent of seeking social face may vary, the motivational gravity to possess and maintain personal face is unquestionable.

To a significant degree, face and facework constitute the basic ground rules that structure and constrain much of Thai social life. The cultural model of Thai face and the prototypical face scenario I propose is an attempt to identify and elaborate this logic of Thai face, that is, the Thai face game. Such represents a salient component of Thai culture, yet much work remains to understand more fully this still underspecified area.

Part 3

Preserving Face

7

Theological Anthropology and a Christian Understanding of Face

ONCE WE HAVE "REGAINED face," that is, achieved a renewed understanding of what face is, it becomes imperative to create a proper framework within which a healthier understanding of face may persist. Just as in the prototypical scenario of Thai face I propose, once people regain face, they must enact subsequent strategies to maintain that face. This process is essentially one of "preserving face."

This chapter will focus upon several important issues I believe will facilitate such face preservation and maintenance. By this, I do not refer to the face of an individual. Rather, the preservation and maintenance I intend here is for the Thai Christian community, and for the broader missiological community in order to uphold the essential face-relatedness of all relationality and to maintain such as a focal point of reflection. To counter the negative effects of Western cultural and theological prosopagnosia, it is necessary to properly orient a Christian conception of the self. To do so, I will examine recent appraisals of the self in modern philosophy, social science, and especially discussions from recent Trinitarian theology. By doing so, I offer an appraisal that makes room for face and does so by orienting it within an explicitly Christian framework. The cumulative effect of these varying accounts will lead to the conclusion that the self is, inescapably, a relational entity. This notion of the relational self, in turn, reveals the modern Western self for what it is—a myth. Moreover, an account of the self from the perspective of Trinitarian anthropology demonstrates that the modern Western self is not simply a fiction but, worse, an idol.

To demolish this idol of the modern Western self is a particularly important step for this project. As I noted in chapter 2, a significant part of the prosopagnosia problem is a consequence of a particular version of the self. That is, this type of cultural and theological prosopagnosia is predicated upon this modern Western self. Yet, what if the proper way to conceive of the self is not in terms of essence or substance? What if these philosophical, theological, and psychological traditions from the West have obscured important dimensions of the self, dimensions that may be critical for a more adequate understanding of the human person? What if the self is fundamentally a relational entity? Indeed, many recent discussions about the self have concluded as much. What would be the implications of conceiving of the self in terms of its sociality and relatedness? What influence would this have on the pervasive prosopagnosia, particularly if this cultural and theological malady depends on this distinctly Western notion of the self? Clearly, to move beyond the modern Western conception of the self would remove those hesitations and objections toward face, which inhere in that particular self paradigm. In doing so, the relational self I propose instead provides a natural way of taking up the issue of face. First, however, I must now turn to various critiques of this traditional Western formulation of the self and the implications for face such critiques necessitate.

The Self and Relationality

In his 2003 work, *Reforming Theological Anthropology*, LeRon Shults surveys a shift in modern thinking, what he designates the "turn to relationality." In particular, he highlights how perspectives from contemporary neuroscience, philosophy, and biblical studies call into question the assumptions of "substance ontology," which have dominated the discussions of the self in the West since the time of Aristotle. Specifically, his work brings into focus a way of viewing the self that is fundamentally distinct from that which I have traced in the preceding section.

If Kant played a significant role in the hyper-individualization of the self, he also contributes, in an ironic twist, a key ingredient to the undoing of the modern Western position. Kant's philosophy reverses the general notions of the objective world and human subjectivity, placing human subjectivity at the center of interpretation and knowing. Of central importance, however, is the way Kant significantly alters the age-old ordering of categories by assigning relationship a much higher level of priority than did Aristotle and most subsequent Western philosophy. As Shults notes, it was

> ... Kant's explicit critique of Aristotle's treatment of relationality [that] provided the impulse for a series of philosophical developments that would open conceptual space for the rapid advancement of dynamic relational hypotheses in physics, psychology, and the other sciences that shape our culture. (2003:22)

This dynamic relationality has variously influenced modern views of the self. Conceived of along these terms, the person is essentially a relational self where the category of "human being" involves necessarily a self related to other selves (Ury 2001:268). This relational self is generated through communication and relationship, a socially constituted self. It is this conception of the self from the perspective of relationality I now wish to explore. To do this, I attend to a critique of the modern Western version of the self through engagement with three perspectives—that of contemporary philosophy, social science, and Trinitarian theology.

The Self in Face Theory and Self-Presentation Theory

Both face theory and self-presentation theory postulate that human selves are occupied profoundly in every social interaction with the projection of symbolic information regarding the self. If these perspectives are accurate, then face is not some ancillary or optional feature of the human person. Face, by this account, emerges as a foundational dimension of human relationality and identity construction.

Contemporary Philosophy

A fundamental assertion of much current philosophical thinking is that the self only exists as part of a larger relational framework. "One is a self only among other selves. A self can never be described without reference to those who surround it" (C. Taylor 1989:35). This is so because the basic question of the self (i.e., "Who am I?"), is answerable only by reference to the way that every person is embedded within the broader context of human relationality.

> I define who I am by defining where I speak from, in the family tree, in social space, in the geography of social statuses and functions, in my intimate relations to the ones I love, and also crucially

in the space of moral and spiritual orientation within which my most important defining relations are lived out. (1989:35)

This view posits an essential dialectic involving the intertwining of the we—and I—experience. I exist only as I interact with, am formed by, and respond to the other. This does not mean a fusing of the self and other. To think of a self in this manner does not require a demolition of the ontological distinctions between self and non-self. Yet the fact that the self does indeed hold to its own positions and stances, stances that many times resist or reject the stances of others, is possible only as such stances and positions emerge from a self embedded in specific social understandings, that is, traditions (1989:39).

To speak of this type of self follows the narrative mode of self in the thinking of Alistair MacIntyre. For MacIntyre, these social traditions are the stories, the narratives within which we find ourselves. The self then is properly a narrative self—"The story of my life is always embedded in the story of those communities from which I derive my identity" (MacIntyre 1985:221). Taking MacIntyre's famous statement about ethics and narrative and modifying it to fit this discussion of the self, we might say then that I can only answer the question, "Who am I?" if I can answer the prior question, "Of what story or stories do I find myself a part" (1985:216). That is, the identity of the self is only conceivable as part of a larger community whole. This means then that issues of the self and embeddedness in community intertwine inextricably, "indicating that any philosophy of the self will at the same time by a philosophy of society and community" (Schrag 1997:90).

Relationality is also essential for the constituting of the self, for relationships function as a sort of film laboratory, developing a gradually forming picture of the self. The emerging portrait of what any given self is occurs through a "shift of focus from the self as present to itself to the self as present to, for, and with the other" (1997:78).

> The self in community is a self that is situated in this space of communicative praxis, historically embedded, existing with others, inclusive of predecessors, contemporaries, and successors. Never an island entire of itself, the self remains rooted in history but is not suffocated by the influx of historical forms and forces. The communalized self is in history but not of history. It has the resources for transcending the historically specific without arrogating to itself an unconditioned and decontextualized visions of the world. (1997:109)

Such a self in contrast to the modern Western a-contextual self, is profoundly relational.

An issue critical to understand the constitution of identity and self properly is the Wittgensteinian distinction between avowals and ascriptions (Penman 1994:19ff.). Wittgenstein contends that our notions and conceptions of the self are generated in a different way than are other general notions. It is through the concepts of avowals and ascriptions that Wittgenstein distinguishes this difference. Avowals are first-person designations of psychological concepts (e.g., "I am hungry," "Yesterday I felt rather put off by her words"). We may claim these descriptions to be accurate yet they are never amenable to the observation of others. No other person can ever know in any direct fashion that these assertions are in fact true. Because of this, avowal assertions of the self are necessarily without criteria. That is, there are no automatic criteria to establish whether in fact states of self-avowal are as we say they are or are mere fabrications. I have no neutral standards to check your avowals against what they claim to be. These remain forever a possession of the individual self.

Ascriptions are statements of a fundamentally different kind. "Look at my red car" is a statement to which others may advance opinion based on communally held criteria. What vehicles count as a "car" and what constitutes the color "red" are things upon which people can and do agree. Thus, ascriptions admit to publicly verifiable criteria upon which others may assent or reject the ascriptive claims. I do not have to take your word for it. Ascriptive assertions can be debated and eventually accepted or rejected based upon community standards that transcend the individual self.

Not only are avowals and ascriptions fundamentally different types of designations. Critical for this discussion of the self, we must also note how we acquire avowals and ascriptions differently. That is, first-person avowals are only possible subsequent to learning second-person ascriptions. I cannot meaningfully assert internal states (avowals) without first being given the language for such self-designations through relationships with a community of others. We acquire a sense of being "hungry" or feeling "put off" not by someone pointing to examples of these or by innate personal knowledge but "by a reliable public expression" of what these actually represent (Mühlhäusler and Harré 1990:99). It is in this public avowing that the first-person utterance functions as a "substitute for, or complement to, a natural expression" of our feelings (1990:99). Our sense of self (who I am, what I feel), then, is a result of our interaction and appropriation with the ascriptive language of others.

This is a critical point and one that essentially deconstructs the myths commonly associated with the modern Western individual self. The sense of self or personal identity, that is, who I think and feel myself to be, is largely the result of our interaction with others. As Penman notes, it is only "through being given these labels, or ascriptions, as the second person in a dialogue that we can later take them on in the first person and avow that that is what we are" (1994:20). It is more accurate to think of the self, then, as constituted by relationality, through communication with others rather than something independently generated or a particular set of unique and inherent individual characteristics. Contrary to the notion of the modern Western self, those things that we take to characterize our most personal, internal essence are in fact functions of relationality.

Framed within these contemporary philosophical notions, a picture of the self emerges that is a deep, many-tiered, and complex reality rather than a one-dimensional conceptualization that an essentialist version requires (C. Taylor 1989:29). The human self is constituted not by substance or essence but "though discourse and action . . . within a community" (Schrag 1997:77). This type of self is not simply embedded in relationality, an individual self that happens to exist in a relational context, but is a self that from its very inception is essentially constituted by its relations.

Social Psychology

Modern social scientific discussions of the self affirm this same point, that is, the self is a multivalent and socially constructed entity. It is perhaps the "symbolic interactionist" approach of George Herbert Mead that captures this most famously. Mead's distinction between the "I" and the "me" advanced the construct beyond that taken by the earlier work of William James. In particular, Mead's approach emphasized a much more complete account of the way the social environment was responsible for constructing the self. Mead maintained that the self was constructed through a process of projecting the self onto others. The "me," that is, the social aspect of self, meets in social space the varying stances taken by others. The "I," that is, the principle of action and impulse, responds by reflexively processing these social messages about the "me." The act of thinking, then, is an inner conversation between a "generalized other" and the "I" (Grenz 2001:308). The unity of the self is constituted by the function of the "I" as a sort of repository containing all the previous "mes."

The result of Mead's approach is a self that is not an inherent property of the human person, as is for example the human heart or a person's faculty of hearing. This self does not function as the "essence" of a person like the self of the modern West.

> The self is something which has a development; it is not initially there at birth but arises in the process of social experience and activity, that is, develops in the given individual as a result of his relations to that process as a whole and to other individuals within that process. (Mead 1964:199)

Such a self has its genesis, then, not in the boundaries of the discrete individual but in the dynamic flow of relationality in social space. "The self, as that which can be an object to itself, is essentially a social structure, and it arises in social experience" (1964:204). The self, from the symbolic interactionist perspective, is a thoroughly social self.

Once a self has come to be, it is possible, Mead contends, to become an isolated self set in its own social experiences and world, but it is impossible to conceive of this same self as coming into existence, at least initially, except as a part of social experience and relationality (1964:204). So then, a person can completely withdraw from all forms of sociality but their very ability to function as a self, even in their decision to withdraw from relationality, is predicated upon the prior notion of self formed by and based upon the relationality they now choose to reject. Thus, the very existence of a thing called the "self" is predicated upon the social relationships that constitute its social environment.

This self then is variably revealed in social interaction. That is, the social context is fundamentally determinative of how this socially constructed self appears.

> What determines the amount of the self that gets into communication is the social experience itself. Of course, a good deal of the self does not need to get expression. We carry on a whole series of different relationships to different people. We are one thing to one man and another thing to another. There are parts of the self that exist only for the self in relationship to itself. We divide ourselves up in all sorts of different selves with reference to our acquaintances. . . . There are all sorts of different selves answering to all sorts of different social reactions. It is the social process itself that is responsible for the appearance of the self; it is not there as a self apart from this type of experience. (Mead 1964:207)

Mead's point is well taken—we all maintain a hierarchy of multiple identities, not a singular, monolithic one. The context for all activity of the self is in social space, and it is the varying contexts of that space that determines how and when these different identities emerge (Stets and Burke 2003:135).

Other theorists emphasize this social constructivist account of the self and the critical role that language, social context, and relationality play in its constitution. Thus,

> . . . any sociopsychological image of the self, in fact the very possibility of self-concept, is inextricably dependent on the linguistic practices used in everyday life to make sense of our own and other's actions. (Potter and Wetherell 1987:95)

The self must not be conceived of as "an object, but the leading concept of a theory of what one is as a person" (Mühlhäusler and Harré 1990:89). Such a self is not an inherent property of the person. Our sense of being a self is "not a natural object, but a cultural artifact. A person is a being who has learned a theory, in terms of which his or her experience is ordered" (Harré 1984:20).

From a modern social psychological perspective, the self is a product of social relations. It is not an inherent property of personhood present at birth, but emerges in social interaction, the product of a multitude of differing social forces.

Trinitarian Theology

Any attempt to sketch the vast number of dimensions in the resurgence of Trinitarian thinking certainly exceeds the boundaries of a single treatment. Thus, what follows is a modest and admittedly incomplete summary of important elements in recent Trinitarian thought. Specifically, I want to trace how the doctrine of the Trinity and the relationality that is part of the being of God affect discussions of the self and therefore of face. This, Trinitarian theology does by revealing the inadequacies of non-Trinitarian accounts of the self and by underwriting the human self with the essential dimension of Trinitarian relationality. An understanding of the self from the perspective of Trinitarian theology provides both a devastating critique of the modern Western self and a necessary corrective to the ephemeral self that emerge from notions of a purely social self.

The various discussions regarding how early Christian thinkers viewed the notions of substance, relation, and personhood attest to the continued debate about the exact shape of these early theological formulations. Many (Gunton 1997; LaCugna 1991; Shults 2003; Ury 2001; Zizioulas 1985) argue that the earlier ante-Nicene Trinitarian view advocated a substantially personal and relational view of God. It is in post-Nicene Trinitarian reflection that an ontology of substance replaced this earlier relational emphasis. The earlier emphasis on threeness thus eventually gave way to concerns with oneness (Grenz 2004:151). While the exact contours of earliest Trinitarian thought remain an issue of contention,[1] it seems safe to assume along with Gunton that by the time of Augustine a solidly conceptual and ontological framework for understanding not only the Trinity but also the human person was the dominant view (Gunton 1997:42). Tertullian's well-known formulation *tres personae una substantia* captures such a move toward static categories of substance. This "Latin formulation disposed Western theologians to emphasize the one divine essence or substance, rather than the plurality or threeness of persons characteristic of the East, and to emphasize the joint working of the three, as the one God, in creation and salvation" (Grenz 2004:9).

Yet, it is undoubtedly the Trinitarian formulation of Augustine that became the "fountainhead of most Western theology of the Trinity" (Gunton 1997:89) and dominated subsequent Western theological treatment of the Trinity. The influential threefold analogy of being, knowing, and willing found later expression in the notions of the mind, its self-knowledge, and its self-love (Grenz 2004:9). It was thus the inner human soul or self that Augustine used to base his explanation of the Trinitarian persons. Thus, the Trinitarian theology of the West paralleled the notion of the self already traced. That is, a growing individual and rational interpretation of selfhood began to take on notions that are more static.

Relationality

Theology after World War II began to focus on the nature and significance of Trinitarian theology. In particular came a renewed interest in the category of revelation and a pressing need to reassess the concept of human nature. This is clear in Barth, the theologian more responsible for the revival of twentieth-century Trinitarian thinking than any other (Grenz 2004:34), followed by Karl Rahner. Together Barth and Rahner stand as

---

1. It remains a point of debate among theologians and historians over the true causes of decline of Trinitarian theology. Some locate this in Augustine, others find Aquinas culpable, and still others point the guilt finger at all patristic and medieval theology (Grenz 2004:13).

the two towering figures of the twentieth-century Trinitarian renaissance. Others have made key contributions to this renewed interest, which has only increased in recent years.²

This revival has had a significant impact upon twentieth-century theology and has occasioned a shift of profound significance. This shift is evident in the nearly axiomatic status the notion of the essential relational nature of God has assumed. Regarding this, David Cunningham notes that

> . . . although contemporary trinitarian theologians vary enormously in the degree to which they are willing to renounce their allegiance to a metaphysics of substance, they seem to agree that more stress should be placed on the claim that God is *relational*. (1998:26)

It is not as if the notion of relationality is a concern that is brought to theology exclusively as a result of the relational shift apparent in other disciplines. In fact, the recent revival of interest in Trinitarian theology from a more relational mode is often directly associated with the inherent, albeit often neglected, dimension of relationality embedded in the early Christian tradition. So, for example, many contemporary thinkers seek to appropriate this relationality by a reexamination of the early Greek fathers. This reappropriation has focused particularly on the Eastern church, for many contend the earlier Eastern fathers preserved a much more relational view of God and the self than did their Latin counterparts.

Trinitarian Theology and the Self

What does it ultimately matter how we conceive of the interrelations of the Trinity? First, since Augustine exhibits a strong tendency toward neo-Platonic conceptions in the development of his anthropology, such categories tend toward the static and do not easily admit to relational notions. In addition, because of dualism in his thought, embodiedness for Augustine cannot be central to humans being in the likeness of God. Static notions of substance combined with categorical priority assigned to a non-material essence of the person (the soul) produce a combination of philosophical

---

2. Grenz notes the quip from David Cunningham that questions whether, with such overwhelming attention, the modern preoccupation with Trinitarian theology is less a renewal and more a "bandwagon" (2004:1). See also Gunton's wry remark in his preface to the second edition of his book on Trinitarian theology (written just six years after the first edition) that "Suddenly we are all trinitarians" (Gunton 1997:xv). Of note are Jürgen Möltmann, Wolfhart Pannenberg, Leonardo Boff, Catherine Mowry LaCugna, and Thomas Torrance. For a helpful survey of the theology of these thinkers, see Grenz 2004.

and theological commitments that ultimately, whether intended or not, resists relationality.

Unfortunately, such non-relational views run the risk of making the doctrine of the Trinity irrelevant. Gunton makes it clear why this is so. He notes that since in the traditional Western view,

> . . . relations are qualifications of the inner Trinity, and not relations between persons, it becomes difficult to see how the triune relatedness can be brought to bear on the central question of human relatedness. God's relatedness is constituted in terms of self-relatedness, with the result that it is as an individual that the human being is in the image of God, and therefore truly human. The outcome is another, theologically legitimated, version of . . . individualism. (1997:102–3)

Not at all subtle, the hidden danger of non-Trinitarian thinking is an individualistic notion of the self that at the end of the day underwrites individualism.

Theologian Alistair McFadyen elaborates on the serious consequence of holding to a-social or less relational conceptions of divinity (1990:25–31). To conceive of God as a single, undifferentiated, and essentially unrelated subject leads inevitably to a self-generating and self-enclosed God (1990:25). God then "becomes . . . the archetypal individual: impassible and apathetic" (1990:25). Relations cannot be determinative of such a divine being. Ultimately, all communication and relationship must be one-way, moving outwards from the singular God, potentially affecting others but not that of Godself. The anthropology that follows from such a version of monotheism is one where relationship is neither constitutive nor determinative for identity. This is so since the person is either subject or source of communication. Relationality and the identity of the person are related only accidentally or incidentally. This anthropology effects "an individualism in which the person is a closed circle of communication engaged in a cyclic orientation on oneself through oneself for oneself" (1990:26). In this view, individuals, in the end, are self-constituting entities.

This lies in radical contrast to a relational Trinitarian mode that produces a notion of the individual for whom relations are truly formative and constitutive of being. This is because the persons of the Father, Son, and Holy Spirit are neither modes of being nor separate and discrete entities but rather "Persons in relation and Persons only through relation" (McFadyen 1990:27).

Recent Trinitarian thought challenges asocial and individualistic conceptions of God and the human self, arguing instead for a relational notion of Trinitarian personhood. Ury notes three important ways such thinking positively informs the modern discussion of the self. First, thinking in a social Trinitarian mode challenges static or passive notions of God that can result from the application of overly rational notions to God. Second, contra modern Western thinking regarding the self, a Trinitarian view of relationality implies that for both God and humankind, personhood is essentially interpersonal. Third, to view divine personhood through the lenses of relationality challenges traditional notions of power. In the mode of Trinitarian relationality, all power, including the power of God, "is found in deference, in seeking the other's glory, in bestowing honor on another" (Ury 2001:280). Because "persons and community are equiprimal in the Trinity" (Volf 1998b:409), the relational self, viewed through the lens of Trinitarian anthropology, is also an ecclesial self. This Christian version of the human person does not merely consist of individual selves in relations, but a communal self, the new humanity in communion with God (Grenz 2001:312).

Being as Communion

Particularly helpful for this discussion is the work of Orthodox theologian John Zizioulas. His theology represents a thoroughgoing application of the notion that the self is a fundamentally relational entity. Indeed, so forcefully and successfully has Zizioulas argued his position that his basic idea (the so-called Zizioulas Dictum, which stipulates we must understand "being as communion") now ranks in importance of the same order as other commonly accepted Trinitarian principles (e.g., Rahner's Rule) (Grenz 2004:134). His "neopatristic synthesis" draws primarily from the theology of the Cappadocian Fathers. It is upon these fundamental philosophical and theological moves by the Cappadocians that Zizioulas forms the basis of his Trinitarian theology and ecclesiology of person.

Much of the theological controversy in the first several centuries, Zizioulas contends, was the result of the Hellenistic philosophical association of substance with hypostasis that subsequent early Christian thought assumed (Zizioulas 1985:36). The Cappadocians moved beyond these traditional Greek definitions current in their day. Instead, they related the notion of hypostasis directly with the person itself. In this way, the

Cappadocian theologians opened a new way of conceiving not only the human person but also God as three persons.

According to Zizioulas, we should not conceive the being of God in terms of essence or nature. Rather "the being of God is identified with the person" (Zizioulas 1985:41). Such a view is possible, since for God, the category of person precedes that of being or essence. Yet, God's being as person is not like the isolated individual person of the modern West. In contrast to traditional formulations, God *is* not in terms of individual substance, but rather in terms of a plurality of person. God's being consists of three persons who live in ecstatic and exocentric communion. Divine being is communion and a relational event. God in and of himself is an "event of communion" (1985:15). Such is a community that reaches out beyond itself in the mutuality of perfect relationship.

This means that, in contrast to a view that holds pure substance or an isolated monad of pure actuality, love and communal life represent the highest principle and true mode of God's being. To say "God is love" is not to express a single property of God, simply one of many divine attributes. The notion of divine love represents the very constitution of God. Love, expressed in the ecstatic communion of persons, becomes the "supreme ontological predicate" for God (Zizioulas 1985:46). Zizioulas argues that it was this early Eastern notion of the relational nature of personhood that subsequent Latin theology eventually obscured and ultimately lost.

Such a view of Trinitarian personhood forms the basis for Zizioulas's theological anthropology. Central to this anthropology is the notion of a communal ontology of personhood that begins not with substance but with communion (Grenz 2004:140). This lies in stark contrast to the more static Western notion of person (i.e., "the self-existent substance . . . determined by its inherent boundaries" (2004:139). The communion into which God draws people, thus constituting them as true persons, is no generic community. It is the community of the triune God. True personhood, then, from the perspective of Zizioulas, is an ecclesial fact (Zizioulas 1985:15). Those who belong to the church are not merely human beings, a category designating simple biological fact. Instead, those "in Christ" take on the nature of "ecclesial being." This involves individual selves who are transformed into true selfhood only by being constituted as "ecclesial selves." Conceived of in this way, the Christian ecclesia is nothing less than a distinct mode of being (1985:15).

From this perspective, the person is no longer "an adjunct of being, a category that we *add* to a concrete entity once we have obtained its ontological hypostasis. *It is itself the hypostasis of being*" (Zizioulas 1985:39). Thus, the person represents the ultimate ontological category, and such personhood is essentially relational. "To be and to be in relation becomes identical" (1985:88). This particular type of relationality undergirds all the theological proposals of Zizioulas including his ecclesiology, soteriology, and anthropology.

For Zizioulas, the fall consists in the "truth of being" acquiring priority over "the truth of communion" (1985:102). That is, fallen human existence becomes simply that of biological necessity rather than the true communal and relational personhood inherent in God's creational intent, that is, the *imago Dei*. Thus, after the fall, human personhood is perverted and people exist only as "individuals." This notion of the individual is humankind in a natural, biological state. Lostness is a condition of futility where humans exist as purely biological individuals. Death and sin are constitutive of such a state. At its core, however, human life outside of God is the existence of the human inclination that strives toward true personhood (i.e., communal being) but ultimately fails to attain to it since such is impossible except through the salvific act of God that constitutes us as true persons (1985:52).

From this perspective, Zizioulas conceives of salvation as "an ontological deindividualization that actualizes their personhood" (Volf 1998a:83). This deindividualization and personalization does not happen to the solitary individual—it is an ecclesial dynamic. This occurs by inclusion into ecclesial communion. The church, then, is the locus for salvation and true being, that is, personhood. Baptism is the concrete death of the individual and the birth of the person (Zizioulas 1985:88) as individuals are incorporated into a network of relationships (1985:90). Salvation, as an ecclesial phenomenon, means that in becoming a member of the church a person becomes an image of God and comes to exist in the same mode of being of God (1985:15).

Zizioulas offers a thoroughgoing Trinitarian anthropology of the self that posits relationality and community as essential components of the new self that occurs "in Christ." His approach represents an important voice among the growing number of Trinitarian proposals that seek to articulate theological anthropology in a more relational mode.

The Imago Dei

The difference that a relational Trinitarian perspective makes is also particularly evident when we examine the critical anthropological notion of the *imago Dei* and the related concept of *perichoresis*. As is the case for much of Western theology, the point of departure for the Western theological discussion of the *imago Dei* is Augustine. Augustine's conception of the image as the rational powers of the self represents the primary thrust of most early Christian teaching regarding the imago. Though the image as "rational element" does not exhaust the teachings of the early theologians, it formed the central emphasis of early Christianity (Shults 2003:225). The notion of the self as primarily a thinking entity continued to exert great influence in medieval theology. For Aquinas, the image is our essential nature, the human rational soul. Yet, as Grenz aptly observes, the problem with such models parallels that of the problem of the modern Western self. That is, to view the image as something that exists within the confides of an individual soul parallels the more general problem inherent in the move to posit a self as a being that exists prior to relationality (Grenz 2003:322). As I have already noted, such is theologically problematic.

In contrast to such configurations that look at the image in terms of its constitutive elements or ontological substance, recent interpreters have proposed various alternatives.[3] Some (e.g., Barr, Wellhausen, von Rad) have proposed that the *imago Dei* is a functional reality, seeing the image as related to purpose and task. Thus, humankind receives dominion over the earth to function as God's ruling representatives. Others (e.g., Buyer, Brunner, Tillich) offer an existential understanding, emphasizing humanity's enduring penchant for seeking transcendence and meaning. Still others (e.g., Moltmann, Pannenberg) advocate an interpretation that is eschatological, seeing the image as an exocentric impulse that points toward a future destiny. All these have in common an opposition to viewing the *imago Dei* as something contained within the characteristics of the individual self.

A Trinitarian perspective moves the discussion of the *imago Dei* in a distinctly different trajectory. A view from the perspective of Trinitarian relationality challenges the traditional Western notion of the image as something inherent in the qualities or internal attributes of a person (e.g., reason, consciousness, will) by placing the image firmly within a framework of the relational self. Since God is not primarily a single, distinct subject

---

3. For a helpful survey of these, see Shults 2003:226–40.

possessing discrete internal attributes but is a community of persons, the image of God would then imply such relationality (Ury 2001:88). Thus, the contemporary awareness of the relational nature of God and the ecclesial self "suggests that the divine image is a shared, communal reality. It implies that the image of God is fully present only in relationships, that is, in 'community'" (Grenz and Franke 2001:200).

McFadyen comments on such a relational notion of the *imago Dei*. In the divine inter-Trinitarian life, relations between persons constitute identity. These relations are not generic, however, but relations of a particular quality that involve self-effacing love and mutual glorification. It is through this specific kind of relationality, a profound mutuality between divine persons, that God constitutes Godself. The implication is that humankind stands fully as the image of God only when approximating this type of Trinitarian identity construction and this particular quality of relationship. The *imago Dei*, from this perspective, involves ex-centricity, dialogical address, and reciprocal response.

Two important consequences follow from this. First, renewal of the *imago Dei* is a critical component to reappropriating full personhood. Whether this occurs as an "individual" (Zizioulas) or as a potentially full person (Volf), it is certain that we do not gain full and true identity outside of reclaiming God's creational intent for human personhood. Humankind gains true dignity and face only by becoming fully human, that is, by being constituted as the *imago Dei* according to the creational intent of God. As Frederick Aquino observes, this means then that

> . . . God's creational goal for human life is not an "autonomous existence in which (humankind) finds the reference point of life in something other than the very life of God. This is idolatry, which leads to disintegration, confusion, and an improper knowledge, both our knowledge of God and self-knowledge (Rom. 1). The proper mode of existence is rooted in the very life of God, which has been presented to us in the coming of the Son of God (Phil. 2:5–11). However, humanity's "role in the created world can be fulfilled only if [it] keeps intact the 'image' of God which was part of [its] very humanity from the beginning." In other words, the proper dignity and honor of human personhood lies in the appropriation of what God intended us to be, namely, moral human agents who reflect the very life of God in the world. As John Meyendorff points out, the "image of God is not an external imprint, received by [humanity] and preserved by human nature

as its own property independently of its relationships with God. Image implies a *participation in the divine nature*." Communion with God, then, enables humanity to realize the apex of human dignity and honor. (2000:43)

The second consequence follows directly from the first. The locus for this reconstituting of the image is the ecstatic communitarian life of the Christian ecclesia. This renewal of God's image or likeness in us cannot happen as a solitary, isolated event. To be reborn into the image of God is to become a communal being. This necessarily follows from the ontology of personhood explicated by Zizioulas. That is, a communal ontology necessarily leads to identity as "ecclesial self" (Grenz 2001:332). If personhood precedes being, and such personhood is inextricably tied to relationality, the process of regaining our true humanity and personhood (i.e., being saved) means being integrated into the communal life of the Trinitarian being of God and sharing this ecstatic existence in the community of the church. The self or human person is not a solitary being (contra Western individualism), a rational thinking substance (contra Western rationalism), or an immortal soul (contra dualism). The true self is constituted by relationship and mutuality.

This ecclesial self is not just a product of theological speculation but is profoundly biblical. Grenz, drawing upon insights from biblical scholar and historian Tom Wright, notes that "a crucial but routinely overlooked dimension of Paul's understanding of the connection between the new humanity and the *imago Dei*—namely, its corporate character." He continues regarding the holding of honor (glory) and mutual transformation of believers in 2 Corinthians 3:18, that

> . . . at work here is no mere private beholding leading to an individualistic "me-and-Jesus" understanding of the believers' transformation. Rather, just as the eschatological goal is the general resurrection, the complete transformation of believers as a shared experience, so also the inbreaking of eschatological power into the present constitutes a corporate people who are all in Christ and consequently who are all being transformed into the image of God who is Christ. (Grenz 2001:250)

This vision resists reductive individualism and the idea that personal identity emerges from a self-focused turn inward. This produces a fellowship that is fundamentally relational—a mode of relationality that maintains a communal character and corporate identity. This does not eradicate the individual into a protean, communal being. Rather, the ecclesial self represents a dynamic of plurality, not homogeneity (2001:333).

Trinitarian Identity

Assuming a Trinitarian account of the divine self, we come to understand that the conception of an unaffected divine monad should never intrude into the Christian account of God. A dynamic and relational God is not a static being but is open to change. That is, both creation and redemption provide opportunities for something new to enter the experience of God. A relational God is open to change, though this of course does not imply complete malleability. Though certain postures that God takes and specific divine commitments remain unalterable because of God's covenant faithfulness, the Trinity does accommodate change within itself, particularly the type of change implicit in Trinitarian relationality.

The notion of the self that emerges from such a view of God is not an individual who functions as a discrete and internally centered subject. Such a self, rather, is inherently linked to others and the social structures of the communities in which it exists (McFadyen 1990:70). McFadyen, drawing upon social-constructionist thinking, notes that this self is not

> ... some internal organ of identity, but is understood in communication terms as a way of organizing one's life and communication in a centered way. It is not something one has so much as something one does, which a person learns in social interaction. (1990:70)

This view of the self requires that personal identity must relate directly and intimately to the identities of others and our relations with them. It is the call of others and our response to such calls that constitute us as persons. In this way, it is impossible to think of the self as a discrete individual, an isolated entity, or an autonomous person constituted exclusively by unique internal characteristics. The *imago Dei*, understood from a relational Trinitarian perspective, assumes this very kind of identity construction.

Volf's discussion of Trinitarian theology and human personhood in his article "'The Trinity Is Our Social Program': The Doctrine of the Trinity and the Shape of Social Engagement" (1998b), involves critical matters regarding such identity. In particular, he draws upon Regina Schwartz's notion of "hard identities" that are forged in the antithetical opposition of selves over against other selves. A notion of divinity that rests upon a single, omnipotent subject will inevitably result in a hard, possibly even violent, "we are 'us' because we are not 'them'" approach. It represents an approach only possible by assuming the notion of the self as an isolated, monadic, and a-contextual entity.

A Trinitarian approach, however, contends that the Trinitarian relations are not something that self-standing persons enter into as a collection of discrete individuals. The a-contextual and a-social self of the modern Western individual, which produces the either/or approach Schwartz mentions, is replaced by a both/and identity that views other selves as an inherent part of one's own self. This is so because "persons and community are equiprimal in the Trinity" (Volf 1998b:409). That is, the identity of the self includes the personal individual and its multiplex webs of relationality. In a sense, the self is a composite involving important elements of both self and other.

To illustrate this, Volf draws upon John 7:16, where Jesus states, "My teaching is not mine but his who sent me." How should we understand, Volf asks, the seeming contradiction involved in Jesus's assertion of the teaching being simultaneously both "mine" and "not mine"? Volf resolves the apparent conundrum by drawing attention to two fundamental dimensions involved in relational identity.

First, Volf suggests we must understand identity as an essentially non-reducible phenomenon. Relationships are non-reducible, for we are not our relations but enter into relations already standing outside those relations. This results in a necessary mechanism for boundary maintenance, that is, a way of asserting the self in the presence of the other and deference of the other before the self (Volf 1998b:410). Second, Volf notes that relations are never self-enclosed. This dimensions points to how the other does not exist completely outside the self but enters into the space of the self through its porous and shifting boundaries (1998b:410). The self is itself only by being in a state of flux stemming from "incursions" of the other into the self and of the self into the other. The self is shaped by making space for the other and by giving space to the other, by being enriched when it inhabits the other and by sharing of its plenitude when it is inhabited by the other, by reexamining itself when the other closes his or her doors and challenging the other by knocking at the doors (1998b:410).

It is, of course, possible to stress one aspect of the self–other continuum so that an extreme self-orientation dominates the face of an individual. Likewise, one's face may be enmeshed so completely in the other to the point that the concerns and opinions of others dominate and precludes attention to the self. The value of Volf's assessment, however, is in how he draws attention to the essential dimensions of all identity construction, particularly as it takes place within a Trinitarian framework.

Perichoresis ("Dynamic Relationality")

An important part of the Trinitarian life, and by extension, the ecclesial self, is that of *perichoresis*. This theological notion was first developed by Gregory of Nazianzus and subsequently followed by the other Cappadocians. Applied to the Trinity, *perichoresis* meant that there was an active and dynamic movement of relationality within the being of God. This movement, or perichoretic dance, asserted that the individual persons of the Trinity mutually interpenetrate one another but do so without a loss of personal identity. The notion provides a dynamic way of conceiving divine unity not as a "Stoic solitude but a perichoretic compenetration" (Ury 2001:274). Thus, "the unity of the Trinity *is* the relationality, and the relationality *is* the unity" (Loder 1998:195). Applied to theological anthropology, this implies that a human self made anew after the image of God is a self of perichoretic love. This is not some sort of generic relationality, but one constituted by the relationality that is basic to the life of the triune God.

It is crucial to remember that the application of the notion of *perichoresis* to the human person is inherently limited by a simple fact—we are not God. As Volf points out, we cannot fully approximate the life of God's self since we are constrained by creaturely and sinful limitation (1998b:404). This does not obviate the possibility of imitating God conjunctively in certain respects though it is imperative to keep the important disjunctive features always in mind. Thus, two important considerations regarding the human modeling of the divine must constrain any talk of perichoretic relations in human community. First, we may apply such Trinitarian concepts as *perichoresis* to humans only analogously rather than in any univocal sense (1998b:405). Second, since humankind is infected with sin and limited by our humanness, we can only appropriate the divine life in ways that are historically appropriate, that is, cognizant that we cannot achieve a complete likeness of God's life prior to the eschaton (1998b:405).

These cautions Volf offers remind us of the inherent limitations in using Trinitarian notions to understand human sociality. Yet, keeping such reminders before us enables us to identify ways that the perichoretic life of the triune God can provides resources for understanding ourselves as the *imago Dei*.

Mutual Honoring

A theological anthropology based upon the perichoretic divine life of the social Trinity is essentially a "glory-anthropology." Here glory is defined not in an essentialist mode but as a category of social honor. Leonardo Boff suggests that the our primary role as people who know God is to join this dance of Trinitarian life, which he describes as loving, sharing, unity, and "eternal doxology" (1988:123). The perichoretic life of God involves the mutual honoring and receiving of honor inherent in the divine persons. This Trinitarian dynamic "involves the glorification entailed in the reciprocal sharing of love" (Grenz 2001:327). In essence, the loving mutuality inherent in the life of the Trinity is an "eternal reciprocal glorification" (2001:327). This infinite dynamism of communion and interdependence (Boff's "eternal doxology") provides a foundation for speaking of honorification as part of the relationship inherent in being an ecclesial person.

If we envision the life of the ecclesial self as constituted by the dynamic, perichoretic Trinitarian love, such a relational, communal identity must be a reflection of the inner dynamic that exists within the triune life of God. Life in a Trinitarian mode is to "share, share and love, love and unite ourselves to the divine Persons in an eternal doxology as it was in the beginning and ever shall be from all eternity to all eternity" (Boff 1988:218). It is in this way that the notion of glory, or more properly, honor, provides a link between the perichoretic life of God and the lived-out existence of the ecclesial self. God's ultimate salvific purpose aims to bring about the eschatological community of love that becomes a reflection of the Trinitarian life of God. Grenz notes this dynamic as well.

> God's soteriological purposes arise out of the glorification of his own triune nature. By establishing the eschatological community of love, the covenant people, God brings into being a new humankind, a people who mirror for all creation the divine character and essence. As his essential nature is made manifest in creation, the triune God is glorified. Rather than a cosmic egotist who demands the opposite quality in his creatures, therefore, he is the triune God who desires that humans mirror his own holy character, which is love. As we live in fellowship, we bring honor to the one who is himself the divine community of love. (1994:489)

The important point here is that the granting and receiving of honor is an intrinsic part of the divine communion, the perichoretic life of God, that undergirds Trinitarian theological notions. Not only is this true regarding the economic Trinity,[4] for if Boff and Grenz are correct this mutual honoring also forms an essential part of the divine life, that is, the "eternal doxology." God acts for our salvation by honoring himself, that is, showing the world the honorable, loving, and faithful God he truly is. In salvation, we are integrated into the communal fellowship that not only results from but also constituted by divine love and honor. We are constituted into the *imago Dei* and acquire the honorable identity of the triune God by participating in the very life of the honorable and glorious God. By living together in loving community, we reflect what God is like and thereby bring honor to him. This reflexive dynamic of honor that exists between humankind and God draws us deeper into the fullness of communal Trinitarian life that is salvation. Being the *imago Dei* then involves in fundamental ways the dynamic interplay of self, relationality, and mutual honor. The essential dimensions of Trinitarian personhood can occur only within a community of love and honor. Mutual honoring, then, constitutes a basic reality of this lived-out community as it mirrors the divine reality of perichoretic mutual honorification.

It is important to understand the essential Trinitarian or communitarian foundation this requires. Without the presence of another, honor easily becomes hubris, self-contained privilege, and self-aggrandizement. The same is true in regards to the Trinity. Honor for a singular monad becomes self-absorption. A binary community produces a clique, a private club, and honor risks becoming an "I'll scratch your back, you scratch mine" experience. It takes a threesome to open to the full mutuality of giving and receiving honor. Viewed in this way, the giving and receiving of mutual honor between the Father, Son, and Spirit constitutes a basic Trinitarian reality, which reaches out to draw others into this loving community of mutual honor.

> Hence, as the Spirit leads those who are 'in Christ' to glorify the Father through the Son, the Father glorifies them in the Son by the Spirit. This marks the glorification of humankind more specifically, because glorifying the Father in the Son together with all creation is the ultimate expression of the *imago Dei* and there marks the *telos* for which God created humans in the beginning. (Grenz 2001:327)

---

4. For example, see John 17 where the reciprocal giving and granting of honor is expressed in Trinitarian terms.

Yet, such is not simply the goal toward which God draws all creation. Mutual honor and glorification are, in fact, constitutive elements of the lived-out experience of the ecclesial self. As McFadyen reminds us, Trinitarian life does not consist in general relationality but relationality of a specific quality. The mutual honoring in perichoretic mode the quality of relationality that is a part of the ecclesial life involved in the self's reconstitution into the *image Dei*. To honor another is to accept, in a fundamental way, their identity and face claims. Acceptance not only ratifies face but also enhances. Face protection, preventing shame of the other and self, is also related to the practices of honor.

The Problem of the Fragmented Self

It is necessary, however, to highlight an inherent problem with the relational self as it stands in the philosophical and social scientific literature. Though the notion of a "consistent" self of "character" that functions independently of social context and relationality is problematic, the pragmatic self of convenience or utility that some accounts provide does in fact describe a real mode by which many selves function. That is, the relational self can easily dissolve in fluidity that freely floats in the ebb and flow of relational dynamics. Grenz notes that a lack of structure is a fundamental weakness of the modern notion of the relational self. Though rightly criticizing the highly substantial, individual, and rational modern Western self, a self formed through social relationships can be "highly decentered and fluid, for a person can have as many selves as social groups." A self that is completely relational is open to the risk of becoming "a bundle of fluctuating relationships and momentary preferences." The end result is "a highly unstable, impermanent self" (Grenz 2001:136).

The caution Grenz issues also parallels MacIntyre's critique of the notions of face and self-presentation in the work of Goffman. For Goffman, success for the self involved in face- and self-presentation is whatever passes for success (MacIntyre 1985:115). Effectiveness in making a successful face claim is what counts as interactive effectiveness. There exists no objective standards of achievement, no larger narrative account within which this strategic self functions.

By positing such face- and self-presentation as the central theme of his face sociology, Goffman embodies a particular dimension of sociality that Aristotle explicitly rejects, that is, a position that views honor (and by extension, face) as simply that which expresses or involves the positive regard of others. For some, honor then consists precisely is the reception of such honorific regard. This is fundamental to a Goffmanesque account, where imputations of merit and "successful" face- or self-presentation are in fact the entire point. As MacIntyre notes, "Goffman's is a sociology which by intention deflates the pretensions of appearance to be anything more than appearance" (1985:116). In such a social world, the self functions without any objective merit or standards for virtue beyond the immediate "success" of presentation in specific social interactions. Such a self, ultimately, consists of nothing but a series of unconnected episodes of successful or unsuccessful self-projection. It is a self content with face regardless of the cannons or codes upon which such face granted.

This type of fragmentary self cannot be the bearer of virtue since "the unity of a virtue in someone's life is intelligible only as a characteristic of a unitary life, a life that can be conceived and evaluated as a whole" (MacIntyre 1985:205). For MacIntyre, a self is a "concept . . . whose unity resides in the unity of a narrative which links birth to life to death as narrative beginning to middle to end" (1985:205). Thus, the unity of self is a narrative unity. All attempts to provide an account of the self and identity apart from the notions of narrative are doomed to failure (1985:218). This is so because the *telos* essential for any sustaining account of the individual self along with the requisite virtues needed to substantiate any version of self all depend upon a narrative framework that can provide this *telos* and an account of that which constitutes virtue.

In contrast to this Goffmanesque sociology of the self, MacIntyre offers an account of an Aristotelian self of virtue. This Aristotelian account posits honor (or face) to be a legitimate human good.[5] Aristotle points out that people ideally honor others "in virtue of something that they are or have done to merit the honor" (MacIntyre 1985:116). That is, proper esteem and acceptance (honor or face) is based upon the prior possession of some virtuous quality. In his *Eudemian Ethics*, honor is not merely positive acclaim from large numbers of people. Rather, true honor is based upon behavior that is truly honorable, that is, virtuous (Aristotle 1952:1232b

---

5. "Worthy is a term of relation: it denotes having a claim to goods external to oneself. Now the greatest external good we should assume to be the thing we offer to the gods, and which people of position most covet, and which is the prize awarded for the noblest deed, and this is honor; that is surely the greatest of external goods" (Nichomachean Ethics 1123b 16-20).

20–22). As Aristotle asserts in the *Nichomachean Ethics*, "honor is the reward for virtue" (1934:1123b 35).[6]

Thus, honor itself is a good only in a secondary sense since it is based upon a prior, and more fundamental, good. This does not make the insights offered by Goffman invalid. Rather, MacIntyre's (and that of Aristotle) account demonstrates how the self implied by face theory and self-presentation theory is inadequate if not rooted in the larger framework of a moral narrative.

How might we ground face properly so that it does not admit to MacIntyre's critique? He proposes the solution—a narrative self constituted by a particular story (the gospel) and circumscribed by a specific set of virtues. Since the Christian story is not simply one story among others, and the community that results from this story not simply one community among others, but the primary or most basic story and community for Christians, the virtues that inhere are to follow the self through all their communities, and various permutations. Thus, a self that exists within the narrative framework of the gospel story finds its necessary *telos* and account of virtue. It is upon these twin dynamics that face can find proper moorings. This account allows for a self that resists the problematic tendencies of the modern Western self yet avoids the fatal collapse of the self into utilitarian fluidity.

Summary

I began this chapter looking at how the perspectives of modern philosophy, social science, and Trinitarian theology speak to the issue of the self and face. What we discovered is that these perspectives call into question the dominant model of the self in modern Western understanding. That is, the cumulative effect of these varying accounts leads us to conclude that the self is fundamentally a relational entity.

The notion of a relationally constituted self, in turn, does not merely open the door to face—it demands any view of the self give serious consideration to the constitutive role face and facework play. This is so since face is not simply a prideful preoccupation with the self, a function of egocentrism, but truly forms a necessary part of all human relationality.

---

6. "τῆς ἀρετῆς γὰρ ἆθλον ἡ τιμή" (Aristotle 1934:1123b 35). Such is also the opinion of Augustine. "Therefore glory, honour, and power-those Roman aims, which the good men strove to attain by honourable means-must be the consequences of virtue not its antecedents" (Augustine 1984:200).

Face obtains in all social contexts including those that are fundamentally hierarchical as well as those that are more democratic or egalitarian. Face is indeed ubiquitous in all relationality. This admission that the self is fundamentally relational, together with an acknowledgment that face is a necessary dimension of all human relationality, provides the bridge that links the notion of face with a relational account of the self.

Viewing the self as a relational entity and, in particular, the *imago Dei* understood in a Trinitarian mode also resists the prosopagnosia that arises from the modern Western version of the self. Such an account of the self forces those who hold a face-oblivious posture to awaken to the ever-present reality of face. The rejection of face characteristic of the face-averse position is possible only as long as one continues to uphold the modern Western account of the self. Once we abandon the notion of the modern Western self, the door opens for a reappropriation of face as an essential function of the relational self.

A notion of the self as a relational entity rather than an isolated individualistic monad reminds us that we always configure our selves, and our faces, to meet the appropriate identity goals we have in differing social situations. Likewise, the notion of a relational self demonstrates that the putative notion of the "true me" that exists as an inner essence independent of our human relationships is illusory. The sense that face is inimical to the authentic self of self-expression also trades upon the idea of an entity that can exist beyond the reach and influence of human relationality. This account has endeavored to show that such a position does not in fact exist. It seems an inescapable conclusion, then, that we all participate in face and self-presentation, whether controlled or automatic self-presentation.

Face can, of course, fall prey to problematic motives or strategies. Yet, such does not necessitate a rejection or aversion to face but simply requires a deeper understanding of the forces and motivations that are involved in various face activity. To view face as simply utilitarian posturing to meet immediate situational success is possible, but not necessary. That face can involve false or duplicitous motives or an attempt to project an image that does not correspond with deep, internal desires is true, but does not obviate face. The Christian narrative together with a Trinitarian anthropology provides coherence to a relational self.

A view of the human person from the perspective of relationality (i.e., the relational self and its Christian counterpart, the narratively constituted ecclesial self) resists the flawed Western notions of face. This relational account requires us to reflect more self-consciously on face and open up this critical area of human relationality for further exploration. As Ury notes, if "the determinative element of existence is divine interpersonal love, then reality takes on a new face" (2001:266). I would like to reverse Ury's statement and assert that by making Trinitarian being determinative, face takes on a new reality.

8

A Theological Framework to Orient Face

IN THIS CHAPTER, I wish to contend that a proper perspective of face would not only constitute a significant correction to widespread face-oblivious or face-averse postures resulting from a cultural and theological prosopagnosia but also serve to guide Christian reflection about face. That is, as a Trinitarian anthropology of the self requires us to acknowledge face, it is critical to move toward a theological framework in which we might struggle with face issues. What would be the components of such a theological framework for understanding face?

I propose that such a framework would provide resources to engage the dominant modes of face that society offers with a dynamic, back and forth movement between two postures—affirmation and reorientation. Informed by Trinitarian assumptions, these two dynamics should guide us by setting the proper boundaries for all face-related thinking and behavior.

I will suggest three orienting motifs that may serve as markers of this boundary. First, face must be circumscribed within a Trinitarian framework. In particular, this means a Trinitarian view of the self and the *imago Dei* that God who has designed us to be face-generating beings. Second, we must frame our Christian reflection on face upon the central biblical notion of the Face of God and Christ. Authentic human face and facework must seek its source in the gracious face of the God who accepts us. God's Face, mediated to us through the face of Christ, fundamentally reorients and bestows upon us a true face of esteem and acceptance. Third, face and other honor-laden phenomena receive significant attention in Scripture and provide valuable resources for reflection upon face. This pervasive honor discourse that occurs throughout the New Testament forms the third orienting motif.

Affirmation

The most basic feature of the theological framework I suggest is the affirmation that arises from a new awareness of the ubiquity of face. The preceding account of Trinitarian anthropology of the self concludes relationality and face are essential elements of ecclesial personhood. Once we accept this to be so, however, still we must subsequently locate face within the creational intentions of God. For, we must choose whether face is an inherent part of God's plan for humanity or whether its origins lie not in creation but rather in the fall.

If we return to Ting-Toomey's notion of face as "identity respect" or "social self-worth," we see that, at its core, face is about the pervasive human attempt to establish a sense of worth and meaning ("esteem") and to find acceptance (esteem that is "social"). These dual dimensions also undergird the theoretical notions of "social face" and "personal face." Possessing face through both increasing public recognition based on culturally specific values or by an inherent quality of humanness assume the fundamental dimensions of esteem and social acceptance.

From this we see that the roots of face lie in the longing for acceptance (community) and affirmation (esteem). It is through diverse face strategies that we express this deep longing to seek and establish acceptance, community, and esteem. We can conceive face, then, as a mechanism that guides the perennial human quest for community and esteem. We project certain faces (identity goals) and desire for a community to ratify them by acceptance and recognition. This desire for harmony is a primary characteristic of human community. As Shults and Sandage note, humans always "hope to belong in a peaceful and joyful pattern of harmonious relations with others" (Sandage and Shults 2003:207). It is through the avenue of face that this harmony is realized. In this way, we see how face functions as a necessary mechanism for all social relations.

The creation accounts of Genesis 1–3 imply all this. There the basic constituents of face, that is, relationality, acceptance, and esteem all find expression within the goodness of God's created order. Within the pre-fall world implied communion and harmony (between God and humankind,

humankind and the world, and humans with one another) and divine assessment of goodness suggest that face derives from creation itself.

Face is implicit in the garden accounts in at least two ways. First, based upon the account of the mutual interrelatedness between sociality and face, the fact that God is from the beginning a God involved in communication and relationality assumes face and face-related concepts play a necessary role in this story. If, again as I have asserted, the image of God is something that is primarily a relational reality, then the fundamental assertion that God created humankind in accordance with the image of God (Gen 1:26–27) again roots face not in a post-Edenic fallen world but in God's good creation.

Yet, face also arises from the way God esteems the human couple and draws them into harmonious community. God addresses them as responsible moral agents, giving them not only work to do (Gen 1:28–30) but also the moral task of choosing to follow God's directions (Gen 2:16–17). God's pronouncement of all creation as good points to the strong sense of esteem and divine satisfaction that flow from this creational activity (Gen 1:31). Prior to the rupture sin brings, pre-fall relationality reflects the fullness of the divine intensions. Together, the relationality and harmony of the Edenic world and the face-giving posture of God toward his human creation all point to the origin of face in divine purpose.

A darker side of face soon replaces the earlier lack of face problematic. The Genesis creation account highlights that the nakedness of the human couple (both physical but also an implied metaphorical nakedness of living an open life with no cause to hide) involved a state of honor, i.e., "they felt no shame" (Gen 2:25). The primordial sin ushers in the loss of face and the attendant experience of shame (Gen 3:7). From this flow the negative face-saving strategies of cover-up, hide, and denial.

As the account I have provided contends, the phenomenon of face is something that derives from both the life of the Trinity and the ecclesial self, the *imago Dei*, to which God calls humankind to recover. God created us as face-creating beings. Though sin and the flesh can take over and dominate it, face itself originates not in our fallen humanness but as a part of the creational intentions of the triune God.

At the most basic level, then, it seems that God has programmed humankind to be face-generating creatures. Face forms an essential God-given dimension of human personhood and relationality. Such an admission does not simply make room for face and face concerns but posits these as essential components of our humanity. To extend the Cartesian dictum in a completely new direction, it is possible to assert that "we are, therefore we face."[1] Thus, face, provides a bridge for our irreducible human desire for harmony and esteem both which can only exist properly in true community. We should conclude then that at a basic level, face is a divine gift that structures our identity and relationality. And it is at this basic level that we can offer a qualified acceptance of face.

Reorientation

This basic acknowledgment of the face-engaged lives we all live is a momentous first step yet such awareness by itself is not enough to move us forward. We must convert this acknowledgment into a critical awareness. That is, though face is a natural product of relationality, like all other aspects of human relationality sin and the flesh can taint it. Because of this, those who operate from a Christian perspective may not simply take face at "face value."

What could anchor the critical task of face reorientation? What I prescribe here is not a set of fixed rules to apply rigidly. Rather, I offer a series of orienting motifs, all deriving from the fundamental perspectives of Trinitarian personhood offered in the previous section. The three foundational loci I propose are as follows: the face of God and the face of Christ, the *imago Dei* understood as the ecclesial self, and honor or glory. These guiding motifs revolve, in turn, around the essential dual dimensions of face implicit in Ting-Toomey's definition. Each of the orienting motifs I propose addresses this dual dimension of face of acceptance and esteem.

It is legitimate to ask why these three particular motifs should function in this way. Is such a selection purely arbitrary? In fact, the three I have chosen to focus on here are compelling precisely because they emerge out of the intersection of the two main areas of this study. That is, the overlap that occurs when we bring together the discussion of the self (in particular, the ecclesial self that relativizes the main face objections from the modern Western perspective) with the notion of face (both human and divine) yields these three specific dimensions. In this sense, these three motifs are quite organic to this discussion and their poignancy for this account is readily apparent. Admittedly, it is likely that other motifs may be helpful for this discussion. Thus, I do not offer these as an exhaustive

---

1. I use "face" here as a verb that includes face-related behavior and conceptualizations

account or comprehensive guide. Yet, it is precisely in the emergence from this overlap wherein their value lies.

The Face of God/Christ

It is perhaps fitting that we should seek to root the human experience of face in notion of the face of God. Both the Hebrew term *panim* and the Greek term *prosopon* designate the literal face of a person. By extension, this comes to represent the presence of a person and eventually comes to stand metaphorically for the person. To know someone's face is thus to know the person. To seek the face of someone is to seek the person. Such language of the face as the person is pervasive throughout both the Hebrew and Christian scriptures.

Contemporary child psychology helps us understand an even deeper level of the significance of face. Studies of early human development demonstrate how the metaphor of face emerges out of the depths of early human experience. The face of the mother mediates her confirming presence to the infant (Loder 1998:90). The face thus becomes "the primal prototype of the religious experience in which one is placed with recognition and affirmation in the context of the cosmic order" (1998:91). To the child the vehicle of the mother's face mediates her comforting presence and love. Our earliest experience with relationality, acceptance, and esteem grow out of this connection with the face of our earliest and most significant caregivers, which in most cases is the mother. The face of the mother becomes a metaphor for comfort, love, and acceptance.

As we continue to mature, this early experience of face continues to exert influence on our lives. Eventually, however, a tension arises because we become increasingly aware of the limitations of the early mother-face experience. That is, the child soon discovers that the accepting, loving, understanding face that they desire is not a continuous one. As much as a child might delight in always being faced by the face of the mother, her face eventually leaves, whether for only brief moments or for longer, and more anxiety-producing intervals. This leads to something that seems imprinted deeply upon the human psyche at a very early stage, that is, an ontological yearning to be faced with a face of acceptance that will not go away. As Loder notes,

> . . . human nature is so constituted that built into its ego structure and implicit in its greatest achievements is a cosmic loneliness that longs for a Face that will do all that the mother's face did for the

> child, but now a Face that will transfigure human existence, inspire worship, and not go away, even in an through the ultimate separation of death. (1998:119)

He goes on to discuss this "longing in persons for a cosmic ordering, self-confirming presence of a loving other, a longing for that which defines what it means to be human and makes us over in its image" (1998:119).

Such lies at the root of a deeply pervasive human "ontological anxiety" (Shults and Sandage 2003:206–21). That is, much of human fear, guilt, and shame are products of an anxiety that derives from a strong desire to belong to patterns of relationality that are peaceful and harmonious. In addition to such acceptance, we also seek value and meaning, to be esteemed and believe that we are worth something. These desires, in part, emerge from the earlier experience of acceptance and esteem that constitutes the mother-face experience. The frustration of such impulses brings about "ontological anxiety" as we seek to establish worth and find acceptance. This of course parallels the very concerns that lie behind the phenomenon of face.

Interestingly, an additional consequence of the modern individualistic self is how such inevitably leads to the legal/rationalistic approach typical in many modern Western contexts. Such an approach ultimately obviates the need to protect other's social esteem since means of relationality, conflicts, and problems tend to be conceived of in terms of moral fairness rather than intersubjective relationality. What stands in contrast to this is the notion of offenses that are dehumanizing in the way they cause dishonor and disrespect. Such a modern rationalized or legal approach often leads to a sense of diminishment of our very self, our worth as human beings. Such devaluing "offers us an anxious taste of the estrangement that is at the core of the human predicament" (Sandage and Shults 2003:65). This too becomes a significant source of moral and ontological anxiety.

The anxiety to fulfill these needs results in the vast human project of establishing face, satisfying face-related needs, and seeking ontological security in sources independent from the Face of our Creator. Yet, the eternal Face of God speaks directly to this basic human and existential longing. It is this Face of God, that is, true divine presence, mediated through the face of Christ, which renders such striving unnecessary. By locating ourselves in the presence of the Face of God, we find acceptance and establish a sure basis for esteem. The Face of God, which meets us in the face of Christ, establishes, in no uncertain terms, that God accepts us in full and esteems us as possessing incalculable value.

Unlike both the mother's face and all subsequent face experiences in life, this Face is a continuous and perfectly consistent one. The Face of God becomes the full reality of what the face of the mother and the face of others is only an intimation. The human quest that lies behind all our face projections and facework must first be rooted in a deep connection with the original and eternal Face of God. It is only then that such may find fulfillment.

This longing finds ultimate fulfillment (or, perhaps, ultimate frustration) in the eschatological Face of God. C. S. Lewis discusses this in his book *The Weight of Glory*.

> In the end that Face which is the delight or the terror of the universe must be turned upon each of us either with one expression or with the other, either conferring glory inexpressible or inflicting shame that can never be cured or disguised. (1980:13)

Lewis goes on to discuss this same sort of human yearning that arises out of the mother-face experience. Such a deep longing for some connection with the universe,

> . . . to be on the inside of some door which we have always seen from the outside, is no mere neurotic fancy, but the truest index of our real situation. And to be at last summoned inside would be both glory and honour beyond all our merits and also the healing of that old ache. (1980:16)

To be greeted and accepted by the Face of God provides the basis for Christian hope of that ultimate honor, that is, to have our own face claims be recognized and accepted before the eternal Face of God. This is the solution to the "old ache," the ontological anxiety that stems from this basic human existential predicament.

Although this deep yearning to be faced by God's true face originates in our earliest childhood experiences, Shults and Sandage utilize the work of psychoanalyst Ana-Marie Rizzuto to explain how images of God are formed by the various relationships throughout the developmental history of each person. Thus, even the various ways we conceive of God and God's identity are, to a great degree, influenced by the ways we have come to know the faces of significant others. This is so since "the faces of relational figures significantly influence our representations of the face of God" (Shults and Sandage 2003:90). In this sense, face in the human realm is theologically generative. The identity of God we come to know depends, in part, upon our prior experiences of relationality and face. Yet, human relationality, particularly our very earliest and formative relational experiences, in turn depends substantially upon our experiences of the faces of others. It is in precisely in the arena of the human face that we come to yearn for, and eventually know the Face of God. And it is through our experiences of human face that we come to image and now the God whose healing Face we come to know.

The ways we image God, then, are determined to a large degree by the metaphorical nature of face. Yet, this ceases to be a strictly metaphorical experience in the incarnation. Jesus becomes the concrete representation of the face of God in historical form. Ultimately, it is in the face of Jesus that the divine presence, the Face of God, comes to us. The only way for us to know God's self is for God to reveal it to us. How does God mediate knowledge of himself to humankind? We do not know the divine fully or internally as subject. We can never know God *as* God, at least not this side of the eschaton. Such remains the possession of the Trinity alone.

Yet, God reveals himself to us, in concrete fashion. As Loder and Neidhardt remind us, "in Pauline theology, God does not make himself known to us apart from the mediation of Christ" (Loder and Neidhardt 1992:295). Therefore, from the perspective of the New Covenant, this occurs through the concrete identity projection, viz., the face of the human Jesus. We have knowledge of the honor and glory of God through the face of Christ (2 Cor 4:6). Face becomes a significant vehicle for the economic Trinity as there is not other way by which God could be present in relationship with humans. The Face of God finds its most complete expression through the face of Christ, the chosen vehicle for the disclosure of divine self-knowledge and love.

There is of course a qualitative difference between the divine face (as God's presence and projected identity) and human face. God's Face, revealed through the face of Christ, is never self-seeking, does not fall prey to the various strategies of self-justification, hubris, or deception that so often seize human face. The ultimate, consistent Face is never driven by the whims and vicissitudes of the varying moods and changing stances characteristic of humans. The Face of God in the face of Christ is one that is completely true, completely loving, and completely for us.

Thus, it is through the face of others that we first come to know the divine Face. This is eventually modified by an experience with the Face of God who meets us through the face of Christ. To have such a "face knowledge," if you will, of God, then, would not imply as if often the case in contemporary parlance a surface or superficial knowledge. Biblically speaking, having "face knowledge" of God is to know the fullest divine self-expression that comes to us through the face, the presence, the projected identity of the Father through the face of the Son by the mediating power of the Holy Spirit. God's face is not something constituted by philosophical speculation but by a relationally constituted narrative within which we come to share, that is, the gospel story of Trinitarian love.

Before one comes to know God, a person's face is inherently limited. Without being remade into the *imago Dei* the natural human face can only rely on the purely human resources available in the self's own structures and those offered us by the surrounding culture in which we find ourselves. Thus, the projection and validation of face, outside of the eternal Face of God, must inevitably fall short of those things for which it yearns.

It is in the experience of being faced by the Face of God that we gain a new and true face. We come to be esteemed and accepted by God and, by extension, his worldwide people. God then, is the ultimate giver of face, yet such is always a true face. Indeed, from this perspective, the acceptance and esteem that come from God forms the only proper source for human face or facework. It is the substance to which all human face-related behavior points. Our face projections are the clues to which the Face of God is the ultimate answer. This is the grand divine facework of the God who faces us with a face of grace and ratifies our innate human face needs to be esteemed (honor) and accepted (community). It is in these ways that the Face of God can function to orient a Christian account of face.

The Ecclesial Self and the Imago Dei

It is the gracious face of God that meets us and accepts us through the face of Christ, which constitutes humankind anew into the *imago Dei*. Thus, our ultimate needs of acceptance and esteem are met only in the face of God. This does not obviate, however, the continuing experience of face in human community. God fulfills this through his revelation of mercy and love through the face of Christ but also through the face-generating relationality that is part of the ecclesial self. The ecclesial self, precisely because it is a social self, links face with the *imago Dei*. It is this link that provides an important dimension to help reorient face within the Christian community.

Again, face relates to approval and inclusion since "respect for face is one way to maintain secure social bonds" (Ting-Toomey and Cocroft

1994:332). That face is an important discussion regarding the notion of the ecclesial self is because face, as an inherent element of all relationality, constitutes one of the basic building blocks of the type of community life, which is the *koinonia* of the ecclesial self.

This means much more than a simple assertion that the proper place to situate face is "in church." For, it is only church understood properly as the multiplex reality of ecclesial selves that face can find proper moorings. This points to understanding "church" as the embodiment of a particular type of life. The notion of the self as the *imago Dei* involves understanding the proper end, the divinely intended *telos* for all humanity, as divinely constituted relationality. This means that we image God by living in community, by not seeking our own face and honor but by esteeming the other, laying down our lives for others in love, establishing our identity and thus our face by reception of grace (Sandage and Shults 2003:241).

Christian community, the new creation where ecclesial selves are being remade into the image of God, is a proper locus for a Christian reappropriation of face. This is so because it is a place of face-affirmation and face-validation. In a sense, the Christian community is a laboratory where the Face of God is distilled into real-life attitudes and practices. It is a place where legitimate face needs are protected. It is a sanctuary where people may escape the often brutal face-denigrating world. In a word, the church becomes a "face-safe place." In a fundamental way, the self-in-community, the *imago Dei*, becomes a community of face-validation and face-support. Being "in Christ" provides a new communal narrative that gives the self-in-community a different identity and new identity goals. It is such identity goals, given as part of the new narrative in which the ecclesial self exists, that should motivate and guide the varying facework strategy choices.

Thus, we imitate the face-affirming God by validating each other's face claims through grace, love, acceptance, and mutual esteem. Making any identity or face claim is, in a sense, an application to others in social space for face-validation. Such is contrary to the "oppositional logic of same" (Volf 1998b:410), the notion of carving out hard and fast individual identities that stand in isolation and, potentially, opposition to each other. Not only is this undesirable but also in fact quite impossible as we accept the account of the essential social and relational account of the self. In this view, face presupposes that the other occupies part of the conceptual space of the self. Thus, community is not just about a "group face," a conglomeration of individuals who in a corporate way aggregate their faces together. Such must involve our recognition that the face and face needs of others, with whom we live in community, are our own concern. Such a view grows not out of individuals who join a social entity but, rather, from the basic notion of the ecclesial self as a new reality in which we all partake in Spirit-empowered unity of life.

Note, however, that it is only the legitimate face needs of people that should find affirmation. A fundamental stance of face-affirmation must never gloss over sin. Thus, the story and *telos* that are apparent in the gospel must always circumscribe our various face postures and strategies. Yet, the gospel does address our real needs, which include our need to live in a growing likeness to Christ, who is the image of God. Thus, attention to acceptance of other's face needs does not nullify the equally necessary program of living in a harmony that is based, not upon a "don't ask, don't tell" approach, but one where acceptance, affirmation, and esteem create contexts where moral failure is not stigmatized. If an affirmation of face leads to contexts where people can live "plastic" lives, where real hurts and fears are repressed, then such is only a façade, a false face. True face and face affirmation must always seek to anchor itself in the true self, the *imago Dei*, into which it has been remade and toward which it grows as a goal.

If meeting the Face of God provides ultimate acceptance, it is through being integrated into the ecclesial self that we become accepting faces to one another and form the appropriate context in which to image God and situate our own face and the faces of others. The self-in-community that is the *imago Dei* can thus function as an orienting motif in guiding Christian face reflection and activity.

Honor

Honor is a notion which many in the Western world often disregard as either an outdated concern of bygone days or else something that is the possession of very foreign cultures (e.g., East Asia or the Mediterranean world). Theologian Stanley Hauerwas reflects on this ambivalence he felt prior to a renewed appreciation of the concept of honor.

> Initially, I had strong reservations about the idea of honor, since historically and sociologically I associated it with forms of life for which I have little sympathy. That my reservations about the idea of honor are not just a personal quirk is suggested by how little honor is used as a working word in our everyday speech—we no longer think of our moral behavior as a matter of honor, but doing

the right, performing praiseworthy actions, or "doing one's own thing." The contexts in which honor is still used are highly regimented and associated with institutions that seem to imply that honor consists in uncritical obedience to the commands of superiors. Thus, to defend the idea of honor or to reassert its importance seems to be either hopelessly naïve or perversely conservative and authoritarian. (Hauerwas 1995:224)

Hauerwas goes on to discuss how he believes honor should play a critical role in any social organization by marking off those attitudes and forms of behavior that are legitimate ends in themselves. Holding to such standards of honor "are significant exactly because they are the way a particular society reinforces and articulates to itself the forms of life that give that society its reason for being" (Hauerwas 1988:225). Honor structures the life of every community, functioning as a critical moral bridge between the self and society (1988:224).

Marilyn McCord Adams argues that in contrast to the general neglect honor has received in Western theology, the symbolic value of "honor/shame calculus" occupies a central place in the biblical story. She notes in particular how social esteem and honor form a powerful source of human meaning and purpose. The denial of that honor, that is, shame, depletes meaning and, ultimately, the sense of human worth (McCord Adams 1999:107). It is honor (glory, praise, and adoration) that will be the currency of heaven (1999:128).

What I contend here is that a deeper appreciation of honor is essential for properly reorienting face. This is true since, at the level of human relationality, honor (i.e., esteem), together with acceptance, lies at the core of face. To be recognized positively as one who possesses legitimate personal face or to gain social face by the aggregation of positive social esteem both presuppose the social category of honor. Such is also true theologically. As I noted in the discussion of Trinitarian relationality, the relations that are a part of the ecclesial self are not simply some sort of generic relationship. Indeed, this relationality is of a particular quality, that of *perichoresis*. This specific quality is none other than the primary perichoretic impulse of mutual honoring. McCord Adams writes about this quality of relationality. "What else can lovers give each other in utopia, what can the blessed trinity offer one another, if not honor, mutual expressions of appreciation, praise, and thanksgiving for who the other is?" (1999:126).

This is true in the most basic sense of face as the projection of a self's identity claim into social space. When any person makes a face claim, (i.e., projects an identity claim in social space) they are hoping for validation of that claim. When we respond to them in ways appropriate to such a claim we are accepting and validating their face. By doing so we inherently honor them and their claim as we grant legitimacy and esteem to their selves and the face that such a self implies.

This mutual honoring that is part of the ecclesial self is essentially face-giving and face-validating. As I honor another as one whom I accept as part of the *koinonia* characteristic of the ecclesial self, I signal a positive response to the face of this other. This is inherently face-generating since by doing so I grant a basic personal face to the other as one whom God accepts and esteems and who is deserving of this most basic-level face assertion. Also, the gradual sedimenting or aggregation of this perichoretic honoring forms the building blocks which, over time, may produce differing levels of social face. Those who continuously apply themselves to Christian virtues gain distinction, and thus positive face, within the Christian community. Thus, mutual honoring stands as a fundamental dynamic for face as well as the type of relationality that forms the ecclesial self.

Sociocultural Interpretation of the Bible

The notion of honor assumes importance not only as a result of a Trinitarian approach. Recently, some biblical scholars have attempted to highlight the importance of reading the Bible from the perspective of the ancient Near Eastern and Mediterranean cultures in which these documents originated.[2] Such studies draw attention to this long-neglected area as a crucial yet often overlooked dimension of the Bible. Utilizing what they term a "sociocultural" approach, these interpreters give significant attention to categories of anthropological analysis.[3] Of particular importance among these categories is that of glory and honor.

---

2. Bailey (1983), deSilva (1996, 1999b, 2000), Elliott (1981), Esler (1994), Lawrence (2003), Malina (1993), Malina and Neyrey (1991), Malina and Rohrbaugh (2003), Neyrey (1991, 1998), Pilch (2000), Pilch and Malina (1998), Plevnik (1998), and Rohrbaugh (1996).

3. Some have raised valid cautions regarding the misuse of social scientific models. Such include, for example, John K. Chance (1994), F. Gerald Downing (1999), Gideon M. Kressel (1994), Louise J. Lawrence (2003), Marianne Sawicki (2000), We should heed these warnings yet the fact that some scholars do indeed misappropriate current anthropological and social scientific models should not prevent us from recognizing the critical role that notions such as honor and shame play in the cultures in which the Bible was written.

Glory/Honor

That the notion of glory/honor constitutes a neglected dimension of modern theology and biblical studies rests, at least in part, upon the specific ways Western theology has tended to view the notion of glory. If pressed, many would not likely be able to give a concrete definition for the word. Those who could, however, would probably offer a definition of glory as a non-moral quality of God (something shiny and visible) or the essential state in which God exists.

In a memorable passage that illustrates this understanding, C. S. Lewis writes of his own difficulty with the term. He notes how glory "... suggests two ideas to me, of which one seems wicked and the other ridiculous. Either glory means to me fame, or it means luminosity." He concludes his discussion of glory humorously, by asking, "who wishes to become a kind of living electric light bulb?" (Lewis 1980:8). Many in the church (where the term continues in hymns, prayers, and Bible readings) would likely provide a nebulous and fuzzy definition along the lines of Lewis's "luminosity." Even in those instances when a concrete understanding might exist there may be a general lack of appreciation, a shoulder shrug and a "so what," since glory does not occupy a prominent place in the modern cultural lexicon of the West. To what then, biblically speaking, does the word "glory" refer?

The findings from this recent attempt to root biblical exegesis within the cultural context of the ancient Mediterranean cultures point to understanding the terms often translated "glory" in the English Bible more as the social and moral category of "honor" (DeSilva 1999a:204). It is true that "glory" in the Bible sometimes clearly refers to the tangible and observable presence of God (e.g., a cloud, fire, or other overwhelming physical manifestation). In normal, non-theological usage, however, "honor" refers simply to something weighty to which people give importance or to something that makes a person impressive and, subsequently, demands recognition (Botterweck and Ringgren 1974:238). The majority of biblical occurrences, then, are more properly translated by terms within the semantic domain of social honor (e.g., name, face, glory, dignity, respect, fame, reputation, prestige, stature, status, prominence) (Koehler and Baumgartner 1995:457).

Even when the notion of glory does admit to an interpretation of visible manifestation, it is better to think of such as the radiance that is a function of the more basic honorableness of God. That is, as a crown or royal regalia is but an outward symbol of the deeper reality of a king or queen's honorable status, so too divine effulgence is but a secondary manifestation of the fact that God is the ultimate and eternal Honorable One. As McCord Adams notes, since God is a being more excellent than which can be adequately conceived, this means that God also occupies a position of being one "whose honor of virtue is necessary and unsurpassable" (1999:127). A predominant emphasis regarding the honor of God is the idea of honor that flows from God to humankind in manifest acts of power. This again highlights the tangible nature of biblical honor. Such is not, as perhaps in Greek philosophy or medieval speculative theology, an abstraction. The honor of God constitutes concrete events and the active rule of God that originate in and point to his honor (e.g., Ps 19:1; 62:7; 145:5; Isa 24:23). Glory (honor) from this perspective constitutes an ethical and social term rather than that of "luminosity" (*a la* Lewis) or divine radiance.

Piper argues that in the book of John the dominant notion of *doxa* (most often rendered in English as "glory") is not that of "divine brightness" or effulgence but the simple sociocultural notion of honor. John assigns to Jesus's death upon the cross the appellations of "glorification" and "lifting up," which are claims to honor (Piper 2001:284). Sociologically, the honor Jesus receives from God by his honorable death counteracts the shame the believing community might experience because of suffering or ostracization (2001:287). What holds true of John in particular is likely true of the Bible in general. That is, modern readers should understand Hebrew and Greek terms traditionally rendered "glory" with the proper cultural nuance of social honor.

Viewing the notion of glory more appropriately as primarily about the moral category of honor opens up new vistas for connecting the biblical texts more closely with normal social modes of human honor. By extension, such brings us to a place where we can then associate these biblical notions more closely with the dynamic of honor that lies at the core of face.

Honor Discourse

In his significant work on honor discourse, David A. DeSilva seeks to highlight the various ways this notion of honor is important in the New Testament.[4] The term "honor discourse" is an apt description since it

---

4. Indeed, DeSilva's body of work that illuminates biblical texts vis-à-vis the values and rhetorical strategies of honor continues to grow. See, for example, DeSilva 1995, 1996, 1998, 1999a, 1999b, 2000a, 2000b.

points to not only the importance of social honor in the biblical texts but also how authors shaped their rhetorical strategies in order to elicit desired responses (DeSilva 1999a:xiv). That is, honor discourse is about the various ways biblical authors use honor language to bring about a desired response from a given audience. Honor discourse constitutes an important rhetorical tool for persuading and forming the Christian community vis-à-vis the surrounding culture that reflects unacceptable values and practices (1999a:xv).

Most helpful is the model DeSilva proposes for understanding how biblical authors use the language of honor (and shame) as part of an overall strategy of persuasion. DeSilva draws attention to the important consideration for understanding how honor discourse involves appeals to *logos* (highlighting how a particular path leads to honor), *ethos* (emphasizing the character of speaker and or audience as honorable), and *pathos* (moving the affect of an audience by their desire for honor) (1999a:207). Biblical authors, DeSilva contends, make ample use of all such rhetorical strategies.

This rhetorical use of honor aims at two primary goals. First, biblical authors in various ways seek to establish or reinforce the constituency of a new "court of reputation."[5] This involves the various strategies authors use to assert that God and God's people now form an alternate court of reputation within which believers should orient their lives.

In contrast to the dominant courts of reputation that exist in the surrounding culture, it is the opinion of God and, by extension, the people who follow God, the Christian community, that form the true standard for judging honor (DeSilva 1999a:27). This function then is simply to reorient the "court of reputation" from one sphere to a new one.

Honor from the perspective of the gospel posits "Christ in us" as the ultimate criterion for honor (2 Cor 13:5–6). The court of reputation, formerly located in various social entities of their surrounding culture, is now reformulated in Christian terms. The court of reputation in gospel mode places God (particularly as expressed through the life and ministry of Jesus) at the center with the Christian community as a secondary, yet significant component. "Insofar as they accept the measuring rod of Christlikeness

---

5. DeSilva provides a definition of "court of reputation" as that group or subgroup which comprises a person's most significant others. One's reputation, honor, and face, are then derivative from living in accordance with the values and ideals of this group. For those whose lives reflect these group-specific values, there is acceptance and honor. For those who deviate, there is disgrace (DeSilva 1999a:5).

and of pleasing God (the church) can become an important source of support and correction for the individual believer" (DeSilva 1999a:136).

Once we recognize God and his people as the proper "court of reputation," the second function of honor rhetoric is to establish and affirm the honor of the Christian community and its members. By doing so, biblical authors attempt to establish the believer's commitment to this alternate court of reputation and to bolster the community's feelings of worth and esteem. Such a "vigorous counter-program" (DeSilva 2000b:105) is essential since members of the dominant forces of the culture around them continue to influence and form the context in which the Christian community lives. Being socialized into the ethos of the new creation becomes key activity for believers in relation to the issues of honor and face, that is, what constitutes honor and face in God's eyes and how the community adopts and reinforces these new norms in its structures and life.

> They must distance themselves from their own primary socialization and regard those who still operate under that socialization in the majority culture's values as unrealizable guides to what is honorable and is dishonorable. (DeSilva 1999a:123)

So, for example, many of the problems in the Corinthian church seem to involve improper boasting and a continued reliance on the cultural norms of the society around them, specifically in the form of dominant honor codes and the generally accepted court of reputation. Additionally, there continues to exist former honor values given by their previous lives in Corinthian society. Thus, "many of the problems stem from the failure of some of the Corinthians to understand that they are rather to acknowledge and reinforce one another's honor in the body of Christ rather than continue their competition with one another for honor in this new 'court of reputation'" (DeSilva 1999a:121).

Investigating honor and face from a biblical/theological perspective involves much more than simply running a concordance search for the term "honor." Rather, a full-orbed approach takes into account both the various synonyms that fall within the honor semantic domain as well as the various ways such concepts are represented under the rubric of honor discourse when these specific terms do not appear.[6]

---

6. This would include, though not be limited to, such terms as opinion, reputation, dishonor, honor, reproach, disparage, outrage, worthy, noble, praise, scorn, and blame (DeSilva 1999a:9). For a slightly different list, see Malina and Neyrey 1991:46.

Boasting

DeSilva draws attention to the important honor-laden concept of boasting, a topic that occupies a great deal of space particularly in Romans, and 1 and 2 Corinthians. To boast is essentially to stake a claim for honor, that is, to hold to something recognized as honorable as one's cause for a boast. Such a dominant cultural activity finds new definition in the Christian community.

Among the important differences is the denial of legitimacy for Christians to struggle for honor by competitive boasting (1 Cor 4:7). Gifts given for the good of the entire community (1 Cor 12:4–11) are indications of "God's patronage of the new community and not a ground for the human patrons to promote their own honor" (DeSilva 1999a:127). Some continue to boast in accordance with the dominant honor codes taken from the world (2 Cor 11:18). They continue a worldly type of boasting, "laying claims to honor or precedence within the community based on God's gifts" (1999a:127). Such individual boasting that claims honor for itself over against others in the community is an offense against the honor of the giver, viz., God. Instead, Christians are to boast because of their new lives in God (Rom 5:11; 1 Cor 1:29–31). The new standard for honor claims is the work God does through his power (Rom 15:17–18; 2 Cor 12:9; 1 Thess 2:19), the cross of Christ (Gal 6:14). It is only in ways that are commensurate with the gospel of grace (2 Cor 1:12) that boasting, making honor claims, can be a legitimate Christian activity.

Zeal

Another significant term for a proper understanding of honor is "zeal," the positive counterpart to shame. Rather than the more recent popular sense of "intense commitment" or "ardent activity," DeSilva highlights the Greek and Roman notion of zeal as emulation, that is, an appeal to one's own desire for honor that moves one to seek the same opportunity for praise (DeSilva 1999a:25). What this points to is the basic drive to ambition, which leads a person to emulate honorable attitudes or behavior. The appeal is to this desire for praise, which results from adherence to honorable virtue. This appeal to the hearer's innate desire for honor and face is made in order to spur them on to virtuous action, thus gaining the appropriate praise. Therefore, the notion of ardent activity is in view but it is an activity that is primarily motivated by an appeal to the hearer's or reader's desire for honor. Paul encourages the Corinthian Christians to be zealous for the more excellent (i.e., honorable) way (1 Cor 12:31—13:1). Christ redeemed a special people who would be zealous, that is, seek the opportunity for honor and praise, by doing that which is good and noble (Titus 2:14). All these appeals assume the desire for honor, now reoriented toward God and the work of the Holy Spirit in God's people. Contemporary readers may miss the important dimension of honor that lies behind all such appeals to action.

New Testament "Makarisms"

A notion that interpreters have generally overlooked but one that highlights the fundamental honor dimensions of the Gospel stories is that of the so-called makarisms in the New Testament.[7] Taken from the Greek term *makarios*, translators have traditionally rendered this notion as "blessed" or "happy." The best-known of these occur in the Beatitudes of Matthew 5:3–11.

K. C. Hanson draws attention to how we must view these makarisms within the honor-shame cultural matrix of the ancient Mediterranean (Hanson 1994:104). Rather than a futuristic or eschatological interpretation (i.e., some future blessed state) or the notion of personal emotional happiness (i.e., happy), makarisms constitute honor-laden value judgments. To be *makarios* is to be honorable or honored. This means that the makarisms are fundamentally "the conditions and behaviors which the community regards as honorable" (1994:100) or "one's self-respect in conjunction with the community's affirmation of that evaluation" (1994:90). These function then to affirm and reify the values that the community holds in highest esteem, viz., that which is honorable. Specifically, this sets up certain behavior as a model for others to imitate. In this way makarisms "draw attention to remarkable people in the attempt to set up their behavior as exemplary, to be learned from and imitated by others" (Kressel 1994:158).

Thus, such leads to Hanson's translation of the makarisms as "how honorable." The point in Matthew 5 is then about Jesus' redefinition of the honor code for his new community. In contrast to the ways society at large may conceive of honor, the proper criteria for honor in God's kingdom involve being poor in spirit, being persecuted for righteousness sake, and being pure in heart. These are affirmations of the type of honorable

---

7. This term together with its cognates occurs some fifty-five times in the New Testament.

lifestyle that obtains within the community that follows Jesus. Jesus subverts the honor code prevalent in society and reorients honorable status and face around a code defined by a new set of values.

This brief overview of honor and honor discourse in the New Testament highlight how critically important this topic was to the early Christian communities. That such is often passed over testifies to the modern oblivion to the importance of face, honor, and shame. A careful rereading of Scripture reveals a pervasive concern with such issues.

Summary

Developing a proper framework within which Christians might reflect upon the basic, yet complex, human phenomenon that is face is an essential step for Christian face "maintenance." Such a framework, I have contended, finds its moorings in the three orienting motifs of a Trinitarian view of the self as the *imago Dei*, the central biblical notion of the Face of God and Christ, and the pervasive honor discourse that occurs throughout the New Testament.

A Christian account of face must recognize the basic face-orientation of humankind as something God has given but also as a human dynamic that sin can infect and despoil. Although face is a good, it is not so absolutely. Christian difference injected into face relativizes the standards of the dominant cultures in which believers find themselves and locates face within a new social order in the new creation of Trinitarian community. This new community provides the virtues, codes, criteria and *telos* that together constitute a new mode for face.

This chapter has, at the very least, set basic parameters for Christian reflection on face. Indeed, there must be serious reorientation of face as the face mode provided by the majority culture around us typically exhibit dimension marred by human sin. Yet, inherent in theologically informed reflection is the recognition that face holds considerable promise as a viable theological resource.

9

Reconceiving the Soteriological Task

IF, AS I CONTEND in the previous chapter, the notion of face holds valuable theological resources, what tangible ways might this materially affect the theology of the Thai Christian community? This chapter is an attempt to probe more deeply the value of face for one particular area, that is, that of soteriology.

The chapter operates around two primary conceptual movements. First, I describe the task of soteriological construction. I do this in some detail since, from the perspective of much modern Christianity, this particular account will in fact involve substantial reconceptualization. To do this I will discuss briefly various atonement theories and then offer an analysis of the nature of the soteriological (re)construction. Second, based upon a particular understanding of how the soteriological task is to be carried out, I will address the issue of atonement in terms of the specific cultural notions of Thai face.

Let me, however, first offer this disclaimer. Some may ask if indeed it is not presumptuous for one who is not a Thai to embark on such a project. That is, is it not illegitimate for a Westerner to dictate to Thais the shape their soteriology should take? Indeed, such would be the case if that which I ventured to provide was a conclusive proposal that the Thai church should follow. This is not, however, the goal toward which this project aspires. Rather, my objective is more modest. I hope to accomplish two basic goals in this discussion. First, by probing both the history of atonement theories and the proper nature of what constitutes soteriological construction, I hope to demonstrate how we must "unhook" the fact of salvation from any particular culture-laden interpretation of that salvation. This is the critical and initial step that must occur for the Thai church to engage the issue of salvation in a more biblically authentic and culturally relevant manner.

The second goal involves exploring the potential resonance of salvation in the "key" of face. My aim is to provide suggestive and evocative trajectories, stopping short of offering a developed soteriological account. This, of course, is a task that properly belongs only to the Thai church. What I offer here are resources to enable the Thai church to enlarge its theological vocabulary and, in the end, more faithfully articulate the gospel, particularly in terms of the face-laden context in which it exists. So, I am not attempting to dictate the terms of what might constitute authentic Thai theology but rather offer provisional suggestions in the form of orienting motifs, designed to provoke the Thai Christian community to more engaged theologizing.

The history of the Christian faith is replete with attempts to understand and explicate the meaning of the death of Jesus. These attempts have differed in various, even profound ways. Yet, this persistent endeavor during the past two millennia to unpack the significance of Jesus's death testifies to the irreducibly basic place the cross occupies in Christian faith and life.[1] In many ways, the story has become the "linchpin" of all Christian understanding (McClendon 1994:198).

The story, however, requires interpretation. Raw data, a simple assortment of biblical texts, is not adequate. A framework must exist that connects this significance to the lives of those who read these stories. This implies the necessity of what some term "a string long enough to tie up all the fact" (McClendon 1994:213). Such a string we term theory. In its Christian version, then, to "tie up all the facts" regarding the cross of Jesus is to formulate what we generally term theories of atonement.

The history of these atonement theories involves explanations of great variety, depth, and richness (McClendon 1994:200). Yet, in the midst of all the diversity and the great importance attached to it, never has the Christian church offered an official orthodox version of atonement.[2] This

---

1. See McClendon, who quotes Kähler that the Gospels themselves are simply "passion narratives with extended 'introductions'" (1994:198).

2. Thus, as Root notes, while christological discussions were being hedged with all kinds of restrictions, talk about soteriology and atonement remained "free and unrestrained" (1989:264).

points to an essential, yet confounding, dynamic involved in all atonement discussion. On the one hand, the church affirms that the death of Jesus is an event that carries ultimate significance for every age.[3] On the other hand, the more one probes and studies the various attempts at defining the nature of atonement it becomes clear that every account differs in certain, sometimes even critical, aspects. The fact of a diversity of approaches to atonement testifies to a basic dynamic inherent in human explanations of the meaning of the cross. The relevance of the cross is neither self-evident (it requires interpretation) nor universally applicable (what "works" in one context seems irrelevant, possibly even heretical, in a different context). As people inevitably seek meaning in these events to apply to their present situation, what emerges are differing accounts that are more or less persuasive for a particular group of people (Fiddes 1989:220).

To speak of the meaning of the cross is surely to speak of God's decisive act of salvation. Yet, to speak always assumes a contextual speaking, one that occurs in a specific place and time and uses contemporary idiom, reasoning, and persuasion. These twin poles of universality and particularity, involved in all formulations of atonement theory and soteriology, produce a tension aptly described by the proverbial "enigma wrapped in a mystery." How to deal with this tension is the focus of the present chapter. And, though it will address the issue in various ways, the basic assertion here is that to deal with this tension requires a very specific awareness, that is, that the soteriological task at its core, is essentially a contextual project.

The implications are profound. If all descriptions of atonement and soteriological construction are inherently a contextual enterprise, then a faithful articulation of these doctrines can never be a simple parroting of previously formulated accounts. What is required is a framework that avoids certain pitfalls and perspectives that would ultimately undermine the attempt to produce culturally relevant and biblically faithful renderings of the atonement. Laying out the constitutive elements for such a framework is a significant task of this chapter.

The Terms "Atonement" and "Soteriology"

The meaning of the term "atonement" itself is an issue to which we must first attend. The term was conceived by William Tyndale in 1516 to trans-

---

3. As Paul S. Fiddes asserts, "the Christian doctrine of atonement affirms that the story of the death of Christ has universal meaning, an inexhaustible relevance for the human condition" (1989:220).

late the Latin *reconciliatio* (McGrath 1993a:20). Etymologically, the word is a conflation of the terms "at" and "onement," that is, the state of being one. Essentially, then, atonement is about unification or coming together (McClendon 1994:199). Originally, the term was primarily about the goal of the cross, that is, what the death of Jesus accomplished. In contemporary parlance, however, this original focus of meaning has changed. Today, atonement now means something like "to make amends for an offense" or "to offer satisfaction for a wrongdoing."

Protestant circles over the past few hundred years, however, have defined atonement even more narrowly. Theories of atonement have come to represent extended descriptions of the manner or mechanics by which Jesus's death saves humankind (McClendon 1994:199). In essence, such theories deal with the *how* of the fact of atonement. Yet, much of contemporary Christian thinking regarding salvation has associated the term "atonement" with a very specific theory, that is, one of sacrifice and penal substitution.[4] This contemporary usage points to a collapse of the earlier notion of goal or end (i.e., coming together as one) with a particular means, a *how*, by which atonement "works." This, we will see, represents a significant shift that carries serious implications.

In contrast, modern theological circles increasingly use the term "soteriology" to refer to that which was formerly designated "theories of atonement" or "the work of Christ." Yet, soteriology moves beyond the more limited concern of the *how* and deals with the much broader area of the nature of salvation itself (McGrath 1993b:616). Though there is a legitimate analytical distinction, ultimately it is not possible to discuss atonement and soteriology properly in isolation from one another. Formulations of atonement theories represent a single, albeit significant, component of the broader task of soteriological construction. Each depends on the other since to a large degree their concerns overlap. As such, I will address both issues in this chapter.

Metaphor and Narrative

Christians throughout the ages have devoted vast amounts of energy to explicating in precise form the nature and mechanics of the atonement (Carroll and Green 1995:114). Yet, the New Testament, in stark contrast,

---

4. Tambasco 1991:12. See also Bartlett 2001:3, where he notes that the phrase "atonement doctrine" now generally means "sacrifice, expiation, propitiation, penal substitution, vicarious suffering, satisfaction."

is surprisingly unconcerned with any precise description of such issues. Specifically, Paul, upon whose writings Protestant formulations of atonement theory depend heavily, never expresses the exact character of the cross. Rather he focuses on the results of the cross,[5] doing so with various images drawn from both his contemporary culture and also the Hebrew Scriptures. As one who wrote pastoral letters and not dogmatic theology, Paul focused on the practical concerns of ministry and mission and seemed not overly concerned, at least in his writings, with filling in explanatory gaps for a full-blown theory of atonement (den Heyer 1998:45–46). This lack of attention to precise definitions of *how* the death of Jesus brought about the salvation of the world is also evident in the earlier strands of the Jesus tradition (Green and Baker 2000:17). Such seem far more interested in affirming how the death of Jesus demonstrated the fact of that Jesus is Messiah. Without defining in any precise manner the way the cross effected the salvation of humankind, what the New Testament texts do offer is an assortment of dynamic metaphors. This "dazzling array of colors in the mural of Paul's theology of the cross" (Carroll and Green 1995:114) produces an almost chaotic sense where New Testament metaphors "come tumbling over one another, influence one another and are interwoven with one another; they complement one another, but also contradict one another at the same time" (den Heyer 1998:130).

If the New Testament offers multiple and dynamic metaphoric images rather than lengthy explanatory definitions, then it is proper first to understand the nature of metaphorical language. Yet, a tight, concise definition is difficult since metaphor is such a pervasive feature of language. Aristotle defined metaphor as "the application of an alien name by transference" (Gunton 1985:132). Metaphor may be alternately defined as "teaching an old word new tricks," "a calculated category mistake," or "an affair between a predicate with a past and an object that yields while protesting" (1985:132). The basic idea then is the use of an existing concept to communicate a new meaning not explicit in the former concept.

---

5. Marshall notes that "Paul's vocabulary expresses the results of Christ's death rather than its character, and this fits in with New Testament thought in general, which is more concerned with the nature of salvation than the precise way in which it has been achieved" (1990:250).

The Effects of Rationalism on Metaphor

The rise of Enlightenment Rationalism essentially displaced an earlier view of language that granted value to the expression of truth through metaphorical descriptions.[6] It is the doctrine of atonement in particular that suffered most from this influence rationalism had upon notions of human language (Gunton 1989:2).

The trouble was not with the existence of metaphor per se. Indeed, it is scarcely possible to write a sentence without employing language of some symbolic nature. Rather, what developed was the belief that metaphorical language merely performed the function of linguistic decoration and enhancement. Therefore, when metaphors were used it was widely believed they could not communicate genuine truth since such truth only exists in literal statements. Metaphor was thus thought to be primarily non-cognitive, subjective, and emotive. People came to view cognitive, propositional, and supposedly "objective" language as superior and, ultimately, the only reliable vehicle for expressing truth. Indeed, this legacy continues to the present as many in the positivist tradition still view metaphor with great suspicion as fundamentally inadequate to express truth and properly describe reality.

Conventionalization, Literalization, and Myth-Making

This type of Rationalist thinking paves the way for the phenomenon of equating metaphor and myth and the resulting tendency to collapse metaphor into literal descriptions. When a metaphor becomes a conventional term, it begins to dominate in everyday language. People continue using it until contemporary language eventually takes the (former) metaphor literally. This "literalizing" tends to happen in a progressive series of steps. First, the term comes to enjoy sufficiently wide currency of use. Next, its usage transposes from metaphor to "dead metaphor." Finally, what was once simply a metaphor becomes a literal description (Chryssides 1985:152). This phenomenon of language in a rationalist mode becomes true of theological language in general and metaphorical descriptions of atonement in particular.

---

6. Whether Kant's moral rationalism (the rational, moral will replacing the cross as the center of salvation), Schliermacher's rationalism of experience (that is, doctrines are more about what happens within the human heart than any reality of a transcendent God), or Hegel's conceptual rationalism (that is, truth mediated through "purified" concepts), the end result was that metaphor was demoted to second class in its value for expressing truth (Gunton 1989:6–17).

Gunton describes this tendency, particularly evident in modern rationalist thinking, of how a metaphor or imaginative construct of any kind actually comes to be identified with the theory it helps to create. Such a move results in what Gunton terms as "myth" (Gunton 1989:64). So, for example, Descartes described the universe *as if* it were a machine. This becomes a myth, however, when speakers take such language as literal description, understanding the universe to actually *be* a machine.

Such myth making and literalizing essentially conflates metaphor into literal descriptions. Often, then, when people offered theories as to how the cross does what it does, these theories often came to occupy a quasi-orthodox position or definitional priority among Christian thinkers. Once the metaphor ascended to such a place, it was a simple step to view what was in fact a contextually constructed explanation as actually constituting *the* definition of atonement. This is, as C. S. Lewis puts it, to confuse the theory with the thing itself (Lewis 1952:46). The specific problem with such a phenomenon is that the work of Christ and the multiplicity of biblical images used to describe it become captive to one particular perspective.[7]

An illegitimate straining for implications is an additional problem that results from improper use of metaphor. In order to construct any of the major theories of atonement, people inevitably move beyond the actual metaphors and look for ways they might infer more fully what "really happened." Given the inherent limitations of metaphors, however, such an attempt is problematic. A metaphor in itself is seldom wholly descriptive (Gunton 1989:47). Indeed, metaphorical language frequently precludes reliable inferences (1989:148). If a person speaks literally then the hearer is entitled to all the logical inferences necessarily entailed by the proposition. The same is not true when metaphor is used. The analogy presented by a metaphor is not meant nor cannot parallel in every way that which it is describing. To do so is indeed shaky since it is never certain whether such inferences are present in the metaphor or not (1989:149). The problem here is one of pressing too far and demanding more literal sense than a metaphor is capable of providing. This stems from another basic misunderstanding about the nature of metaphors, that is, metaphors are not intended to function as comprehensive explanations of truth but rather as heuristic aids to the perception of truth (Lyall 1984:186).

---

7. This position owes its prominence not so much to biblical or theological rationale but cultural preference, that is, an inclination towards legal-judicial images.

George D. Chryssides notes the example of the metaphorical description of electricity moving through a wire as "a flow of electrons" (Chryssides 1985:149). This metaphor transfers to the concept of electricity connotations normally attributed to fluids. This holds up fine to a point. A break in a wire carrying electrical current stops the connective flow of electricity as a break in a pipe stops the flow of water. One must guard against pressing the metaphor too far, however. Thus, even though a break in a water pipe will inevitable fill the room up with water, a room where an electrical wire has been severed will not become saturated with electricity. Pressed too far, the metaphor breaks down and leads to inferences that are certainly false.

It is axiomatic that language can only and must always communicate by borrowing and altering existing words or ideas. There can be no simple conception of the fit between words and world for when speaking one always draws upon previously existing concepts and terms to express newer meanings. To divide words neatly into two categories then, that is, those that express their meaning literally and those that express their meaning in some other way, is indicative of an outdated and static view of language which is no longer tenable. Metaphor is a necessary "vehicle of discovery" for all new understanding (Gunton 1989:31). Indeed, in an ironic way, metaphor is actually superior to so-called literal descriptions because such in fact mirrors the indirectness of all our knowledge of the world (1989:37f.). The power of metaphor is clear in its transformative power. Not only does metaphorical language illuminate that which it describes but also in a reverse way, actually functions reflexively, redefining the original term itself (1989:78–79). Metaphor changes our way of thinking and our world and is indispensable for all communication.

Since all language, particularly metaphorical language, functions in this way, the tendency to insist that biblical terminology be either metaphorical or literal is wrongheaded on two accounts. First, it ignores the basic function of metaphorical language. It also introduces a "polemic into our understanding of the New Testament confessions of the meaning of the death and resurrection of Christ which is more akin to modern philosophical presuppositions than to biblical modes of expression" (Driver 1986:17). To demand concrete and rational explanations, is to totally misunderstand the nature of language about God. Even more than empirical realities, the realities of the spiritual world strain the limits of human language. If it is not only beneficial but also necessary to use metaphors to communicate about the more mundane matters of electricity, sports, and human relationships, how much more must we rely upon metaphorical language to describe transcendent realities such as God, heaven, and atonement?

Religious metaphors do permit theological inferences and indeed invite such. In fact, the better the metaphor the more pregnant it will be with possible implications. Inferences from metaphors, especially theological metaphors, however, can only function in a limited and tentative way. The more inferences drawn the more risk there is and the more likely there will be disagreement over the extent to which implications should be drawn. To take such a system or theory (built upon deductions drawn from that which by its very nature is limited in ability to yield such inferences) and absolutize it as the exclusive biblical explanation is certainly illegitimate.[8] To construct systems to illustrate is proper and helpful but to compile such inferences into a theory that lays exclusive claims upon "how it works" is neither helpful nor legitimate. Ultimately, as Gunton observes, such a view is "at least a simplification, at worst an intellectually disastrous misunderstanding of language and how it works" (Gunton 1989:27).

Metaphor and Contextuality

Conflation and literalizing lead to the loss of contextual awareness. When we conflate God's work through Christ on the cross with our descriptions of that work, the resulting explanation is easily assumed to possess a universal validity. That is, if one particular description constitutes *the real* description, it becomes the truth about the cross for all places and all cultures. Such a-contextuality, in an ironic twist, is profoundly contextual and results in a damning contextual frozenness. That is, we move unchanged the theories or approaches compelling in one context to a quite different context. Once such occurs (i.e., the theory assumes a central role as the "real explanation"), we force other biblical images or alternate theories to orbit the "orthodox" theory or metaphor in a merely subsidiary fashion. In practice, it is easy for people to view this "orthodox" definition of salvation or atonement as all but exhausting the full significance of the cross. The theory defines atonement. It *is* the meaning of the cross.

This obscures a basic dynamic of all metaphors, which, by their very nature, are contextually specific. Each image works properly within a

---

8. "Subsequent Christian theology has often fastened on to some of these models of atonement and absolutized one (or more) of them. However, such a restricted view is never that of the New Testament writers" (Tuckett 1992).

specific context "where a shared encyclopedia can be assumed" (Green and Baker 2000:20). Because of this intrinsic contextuality metaphors can function successfully only in a context of "shared socio-historical presuppositions" (2000:94). When religious metaphors fail to connect, it is often because interpreters uproot one metaphor from its context and naively transplant it into a completely new environment. If it is the case that a new environment does not share the conceptual presuppositions of the original context from which a metaphor came, the metaphor will likely lack cogency. To do such with metaphors of atonement is to simply parrot the terms that, belonging to another age, may in fact prove dead and void of meaning in a new context (2000:20).

As Paul worked in different communities, his theological language contained a contextual dynamic. This is clear as he moved between the story of Israel, reflected in and interpreted by the advent of Christ, and the exigencies and settings of his audiences. In this way, he adopted language and adapted it to the context, producing an ongoing conversation that sought a fit with the specific circumstances to which he wrote. Indeed, language used to describe the efficacy of the death of Jesus always depends, to a large degree, on the specific contextual needs Paul addressed (Carroll and Green 1995:266).

So then, both the conflation of metaphorical and literal and the straining for inferences often obscure the language of atonement. The metaphor of sacrifice, for example, gained preeminence at a particular time. Theory began to develop as to how Christ's death functioned as a sacrifice. Eventually, these theoretical speculations, usually propositions that offered literal description, eclipsed the original metaphor and became *the* description of atonement. Included in this might be certain implications derived from cultural notions of sacrifice not faithful to the original intention of the biblical metaphor.

Such essentially freezes theories of atonement into a confessional fixidity that often, in the minds of those who favor the particular theory, exhausts the meaning of the cross. Theory is conflated with fact, blurring the fundamental difference between the *what* of the cross and the *how*. Thus, theories of atonement lose their heuristic function as explanations and become literal descriptions of what really happened. Such "mythmaking" has been particularly endemic among post-Enlightenment theology. Following this literalizing tendency is the possible inclusion in the new literal description of improper implications. Such has significantly muted atonement and limited its relevance to a considerable degree. Surely, this is not the proper mode by which the church should carry out the soteriological task. The position advocated here is that to conceive of any formulation of atonement as a literal or fixed description is to profoundly misconstrue the proper nature of the task of soteriological construction.

Narrative

To think about atonement theory it is essential to understand the nature and function of metaphor. Yet, an additional and associated issue, equally important for this discussion, is the proper relationship between soteriological construction or atonement theories and the concept of narrative.

At one level, narrative may be associated with the form of story. In its most basic sense, however, a narrative is a specific type of story that presumes two states and an event that transforms the first state into the second (Root 1989:263–64). Viewed in such a fashion, the New Testament account of salvation through Christ forms perfectly such a narrative pattern. That is, the work of God in Christ (the event) transforms the human predicament of lostness or separation from God (a prior state) into salvation (a new state). If the biblical story of salvation clearly assumes this prototypical narrative form, the task of soteriology becomes a narrative task (1989:267).

Each specific formulation of atonement theory assumes a specific narrative movement between two states bridged by the cross. Each of the different theories defines these states in various ways. These specifically defined states each assume a different way of framing the mechanics of how the cross accomplishes the new state of salvation in Christ. Tuckett's comment is pivotal:

> Very different models and categories are used to describe the "lost" condition of the human race prior to Christ. Different descriptions of the human situation inevitably lead to different explanations of how this has been altered by the work of Christ. (1992:518)

The *Christus Victor* approach assumes a state of enslavement transformed into freedom accomplished by a power event. Anselm's substitutionary view assumes a state of indebtedness transformed by release due to a sufficient offering of honor. A penal view of substitution assumes vicarious punishment that relieves a state of guilt by forgiveness.

Such narrative construction of soteriology, however, cannot rest content simply to repeat the biblical data. The essential task of soteriological construction is to explicate the significance of the biblical story for a particular context. Because metaphors constitute the fundamental building blocks of the narrative shape give the story of the cross, the significance will be one based upon the mutually shared, contextually specific cultural lexicon. Such significance is always a function of the dynamic interrelations between this story and a specific context (Root 1989:265). Simply put, atonement theories are extended narrative descriptions of the story of Jesus describing in a specific context how *this* story is *the* story of redemption. Contextually viable narrative forms of the story of Jesus are constructed in this dynamic interplay between the New Testament metaphors and a particular context. It is in this way we carry out the soteriological task.

This understanding of soteriology as narrative resists a prevalent practice of simply rehearsing biblical texts and parroting previous atonement formulations. New contexts always demand new forms of the story. The work of soteriology is one of narrative *redescription* (Root 1989:275–76). Such is impossible, however, without the creation of new versions of the story, that is, redescriptions or recastings of the story of Jesus in new contextual forms (1989:276). This does not mean, of course, that previous formulations or theories will hold no currency in a different context. It does mean, however, that we may never simply assume such adequacy. Interpreters must always guard themselves from the potential to assume that previous approaches will speak in a new situation.

According to Michael Root, such narrative redescription must necessarily include certain elements (1989:277). First, narrative redescription must always relate to existing patterns of thought or new ones that can demonstrate contextually compelling force. It is within such patterns of everyday existence that the significance of the story arises. Also, there must exist a dynamic interplay between, on the one hand, the uniqueness and fixidity of the events of Jesus and, on the other, the need to find more general cultural patterns that demonstrate the significance of the Jesus story. Finally, all such narrative redescription will be "fitting or appropriate, not necessary" (1989:277). Soteriological construction will be a matter of faithfulness or appropriateness judged by persuasion rather than any indubitable logical demonstration.

In many ways the ideas McClendon offers parallel those of Root. He too emphasizes the importance of narrative for understanding atonement but contends, against the practice of much contemporary Christian practice, that the ultimate narrative framework within which these images must exist is not theories, but the gospel story itself (McClendon 1994:227). McClendon conceives of theories of atonement as a contemporary sort of *midrashim* that enlarges the biblical story into contemporary relevance (1994:230–33). If we ask which theory is the correct one, the proper answer is at the same time both "none" and "all." Not any one culturally specific theory is "right." None are completely adequate alone nor are any appropriate for every context. Yet, all are "right" for each sheds light (albeit different valences and trajectories of light) on the one story of Jesus and God, the story that undergirds every expression of the Christian faith (1994:232).

What may we conclude from this brief survey of metaphor and narrative? First, we must acknowledge that every attempt to articulate the atonement, whether as a metaphor or narrative, is only a partial description. No single formulation can hope to account for all the biblical materials nor can any single approach accommodate the multiplicity of human struggles that the cross must address. This is because though each theory may legitimately appeal to different strands of New Testament teaching, no single theory can completely exhaust all of these biblical resources.

In this sense, then, any theory of atonement must be of necessity provisional, always subject to revision. Each specific configuration of atonement is contextual, dependent upon culturally specific language and logic. Metaphorical language, employed in service to particular contextual needs, is always designed to communicate for a contextually specific audience, informed by the particular circumstances that dictated their writing (Carroll and Green 1995:114).

The Radical Contextuality of Atonement Theories

There is another reason we should regard all soteriological formulations as provisional. Each metaphor, theory, or redescription contains within itself inherent tensions. As McClendon notes, it is "not possible to line up even one set of New Testament writers behind any one 'theory' without embarrassing anomalies" (McClendon 1994:266). Such is even more apparent when biblical writers mix metaphors (e.g., Cor 1:13–22, where the author conflates military, *Christus Victor*, redemption, legal, and sacrificial images). There will be times and places where these tensions, though perhaps acknowledged, will be bearable and tolerable. Yet, new contexts will arise that cannot endure such tension. When this happens, newer formulations that are more cogent become necessary.

The existence of such tensions points to the paramount importance of the relationship between social context and theories of atonement. McClendon astutely observes how each general approach to the atonement was ultimately dependent upon cultural assumptions for its cogency and legitimization. As these assumptions are displaced or change, so too does the cogency of the theory that depended upon them. If it is in its atonement theology the contextual rootedness of the New Testament is most explicit (Green and Baker 2000:88), it should come as no surprise that every formulation of atonement theory is by definition essentially contextual.

Early Ideas of Atonement

For example, the notion of *Christus Victor* originates from a minority pre-Constantinian church. Such was a persecuted church that had no social standing, and generally viewed the state as an oppressive power. In such an environment, "Christ's Victory over the powers heralds the triumph of a community that is socially relevant even when outwardly diminutive and despised" (McClendon 1994:202). Even the gradual demise of the doctrine was a function of contextual factors. The original formulation of *Christus Victor* lost its potency as an interpretation in the context of a Constantinian church. Such was not because people ceased believing in demons or stumbled over objections to tricking the devil. Rather the fundamental reason that *Christus Victor* fell out of use was that the church, in a Constantinian context, had lost its sense of confrontation with the world (Weaver 2001:86-87).

A church that no longer confronted the empire but looked to it for support, protection, and intervention on its behalf needed a new way of thinking about salvation (Weaver 2001:87). The context changed and with it, certain fundamental assumptions about the world. In that new context, certain formulations of atonement theory (viz., *Christus Victor*) no longer held its previous persuasive power. The ransom theory, too, ultimately failed by becoming too literal and too dualistic, things later interpreters could not tolerate (Gunton 1989:88). The various ways Christians conceived God trapping the devil were often wildly speculative. The inherent ethical challenges of a God who wins by deceit also proved an obstacle. An additional problem for later generations was the notion of "double allegiance" (i.e., the notion that humankind could owe certain obligations to both the Devil and to God), which was no longer tenable in the feudal society of Western Europe where the feudal lord (and, it was assumed, God) held complete power (Grenz 1994:342–43). As contexts changed, so did the appropriateness and believability of the ransom version of atonement.

Anselm and Satisfaction

What is true for early versions of atonement is no less true for later formulations. Anselm offers the first fully formed atonement theory, and also the first that can be properly termed "Western" (Tambasco 1991:14). Many of the earlier legal notions involved in discussions of salvation found explicit expression through his version of satisfaction. Gunton, discussing the introduction of legal thinking into the Western church, quotes Harnack's assessment:

> Here, as in almost all departments of activity in the Latin Church, it was of the highest moment that Tertullian, the jurist, and Cyprian, the ecclesiastical ruler, were the first Latin theologians. Disinclined for philosophical and strictly religious speculation, and dominated by a prosaic but powerful moralism, the Latins were possessed from the first of an impulse to carry religion into the legal sphere. (1989:85–86)

Though often associated with the penal view, Anselm's ideas are distinctly different. Yet, in ways similar to the Reformers, Anselm's theory depends upon a culturally specific notion of universal justice (Gunton 1989:89). For Anselm, however, the answer to the problem inherent in humankind's sin is *not* the exaction of a penalty, as in later legal formulations. For Anselm, there existed a difference between the notions of *satisfactio* and *poena*. These in fact existed as alternatives to each other. The Son's offering on the cross satisfied the Father's impugned honor. Consequently, there is no need to exact the owed tribute, or punishment. God is thus free to withhold imposing a compensatory penalty against guilty sinners (1989:90). Jesus, contra later penal theories, is not punished in our stead but rather offers perfect satisfaction on behalf of humanity. In this way, Anselm's approach legitimately constitutes a satisfaction, rather than a penal, view of atonement.

For Anselm, the legal framework that formed the bedrock of his approach to atonement was a part of the larger fabric of medieval European society.⁹ The feudal system, personal honor, justice, and retribution were givens Anselm could assume and upon which he could legitimate his theory of satisfaction. What to many moderns is an obstacle is precisely what made the theory so attractive to the early proponents.

Penal Substitution

I now come to the approach to atonement and soteriology that requires the greatest attention for this chapter since it has provided the bedrock for much modern Protestant soteriology. This is the penal substitutionary view of atonement. Regarding the great currency this view has enjoyed in recent Western Christianity, Joel B. Green and Mark D. Baker note that

> The affirmation that "Christ died for our sins" has, in the last two centuries, increasingly been articulated in the form of the doctrine of "penal substitution" or "satisfaction": Jesus satisfies the wrath of God by enduring the punishment we deserved on account of our sin. In fact, for many American Christians "penal substitutionary atonement" interprets the significance of Jesus' death fully, completely, without remainder. (2000:13)

Indeed, since the mid-sixteenth century, the penal version of substitutionary atonement has gained the ascendancy and become the quasi-orthodox and most widely accepted theory among Western Protestants and evangelicals (Grenz 1994:345). It enjoys, as Anthony Bartlett notes, "a privileged, even sacred status in the Western theological cannon" (Bartlett 2001:76). In much modern Protestantism, this approach has come to enjoy the status of being *the* biblical explanation of the work of Jesus on the cross.

Yet, despite operating as the "biblical" definition of atonement for much modern Christianity, penal substitutionary atonement is an account that requires a very specific cultural lexicon. In particular, a penal substitutionary account of atonement rests upon a particular legal notion of retributive justice (McClendon 1994:205).

The social context of newly reforming European justice systems sets the stage for early Protestant leaders to explicate their theology, and in particular, the doctrine of atonement, using contemporary and compelling legal notions (McClendon 1994:207).¹⁰ In such a context, it was important

---

9. "The Cur Deus Homo was the product of a feudal and monastic world on the even of a great transformation" (Southern 1990:222).

10. As McClendon notes, it is surely no accident that, though the term "payment" had been used before, it was not until this period of a reformed English justice system that

to demonstrate that even God did not act arbitrarily but lived under the demands of his own legal framework (i.e., his own righteousness). Such is clear in Calvin. Thus, "The absolute place that Calvin gave to law is understandable in the political context of his time, where the authority of law could operate as a check upon the arbitrary behavior of earthly princes" (Fiddes 1989:103). In a creative and contextually relevant manner, these thinkers formulated a theory of a God who must necessarily exact punishment according to the divine law.

This is a substantial change from the earlier approach of Anselm, who proposed the satisfaction of divine honor eliminated the need for the imposition of penalty. Calvin, collapsing this Anselmian distinction between satisfaction and punishment, formulated a theory of a God who must extract punishment to be satisfied. So, "from Anselm onward penal substitution simply leaps the formal steps of satisfaction, moving at once to the point of wrath that lies behind the whole, and making Christ bear this passively rather than offering compensation actively" (Bartlett 2001:85). In Calvin and other proponents of penal satisfaction, there is an unfortunate tendency to conceive of the relationship between humans and God as fundamentally one of legal obligations (Gunton 1989:86). In particular, this meant a Western legal framework.

Such culturally specific notions are clearly evident in the work of senior evangelical spokesperson and penal substitutionary atonement advocate J. I. Packer. Though Packer contends penal substitutionary atonement is a purely biblical viewpoint, the very language he uses to advocate this approach betrays how this theory is actually a conflation of Western legal notions with the biblical language of justification.

Rather than the biblical background he claims, Packer's definitions of righteousness and justification actually derive more from Greco-Roman notions. Righteousness, he asserts, is "that quality in God whereby he always does what is right . . . giving to every man his due" (Packer 1980:127). Packer notes that such "was Aristotle's definition of man's righteousness and it is the fundamental biblical view of the righteousness of God also" (1980:127). The outworking of this divine justice occurs on the cross. There, justice is done because sin is punished, as it deserves to be (1980:129). This is possible due to "satisfaction," an aspect of righteousness described in Roman law where claims are met (1980:128).

---

the terms were used in a juridical sense. Likewise, both Calvin and Luther, two advocates of such a theory, were also lawyers.

Indeed, it seems Packer and other exponents of this approach offer a profoundly Western legal framework as an interpretive matrix for understanding the law of God, sin, and atonement. The intimate connection between the penal satisfaction theory of atonement and systems of retributive justice is clear (Weaver 2001:3). That is, a requirement to inflict punishment on the perpetrator of a crime in order to accomplish justice is basic to a penal substitutionary view. Punishment is a quid pro quo arrangement, an act of vengeance, in which pain is inflicted on the perpetrator in compensation for the pain they have inflicted (2001:180).

This requirement of retributive justice is then transferred to the realm of human sin, relationship to God, and eventually the work of Jesus on the cross. Thus, according to penal substitutionary logic, human sin produces a legal guilt and such guiltiness makes us accursed before God and subject to legally appropriate punishment. God, who loves humankind, desires for intimate fellowship with humanity. Yet, sin and guilt must be punished and so this breach between the human and divine remains.

Indeed, it is this polarity between the justice and love of God that forms one of the primary tensions in the penal satisfaction view. Such is the quandary of how God can be justified in admitting sinful humanity into fellowship with himself. God's own justice (the need to punish the guilt of sin) and love (the desire to maintain relationship with sinful humanity) exist in tension. Penal substitutionary theory becomes the logical outworking of this opposition (Bartlett 2001:85).

The solution the penal view provides enlists biblical notions of sacrifice in support of its contention that sin must be punished. The death of Jesus on the cross represents the supreme sacrifice. Jesus experiences this accursedness and punishment on behalf of humankind, exhausting the divine requirement of punishment that was properly ours to bear. Such a sacrifice functions according to the canons of retributive justice (sin is justly punished) and propitiation (a sacrifice that satisfies God's anger and opposition toward sinful humankind). Though often assumed to represent *the* biblical understanding of the death of Christ, the logic and conceptual cogency of the penal substitution view cannot be extracted from the specific, Western cultural conceptions that undergird this view.[11]

11. Such is not simply a Western phenomenon, however. Others from non-Western contexts also hold to such thinking. In examining different approaches to salvation explicit in the world's religions, Tokunboh Adeyemo, himself an African, concludes that the true biblical view is salvation by grace through faith alone, understood within a framework of the substitutionary penal view of atonement and a definite need to pacify the

The New Perspective

Properly understood, however, Scripture does not provide the notions penal substitutionary atonement assumes. It is, of course, undeniable that sacrifice plays an important part in the story the reparation of the fractured human-divine relationship. Here, however, the framework is that of the Hebrew law court and the relationship between the gracious God and his covenant people, rather than a Western legal perspective (Gunton 1989:87). In the Hebrew context, the purpose of sacrifice was not to punish but rather to remove uncleanness that pollutes. Concerning this Gunton remarks whimsically that of course no Hebrew would have though a cupful of barley offered in sacrifice was being punished (1989:119–20)! At its core, then, biblical notions of sacrifice no not derive from concerns with punishment or retribution, as penal substitutionary theory assumes. Old Testament scholar John Goldingay contends that an erroneous link between atonement and the notion of punishment arises from a misreading of Isaiah 53:5–6 and 10–12. It is more correct to read the sacrificial notions in Isaiah 53 from the perspective of the Hebrew sacrificial system, not from a punitive perspective (Goldingay 1995:8). This is so since Hebrew religious sacrifice was one of expiation and representation and not propitiation and substitution (Travis 1995:34).

In recent years, a new approach to Pauline interpretation has arisen within the guild of New Testament scholarship that also highlights the essentially modern Western presuppositions that lie behind penal substitutionary thinking. Though lacking formal boundaries, a rejection of many traditional biblical and theological notions gives this school conceptual coherence. In particular, it has arisen as a corrective to certain misconceptions regarding Pauline understandings of justification, law, and works of law.

---

wrath of God (Adeyemo 1983:11). Yung Hwa links the penal view of atonement to a missional orientation, contending that if a penal substitutionary view of atonement is lost "evangelism will no longer be an existential confrontation with a Holy God who abhors sin in all its forms" (Hwa 1989:554). Even in D. A. Carson's edited volume, *Right with God: Justification in the Bible and the World*, a self-conscious attempt to explicate the gospel for other cultural contexts, what is offered is ultimately nothing but a rehearsal of the traditional Reformed penal substitution perspective. Such non-Western yet penal perspectives contend that there continues to be a need for someone to pay the penalty for sin (Sumithra 1992:224), that God deals with humankind fundamentally as Lawgiver and Judge, that righteousness is imputed to humankind while sin and guilt are imputed to Jesus (Unum 1992:252), and that sin is "in one way or another a revolt against God's law" (1992:253).

This "New Perspective" posits that such a misunderstanding has indeed been the case, especially since the time of the Protestant Reformation. For Luther, and subsequent Protestant theology, the doctrine of justification by faith alone was "the principal doctrine of Christianity. The major point of departure for the New Perspective is an assumption that this particular formulation of justification by faith has read the biblical data in ways conditioned by modern Western culture" (Dunn 1988:lxv).

Wright summarizes the traditional Protestant theological package of justification.

> People are always trying to pull themselves up by their own moral bootstraps. They try to save themselves by their own efforts; to make themselves good enough for God, or for heaven. This doesn't work; one can only be saved by the sheer unmerited grace of God, appropriated not by good works but by faith. (1997:113)

Such an understanding likely owes more to the early Augustinian-Pelagian controversy and the Reformation dispute between Luther and Erasmus than it does to Paul and New Testament teaching. Though not a complete misrepresentation of Paul, this way of reading Paul is at best misleading and at worst, a serious distortion on several points (1997:113).

Such an interpretation is intricately related to a specific reading of the book of Romans. This reading locates Romans 3:21—4:25 as the heart of the letter and, since Romans was believed to be the center of Paul's thought, the heart of Paul's gospel. This section has been thought to consist of (1) a polemic against any form of acceptance before God by human endeavor and (2) a proclamation of righteousness through faith alone. Many assume these two emphases to form the central distinguishing features of Christianity vis-à-vis Judaism and all other religions (Longenecker 1999:59).

Protestants, then, have often read Romans as a compendium of Christian theology, the gospel in microcosm. In doing so, however, proponents of the New Perspective claim they have ignored Paul's own literary and religious background and caricatured first-century Judaism as a religion of "works-righteousness" (Longenecker 1999:59). The point is that "Protestant exegesis has for too long allowed a typically Lutheran emphasis on justification by faith to impose a hermeneutical grid on the text of Romans" (Dunn 1988:lxv). By locating the core of the gospel in Romans, Protestant interpretation has not only misread Paul but also, by extension, misrepresented the gospel.

The Hebrew Law Court, Covenant, and Righteousness

A basic assumption of much modern Protestant reading of Paul is the notion that behind the language of justification was the notion of the law court. Luther and the other Reformers were certainly correct in asserting the forensic dimension of righteousness language in Paul. New Perspective authors argue that, in contrast to Western notions of justice, biblical righteousness language instead implies the Hebrew law court. "Righteous," in the Hebrew law court, refers to "the status [people] have when the court finds in their favor" (Wright 1997:98).

Such a reading relativizes many of the pressing questions regarding righteousness that arose out of the context of Reformed theology. It makes no sense therefore to ask whether the "judge imputes, imparts, bequeaths, conveys or otherwise transfers his righteousness to either the plaintiff or the defendant. Righteousness is not an object, a substance or a gas which can be passed across the courtroom" (Wright 1997:98). Again, "to imagine the defendant somehow receiving the judge's righteousness is simply a category mistake. That is not how the language works" (1997:98).

This law court language is intimately connected with a most basic notion of Jewish theology, that is, salvation as covenant membership. This is contrary to morality defined in terms of Western legal justice the proper way of conceiving the way God relates to humankind. The understanding of the term righteousness in the Hebrew Bible as primarily a notion of relationship in reference to God's covenant emerged at the turn of the century in Hermann Cremer's important work. Cremer argued that righteousness, at its core, is in fact a concept of relationship and not that of an ideal norm as in the Greco-Roman tradition. For the Israelites, "righteousness" was a quality or characteristic "of those . . . who faithfully kept the law that was their delight" and so continued in a covenant relationship with God (Kuyper 1977:252). In contrast, to be "unjust" or "unrighteous" is to act in such a way as to destroy or injure the covenant relationship. What upholds the relationship is "righteousness," again not as adherence to an abstract ethical norm. Rather, such has a fundamentally relational dynamic, that is, those types of actions that maintain covenant fidelity. So then, for God to make one righteous is not to become morally or ethically spotless. Rather, a righteous standing involves the restoration of a positive relationship within the covenant people of God. N. T. Wright summarizes that

> . . . covenant faithfulness in the present is the sign of covenantal vindication in the future; the badges of that present covenant

faithfulness may vary from group to group, but those who wear the appropriate ones are assured that the true god will remain faithful to them and bring them safely into the new world that twill soon be ushered in. (1992:336)

For the judge to act righteously then is to try the case impartially and properly, to support and uphold the defenseless and those who have no advocate. For the plaintiff and defendant, to be righteous is to have the court rule in their favor, vindicating them against the accuser (Wright 1997:97–98). To be "just" or "righteous" for God, then, is to uphold the covenant. This points the fundamental sense of the term when applied to God, that is, God's fidelity to the obligations of relationship, and particularly, his covenantal obligations to save his own people. Indeed, there exists a close connection between salvation and righteousness (e.g., Isa 46:13; Jer 23:6; Ps 40:10) (Tambasco1991:21). Though the demands of the covenant varied (mercy, triumph, faithfulness, defense, steadfast love, law), the notion of the creative and saving activity of God, that is, his righteousness, is basic to all (Tambasco 2001:20). For Paul, the covenant-making God had renewed his covenant. God's righteousness ("covenant faithfulness") means that God will one day vindicate his people by giving them favorable judgment ("justification") as his new-covenant people. It is this kind of righteousness that Paul contends has been revealed in the good news of Messiah Jesus (Rom 1:17).

The crucial point for here is that the authors of the Hebrew Scriptures never use "righteousness" for God's punishment toward his covenant people (Tambasco 2001:21). The forensic dimension in the Hebrew concept of justice/righteousness is not that of impartial justice or of a neutral judge applying the demands of the law and meting out to guilty individuals their due. Rather, the picture in the Hebrew Bible is one of a covenantal partner who upholds the right and defends his special people (2001:22). This is especially true toward the victims of injustice (Isa 58:1–9; Deut 10:18; Ps 146:7). So, "righteousness," from the perspective of the Hebrew Bible, is a transformative and re-creative concept, not a punitive one. Viewed within a Hebrew covenantal framework and not that of Greco-Roman law, the apparent tension between God's love and his righteousness/justice disappears.

The question of the righteousness of God for later biblical and Second Temple Judaism is not, as with Reformed theology, about how sinful humankind can be set right with God. Rather, it was, as Wright conceives of it, a question of "when and how would Israel's god act to fulfill his covenant promises?" (Wright 1992:271). God's righteousness is inextricably bound up with issues relating to the covenant 1992:272). The penal substitutionary view of Paul, justification by faith, and righteousness is contradicted by a more faithful reading given us by New Perspective proponents.

"Works of Law" and "A Righteousness of My Own"

Two Pauline phrases typically assumed to demonstrate the traditional Protestant approach to salvation and indicating a type of works-righteousness are "works of the law" (Gal 2:16; Rom 3:28) and "a righteousness of my own" (Rom 10:3; Phil 3:9). New Perspective scholars challenge this basic assumption. James D. G. Dunn and Alan M. Suggate argue that the meaning of these phrases have more to do with covenantal boundary markers (in a religio-sociological sense) than with any supposed system of earned salvation. The nearest parallel to the Pauline phrase comes in the Qumran writings where "deeds of the law" were what marked out the Qumran community in its distinctiveness from outsiders and enemies (Dunn and Suggate 1994:13). Such concerns would revolve around circumcision and the Jewish food laws. These are precisely the major concerns in Paul's polemic against the opponents in Galatia (Gal 2.1–15). For Paul, "works of law" were those things (e.g., circumcision, dietary practices, Torah as a sociological marker) that maintained the distinctiveness of the Jewish people.

The phrase "works of law" then, does not represent good works in the sense of "man's arrogant striving after self-righteousness" (Bultmann 1951:263–64). For Paul, "works" were not a legalist's ladder, up which one climbed to earn divine favor. Paul, of course, would certainly oppose any such notion but this was not the specific problem in his context. Rather, works of law for Paul were the badges that one wore as marks of identity, of belonging to the chosen people in the present (Wright 1991:201). These sociological identity markers were the all-important signs of belonging to the people whom God would vindicate and redeem. They were the present signs of future vindication. This was how "'the works of Torah' functioned within the belief, and the hope, of Jews and particularly of Pharisees" (Wright 1992:238).

What then is the proper meaning of the phrase a "righteousness of my own"? In the two passages where Paul speaks about his past before the Damascus road experience, he mentions his "zeal" (Gal 1:14; Phil

3:5–6).¹² Dunn points out that such "zeal" was characteristic of Jewish piety, evidenced in an overwhelming desire to do the will of God. This corresponds with the zeal or jealousy of God that point to his exclusive claims upon Israel as his particular possession.¹³ Those who demonstrated such divine zeal used this concept with the greatest approval by "fighting to defend that exclusiveness, by maintaining Israel's distinctiveness as God's own people over against the other nations, the gentiles" (Dunn and Suggate 1994:9).

It is not difficult to recognize that Paul saw himself standing in this same tradition of holy zeal. The pre-Christian Paul viewed the opening up of the gospel to the Gentiles by the Hellenist evangelists as a threat to Israel's distinctiveness as God's own chosen people (Dunn and Suggate 1994:10). For Paul, a "righteousness of my own" did not denote legalistic striving to attain salvation by his own moral effort. Rather, the notion functioned as a badge of honor, a way of holding distinction as God's very people over against other ethnicities and nations. In essence, such operated as a marker of social honor and prestige to which Paul held to tenaciously. Read this way, such a notion does not provide conceptual support for the traditional reading of guilt-based penal substitutionary atonement.

The Individual and Guilt

Traditional thinking regarding justification often assumed guilt and guiltiness (both the felt guilt of a contrite conscience and objective, moral guilt) as the primary human dilemma. In this regard, personal guilt and justification have become mutually reinforcing ideas for much Protestant theology (Jewett 1999:16).¹⁴

The New Perspective rejects such a perspective as the appropriate framework within which we should understand Paul. The obvious problem with this understanding is that Paul never himself writes about his feelings of guilt nor his pre-Christian failure to keep the Law. On the contrary, where he specifically mentions his experience with the commandments of God, Paul's conscience seems quite robust (Gal 1:13–14; Phil

---

12. In Romans 10:3, where Paul is giving testimony on behalf of his own people, there is presumably something of a self-testimony reflecting his own pre-Christian experience.

13. For example, Exod 20:4–5; 34:12–16; Deut 4:23–24; 5:8–9; 6:14–15; Josh 24:19–20.

14. Jewett notes that the traditional Western notion of guilt and forgiveness "stands as the organizing principle in every commentary on Romans that I have studied" (1999:16).

3:6). Paul does not appear to have much trouble at all in defending his ability to keep the commandments and the Law. Many have appealed to Romans 7 as a piece of pre-Christian autobiography, an obvious example of the moral frustrations of a person struggling with the commandments. It was not until earlier in this century, however, that this anthropological interpretation of Romans 7 was effectively undermined and more properly understood as a polemic for the goodness of the Law (Dunn and Suggate 1994:4). Stendahl takes this position and points out that Paul never urges Jews to find in Christ the answer to the anguish of a plagued conscience (1977:78–96). Likewise, he properly notes that the famous formula of Luther, *simul iustus et pecator*, "cannot be substantiated as the centre of Paul's conscious attitude towards his personal sins" (1977:202). Such a reading of Paul rules out the notion of righteousness as God's distributive justice, seeing such as a distortion based upon Luther's misreading of the Latin *iustitia* (Wright 1997:103).

First-Century Judaism

A New Perspective reading of justification also takes issue with another set of assumptions fundamental to traditional Protestant soteriology. This is the picture of a degenerate and legalistic first-century Judaism, a religion of works-righteousness. The Reformers, noting what seemed to be Paul's battles with a type of legalistic religion similar to that of medieval Catholicism, naively equated the practices of their day with those of the Judaism in the time of Jesus and Paul. First-century Judaism was degenerate, it was assumed, precisely because it was legalistic, dependent on human effort, and self-satisfied with the results.[15] Rudolf Bultmann represents this view, boldly stating that the real sin of the Jews was not their violation of God's law but their intention to become righteous in his eyes by trying to keep it. Such follows from "the insight which Paul has achieved into the nature of sin" as "man's self-powered striving to undergird his own existence in forgetfulness of his creaturely existence, to procure his salvation by his own strength" (Bultmann 1951:262).[16]

Advocates of the New Perspective, however, argue that the Judaism of Paul's day was not the type of legalistic religion familiar to Luther. Rather,

---

15. See in particular chapters 3–4 of Klein 1978.

16. Similarly, he states that for Paul the notion of boasting "discloses the basic attitude of the Jew to be one of self-confidence which seeks glory before God and which relies upon itself," viz., "sinful self-confidence" (Bultmann 1951:242–43).

it was for the most part a religion of grace, with human obedience always in response to that grace. E. P. Sanders has popularized the term "covenantal nomism" to describe this type of religion.

> (T)here does appear to be in Rabbinic Judaism a coherent and all-pervasive view of what constitutes the essence of Jewish religion and of how that religion 'works'" which "can be summarized in the phrase 'covenantal nomism.'" Briefly put, covenantal nomism is the view that one's place in God's plan is established on the basis of the covenant and that the covenant requires as the proper response of man his obedience to its commandments, while providing means of atonement for transgression. (1977:75)

This means that the covenant was a product of divine initiative, and the law provided the framework for life within the covenant. The law, in this view, is not the means to get *into* the covenant people, but the means for living *within* it. The function of the law was not to provide a way of "getting in" to the covenant people of God or to earn God's acceptance, though obedience to Torah (yet never perfect obedience!) was a requirement for continuing membership (Dunn 1996:312). The Judaism of the first century understood that "grace is always prior, and that human effort is a response to such divine initiative; that good works are the fruit and not the root of salvation" (Dunn 1988:lxii–lxiii). That is, law was a means of regulating life within the covenant community. It functioned primarily as an expression of the distinctiveness of Israel, in sociological terms, the "identity marker" that constituted Israel's distinctiveness and boundaries (1988:lxix).

The Judaism of the first century understood that "grace is always prior, and that human effort is a response to such divine initiative; that good works are the fruit and not the root of salvation" (Dunn and Suggate 1994:8). The New Perspective undermines the traditional Protestant notion of first-century Judaism and reveals it for what it is, that is, a "gross caricature" (Dunn 1988:lxv). Though acceptance of Sander's work, and particularly his notion of "covenantal nomism," differs considerably, the basic thesis that Second Temple Judaism did not constitute of religion of works-righteousness has been widely accepted. Consensus also exists (though again, the point is not totally undisputed) that Second Temple Judaism did not teach the need for perfection in keeping the law, either to gain entrance into the people of God or to retain one's covenant status (Dunn 1996:312).

In summary, the New Perspective demonstrates how many traditional Western theological ideas (particularly those associated with the dominant modern version of penal substitutionary atonement) owe more to specific cultural notions than Paul or other New Testament writers. Righteousness is not some abstract legal norm equivalent to Greco-Roman notions of guilt and retributive justice.

A Hebrew version views righteousness as a function of God's love, his own commitment to and faithful saving activity toward his covenant people (Wright 1997:110). Such a covenantal view of righteousness and justification no longer requires love and justice to be set against one another, as has typically been the case in penal substitutionary thinking. This removes the tension inherent in much atonement thinking between the conflicting ideas of justice and love. Such is a crucial move for thinking about soteriology in non-Western contexts since the traditional Western doctrine of justification has been so closely tied to particular Western notions of law and guilt. The end result has been a very Western gospel.

Besides reforming the notions of justification, an even more significant contribution of the New Perspective approach is to dislodge the doctrine of justification by faith (as understood from a Lutheran or Reformed perspective) from the controlling center of atonement theory. Justification (rightly understood) may continue to hold an important place within the theological lexicon, but a New Perspective reading reveals justification as simply one of many images used to represent the effects of God's redemptive activity (Hultgren 1985:82; Beker 1990:121). This allows the church to reposition the person of Jesus himself and the gospel announcement of his sovereign kingship as the proper center in gospel proclamation. Wright is emphatic about this very point.

> Let us be quite clear. "The gospel" is the announcement of Jesus' lordship, which works with power to bring people into the family of Abraham, now redefined around Jesus Christ and characterized solely by faith in him. "Justification" is the doctrine that insists that all those who have this faith belong as full members of this family, on this basis and no other. (1997:133)

By doing this, a New Perspective approach opens the way for a more dynamic and multifaceted view of the gospel, salvation, and atonement. A New Perspective approach unchains the gospel from the excesses of traditional Protestant soteriology and allows the gospel to find expression in new and exciting ways in the contexts of the cultures of the modern world.

Summary

The doctrine of atonement has often been a problematic and contentious issue. Yet, it remains a necessary component of basic Christian doctrine. Gunton argues that though it has often been egregiously misconceived there is a continuing need for the centrality of atonement. Even the concept of the justice of God, properly understood, must continue to hold center place in the message of the church (Gunton 1989:101). This is so because the church

> . . . still stands or falls by whether it proclaims and lives by the Gospel of the liberating grace of God, or whether its life degenerates into some form of self-salvation. For that reason, the doctrine of atonement must continue to be at the heart of Christian theology, and the metaphor of the justice of God at the heart of the doctrine of the atonement. (1989:101)

If there is a continuing need for the atonement, might it be possible to dispense with the extensive doctrinal descriptions in which we get lost and entangled? That is, if we continue to affirm atonement must we bother with theories? If the church existed for a thousand years without any formal theory of atonement, could we not do without such today? Could we not simply affirm the *fact* of atonement without the diversion of the *how*?

Though it is certainly the case that the fact of Jesus's work saves humankind and not any particular understanding, there is still good reason to press for a clear and extended articulation of the meaning of cross. For, as Yoder notes, if the theologians do not attempt such a task, the demands of preaching will cause someone to venture a guess. That is, if Jesus and his life remain at the center of the proclamation of the church, then someone will inevitably have to explain how and why the cross was "for us." In the end, if we are not self-critical in our reflection on the cross, we will simply offer "hymnology, the tracts people read, and non-theological literature with its unstated assumptions" instead of solidly biblical and critical deliberation (Yoder 2002:305). Beyond this, there exists an apologetic and evangelistic root as well. If we are missional, there will always be a demand to demonstrate the significance of the gospel for modern people.

Ultimately, there is no way to escape some attempt at explaining the notion of atonement. The only choice possible is that between critical and non-critical soteriological construction. Opting out of theory, then, is in fact not a real option. Most certainly then, we still need the cross and we must theologize about its meaning, including developing extended narrative descriptions that utilize salient contextually specific metaphors and ideas.

This need ultimately arises out of the twin poles of universality and particularity, an inherent dynamic in any biblical formulation of atonement and soteriology. To be truly universal requires a particular shape in a particular place. The good news about Jesus does not function like Islam, which is forever frozen in a specific cultural encoding. Though Islam claims universal scope, it expresses this universality in the form of a single particularity. The gospel is radically different. There are four canonical Gospels, not one. Such points to the eminent translatability of the story of Jesus, allowing specific cultural idioms to play an important role in creating new accounts of salvation. It is precisely because the gospel is universally good news that particular, context-specific formulations are required. And, it is by the construction of soteriology and atonement in particular contexts that the church demonstrates the true universality of the gospel.

This discussion leads to an understanding of atonement theory and soteriological construction that must exhibit three essential and closely related characteristics. These are the dynamic, the missional, and the contextual dimensions of all soteriological descriptions. I will now develop these characteristics.

Dynamic

Though there seems to be an inherent impulse in much evangelical Protestantism to locate the meaning of the atonement in a fixed cultural expression, it is imperative to understand how in fact such thinking hinders the effective communication of the gospel. Yet, the proper response to the need for varied soteriological expressions is not relativism but rather the affirmation of a robust pluralism, centered on the Gospel stories of the crucified Messiah. Interpreters must allow each metaphor to speak on its own terms (Green and Baker 2000:68). Though we must eventually move from individual metaphors to more comprehensive theoretical constructs, there always remains a danger of turning a "choir of New Testament voices into a solo performance" (2000:69). In the final analysis, it is best to heed Margo G. Houts, who contends that there are no easy answers to this challenging task. Instead, as Houts asserts, there are only "theories which try to assimilate a wide array of biblical images, theories which try to explain a mystery, theories which fit some cultural milieus better than others, theories which all have their flaws and glitches" (Houts 1993:1). A singular formulation can never sufficiently explicate the mystery of the gospel. The fundamental dynamism of soteriological construction will always require multiple images and multiple theories to account for these images.

Missional

No New Testament document or any specific version of the story of salvation in the Bible is sufficiently specific to yield a complete theory of atonement or a full-blown soteriology.[17] That this is the case points to the essentially missional dimension of the construction of atonement theories and soteriology. Indeed, the missional nature of the gospel itself mitigates against such, for this would be to freeze the story of salvation by fusing it to only one cultural context. McClendon is surely right when he notes that "a story told in one time and place distorts the work of Christ when dogmatically repeated in a very different time and place" (McClendon 1994:207). Such brings us back again to Gunton's notion of myth. The universal nature of the good news demands new formulations in concrete and particular contexts. Such points to the profoundly missional nature of all soteriological construction.

Contextual

The task of soteriology is to create new metaphors and new approaches to explaining the significance of Jesus' death. In the above account, I have articulated a historical rationale that demonstrates that this is in fact what the church has done through the ages. The metaphors used to describe salvation and dominant theories of atonement reflect substantive cultural changes to which the church responded. Such is a twofold response. First, older configurations would lose appeal as the underlying cultural logic became less compelling. Second, believers created new and vibrant accounts that fit more appropriately the narrative logic of new cultural context.

This illustrates that though we must continue to rely on Scripture for our soteriological construction, we must necessarily move beyond the basic New Testament images to create new culturally relevant constructive accounts of salvation (Green and Baker 2000:88). To do so would mean to become self-critically creative, embracing both the historical practice

---

17. "I need only note that, while the patterns in the text may be able to place limits on soteriological construction, they are not sufficiently specific to dictate a particular soteriology and thus eliminate the need for contemporary soteriological construction" (Root 1989:275).

of the church and "the contextually driven program of biblical authors" (2000:114).

The modern church, however, often has "failed to take seriously the legacy of the New Testament" (Green and Baker 2000:18) and the implications of the necessary connection between favored theories of atonement and culturally compelling narrative logic. Even those who are members of a given non-Western cultural context, however, may not be able to connect deeply with their own culture. For example, Steven Benson paints a picture of the Indian context we ignore at our own peril.

> Yet the foundations of Asian theologies were often laid by Western missionaries even as they laid the foundations of the churches.... Even when the teachers are products of the local culture, their higher education is often in Western institutions or under the guidance of those who were trained in the West. Because of these factors, culturally appropriate theological expression is not necessarily something that is easy or natural simply by virtue of birth on Asian soil. It is rather alarming that nearly all teaching and preaching on atonement in Indian churches uses exclusively the language of medieval Roman law courts even though that setting is foreign to every Indian Christian's experience. (1995:118–19)

Indeed, to restore this early Christian dynamic is nothing other than to provide a concrete answer to their question, "What would happen if our thinking about the atonement took the church's mission seriously?" (Green and Baker 2000:114). To take a missional approach to atonement and soteriology means to seek contextually relevant and significant approaches in ever expanding cultural contexts. Such a missional impulse requires the church to hold in creative tension both the universal and particular dimensions of the gospel, drawing upon the old to create the new and channeling the new to reinforce and sustain the old. This is the true nature of the soteriological task.

In fact, these three dynamics interpenetrate one another and live in reciprocal dynamism. Constructing missionally sensitive theories of atonement requires contextuality, for mission inevitably brings the gospel into new contexts. To do so necessitates contextually viable formulations. Indeed, in constructing such, the task must be a dynamic one necessarily. Static atonement thinking brings us right back to Gunton's myth. To be faithful to its universal impulse, soteriological construction must always be dynamic, missional, and contextual.

As Kärkäinnen rightly notes, the "critical task of Christian theology is to express the living traditions in a way that not only makes sense in the present context but even points to the future" (2004:131). It remains a most urgent task to rethink, restudy, and re-present versions of soteriology that "make sense in the ever-changing world" (2004:131). In other words, the fundamental questions to ask regard the relevance traditional notions of salvation have in the non-Western world and how a reconceived understanding of the soteriological task will enable new expressions in these ever-changing contexts. In this way, Christian theologizing regarding atonement and salvation will find its way into the future.

10

Salvation in the Context of Thai Face

ROBERT JEWETT'S STATEMENT OF how notions of guilt and forgiveness have ruled Western readings of Romans (and, by extension, Paul and New Testament theology) takes on greater significance when we consider soteriology as a contextual project, particularly as it relates to the context of Thai culture and face. Protestant soteriology has typically posited guilt and guilt anxiety as the core human problem and constructed versions of atonement based upon Western legal logic (Kraus 1990:207). The account I have provided demonstrates that though such utilization of guilt may be appropriate for certain contexts, we must recognize that the narrative logic upon which the church in any given age builds its soteriological descriptions is always contextually determined. We may not conceive of these as absolute accounts and apply them universally. A contextually aware account of soteriological description allows us to hold our views of salvation "lightly." This does not indicate a lack of seriousness but rather awareness that these accounts are always products of and suited for specific contexts.

Upon this account, it is possible to free atonement theory from the specific cultural contexts within which we form these theories. To do so mitigates against the unfortunate fusing of culturally specific descriptions (the theory) with the work of Christ (the thing). Particularly critical for this project, to unhook Western conceptions of personal guilt from the controlling role in soteriology is to free the oft-silenced voices of honor and shame, concepts so central to much of the context of Thai face, to occupy a new place in the articulation of contextual theology.

This connection I am making between face and soteriology is not arbitrary. Thai face constitutes a nexus of images and concerns that is, given its importance in Thai culture, potentially compelling and fruitful for contextually authentic soteriological construction. In particular, the prototypical face scenario I propose in chapter 6 demonstrates a narrative structure and logic framed by honor and shame. Since salvation is always about narrative specific logic, one way to understand salvation is to look at the culturally specific narrative logic inherent in a cultural model of Thai face.

Such takes into account important observations Joseph Cooke makes in his critique of the soteriology in the Thai church. The typical Western anguish over guilt, the desire for legal acquittal for misdeeds, and the desire for personal cleansing do not appear to form compelling elements within the Thai culture and psyche (1978:4). Yet, there is a fundamental, albeit often overlooked, area of Thai sociality that helps us in this discussion. Cooke highlights such, noting a

> ... personal element to Thai morality—a sphere where the experiences of acceptance, rejection, shame, honor, condemnation, and forgiveness have relevance. And that element, that sphere, is to be found in the framework of society and in the context of relationships with other people. (1978:19)

Cooke is surely correct in his observation that this type of "relational atonement" is pervasive in Thai culture. It is within this personalistic arena of face (with its associated dimensions of honor, shame, acceptance, offense, apology, and restoration) that we can speak about the experience of salvation more adequately in the Thai context (Cooke 1978:20). Though he does not use the specific language of face (preferring the more general ideas of honor and shame), in essence Cooke's proposal calls for using the logic of Thai face as a contextually specific narrative logic to express the good news.

This chapter represents a discussion of the soteriological implications that exist in an examination of the cultural logic and narrative structure of Thai face. To do this I first highlight how reflection upon honor and shame can contribute valuable resources to the Thai church as they attempt to articulate an authentic Thai soteriology.

Second, I investigate a particular way of conceiving salvation, the doctrine of salvation as union with God, or *theosis*. This soteriological approach provides resources that resonate deeply with many cultural dynamics present in Thai culture. As an approach that originates out of a non-Western context, it provides a view of the work of God in Christ that avoids many Western notions associated with traditional soteriological formulations. An assessment of salvation in the face context of Thai culture that takes into consideration the doctrine of *theosis* can, I believe, contribute stimulating and generative resources.

Shame

Despite the universality of the shame experience, it is a consistently neglected theme among Western theologians and Western missionaries in non-Western contexts (Stockitt 1998:112). Indeed, much Post-Enlightenment thinking in the Western world often had the totalizing effect of not merely depreciating the experience of shame but even subsuming it under the rubric of guilt. Thus, shame was designated a subtype of guilt, one that more often than not was considered a much more inferior reaction to sin than that of guilt (Kraus 1990:208–9). The result has often been that the non-Western world (and even contemporary culture in the postmodern West) has not heard the story of Jesus as "good news" (Green and Baker 2000:32).

The concept of shame as a moral category can provide a fruitful way to understand the cross for non-Western contexts and, particularly the context of Thai face (Kraus 1990:215). If we resist the temptation to view sin in a purely legal mode, it becomes quickly apparent that the Bible also frames the issue of sin in terms of failure, disorder, alienation, and shame. Framing sin in a non-legal mode does not minimize sin, as some might contend. Barth held that sin was the core problem of humanity yet was clear that "within the schema of human destiny in partnership with God, sin as a condition is of much more concern than sin as specific transgressions" (Benson 1995:111). Additionally, the curse of law may also be viewed legitimately vis-à-vis shame and defilement, rather than guilt and legal culpability (Kraus 1990:217). In similar manner, Scripture frequently frames God's judgment in terms of shaming (e.g., Luke 12:1–3).

Because shame is such a dominant component of the face experience in Thai culture, a contextual understanding of soteriological construction demands that relevant atonement thinking must speak with contextual clarity to this issue. Such an approach might emphasize a Christ who was shamed with thorns but crowned with honor and glory. It may also frame salvation in terms of incorporation into the story of Jesus where God sets us in a new place. In this new place, shame is abolished and new identity given. Humankind is "united with the crucified and risen Lord, with (an) identity now given, not through (our) own divisions and failure, but in grace" (Atkinson 1995:264). The exact details of such would of course need to be worked out *in situ*. The point here is that the phenomenon of shame demands to be considered in development of atonement theory in the Thai context where such is a salient cultural feature.

Honor

Framing the gospel in terms of shame, though, is only part of an appropriate response. Reconfiguring salvation positively in terms of honor and glory is a critical move since shame is not "solved" by forgiveness, as is guilt. Rather, the reestablishment of relationship and communication through loving communion and the affirmation of worth of the shamed is what ultimately removes shame (Kraus 1990:211). Honor increases, or makes heavy, the self, while shame decreases or empties it (Bowen 1991:31). Thus, "the healing of shame is accomplished in the restoration of honor. 'Salvation' is making full again the self that has been emptied" (Bowen 1991:32). It is in the experience of salvation that God gives us a new name, affirms our dignity, and re-honors us (Kraus 1990:165). Indeed, such an experience is face-producing as well.

A New Perspective reading of Paul opens up new horizons where the notions of honor may legitimately take a central role. If Protestant readings of Romans, Paul, and the New Testament have been unduly constrained by traditional notions of justification, then by freeing the gospel from this narrow confessional straightjacket a New Perspective approach opens the door for a fresh reexamination of these ideas. If understood within the proper sociocultural context of the honor/shame systems of the ancient Mediterranean world, Dunn's notion of the sociological function of law and works of law as one of privilege and honor makes perfect sense. Viewed this way, righteousness, honor, and glory parallel one another considerably. Terms within the semantic domain of "righteousness/justification" take on a new meaning of "being set right" within a covenantal framework of God's righteousness. Being a full member of God's covenant people is indeed the greatest of honors. If sin is falling short (i.e., existing in shameful inadequacy) of God's honor, righteousness/being justified "is to have such glory and honor restored" (Jewett 1999:12). The effect of salvation is "being honored by God through Christ who died for all, the formerly shamed . . . integrated into the community of the saints where this transformation process occurs under the lordship of Christ" (1999:12).

A major task for contemporary believers would be to reframe theology in terms of honor/shame in order for the gospel to speak with greater clarity and power to such contexts (1999:11).

Theosis: Salvation as Union with God

We must pose the question, then, whether there exists an approach to salvation or atonement that has resonance with the themes mentioned above. Indeed, such an approach is available though it comes in a form not particularly familiar to most Protestants.

In a most succinct soteriological description, Athanasius comments that "God became man, that man might become God" (Athanasius 1978:3).[1] For him, the effect of the incarnation of the Logos was "that he might deify us in himself" (Rakestraw 1997:257). Here, in summary, is Eastern Orthodox soteriology and theory of atonement, alternately knows as *theosis*, divinization, or deification. Admittedly, conservative Protestant and evangelical theology has generally rejected *theosis* as an appropriate way of conceiving salvation. In fact, it does not hold great currency in any Western theological tradition. Yet, *theosis* is not merely an antiquated theological curiosity or the exclusive possession of Eastern Orthodoxy (1997:257).[2] And, as I hope to demonstrate, there are particularly compelling reasons for us to rethink the value of this ancient Christian doctrine.

---

1. Athanasius 1978:§54, 3.
2. Many associate *theosis* exclusively with Eastern Orthodox theology. Yet, though central to the Eastern Orthodox traditions, the theme of sharing in the divine life is present in certain strands of Protestant theology as well. Among the Latin fathers, *theosis* was an important concept. Tertullian, Hilary of Poitiers, Ambrose, and even Augustine and Leo the Great accepted the doctrine, though it did not occupy as central a place as in the Greek fathers (Balás and Cist 1997:339.). A. N. Wilson's work on Aquinas and Palamas reveals that Thomas actually had a much more robust doctrine of *theosis* which in many ways paralleled that of Palamas (1999). Recently it has become clear that Luther had much more to say about divinization than has been traditionally assumed. Norris notes the work of Finnish Lutheran Tuomo Mannermaa, who claims that the Latin *deificatio* and the German *Vergöttlichung* appear more frequently in Luther's writings that does the phrase *theologia crucis* (Norris 1996:421). Indeed, Luther's own concept of justification may have been more similar to *theosis* than that of subsequent Lutheran theology (Kärkkäinen 2004:37). *Theosis* seems to have had a place in the theologies of Wesley and other British Protestants (Rakestraw 1997:264–66; Christensen 1996:71–94), and also appears to have held importance in Anabaptism soteriology (Kärkkäinen 2004:67–72). Due to its presence in all major theological traditions, *theosis* may legitimately be termed a catholic teaching of the church that has been preserved by Orthodox theology (Norris 1996:422.).

At its core, *theosis* is about participation in the life of God. It is an explanation of the Christian's "reintegration into the life of God" (Rakestraw 1997:258). Through the Holy Spirit, the faithful become sharers of divine nature. They are formed in the new life. They put off corruption. They return to the original beauty of their nature. They become participants of God and children of God. They take on the shape of God. They reflect the light of Christ and inherit incorruptibility (Stauropolous 1995:189).

As the term indicates, *theosis* or deification is also about becoming like God. Properly understood, such is a change into a new mode of life—divine life. That is, salvation is not merely a change in status or remission of sins but a restoration of humanity to the creational intention of God. Such theological anthropology views humanity as the unfinished creation of God and salvation as the renewal of the original *imago Dei*. Through baptismal grace, the sullied image is purified and brightened. Such a person is regenerated, gains entrance into the life of the new age, and regains incorruptibility and likeness to God. *Theosis*, understood in such a way, is God's greatest gift to the world and the ultimate goal of all human existence (Mantzaridis 19984:12).

How does this all happen? From the perspective of St. Gregory of Palamas, Christ's human nature was divinized because of its hypostatic union with the Logos of God. Because Jesus was divine, he was able to take into himself the fullness of uncreated divinizing energy, becoming an inexhaustible source of divinizing energy that he transfers to humankind, thereby making them divine (Mantzaridis 1984:33). In this way, the incarnation itself becomes an act of salvation (Ware 1980:103).

This approach diverges from the traditional Western theological approach. Clearly, the Eastern approach to salvation is rooted in a different anthropology than most Western theology. The sin of Adam is understood not so much as transgression of God's law as a deprivation of "divine radiance with which he had been gloriously clothed . . . and corrupted the likeness" (Mantzaridis 1984:22). So then, instead of a Western, Augustinian focus of original sin and the transferal of corrupted human nature, Eastern theology focuses upon two other effects of the fall: human mortality in the form of physical death and the distorted original image of God (Kärkkäinen 2004:21-22).

The immediate consequence of this apostasy was the fall, that is, separation from the living God. Humanity loses the divine gift. Human nature becomes distorted. Death comes. Our subjugation to the tyranny of the devil follows. And thus, we human beings ourselves stand in the way of the divine grace that is poured out upon us. The image of God within us is weakened. We ourselves preclude the possibility of our union with God. We deny the human characteristic and possibility of divinization. The potential of becoming like God disappears and becomes impossible (Stauropoulos 1995:187).

Lacking in such an account is the typical Western emphasis on inherited guilt. Through Adam, sin and death do indeed enter the world. Yet, all humans are morally culpable and guilty because they chose to sin, following in Adam's footsteps. Likewise, the wrath of God, death, and human mortality are not conceived of as retributive punishment but rather function pedagogically. These are intended by God to lead humankind to repentance and reintegration into the divine life. The result of this is to understand the death of Jesus not as a moment of divine satisfaction but rather as the destruction of the power of death (Kärkkäinen 2004:22).

The actual nature of the change involved in humans "becoming God" puzzles many and has often resulted in certain misconceptions. Though the language of humans becoming divine is fundamental, Eastern theologians do not advocate some sort of Christian pantheism or a merging into a divine oversoul. Contrary to the natural suspicions that arise when one first considers deification, the Greek fathers steered ably between this theological Scylla and Charybdis to present a notion of human deification that properly respects God's transcendence while acknowledging the mystical character of his incarnation (Robichaux and Onica 2002:xi).

There is no ontological change into deity. Humans do not *become* God but, rather, by grace and the energies that God bestows, become godlike. Such a careful distinction between the energies and the divine essence of God help safeguard the transcendence of God and keep it from collapsing the biblical human-divine distinction. Thus, the ambivalence many Western theologians have had toward the doctrine of deification is understandable but, ultimately, misplaced. Indeed, many Western theologians have recently overcome this reticence, recognizing *theosis* as a potentially fruitful theological notion. This includes evangelicals (Pinnock 1996; Rakestraw 1997) mainline Protestants (Hinlicky 1997:52), and Pentecostals (Kärkkäinen 2004).

The notion of *theosis* is ancient and has antecedents in ante-Nicene theology. Yet, this doctrine of *theosis* is not just speculative Eastern theology but does indeed have Scriptural roots (Balás 1997:338). The two most frequently cited texts are 2 Peter 1:4 and Psalm 82:6 (John 10:34–35), yet advocates refer to many other biblical passages.³ *Theosis* also closely parallels the notion of incorporative salvation in Paul, for whom the

> . . . prime significance which the death of Christ has . . . is not that it provides atonement for past transgressions (although he holds the common Christian view that it does so) but that by sharing in Christ's death, one dies to the power of sin or to the old aeon, with the result that one belongs to God. The transfer takes place by participation in Christ's death. (Sanders 1977:467–68)

Thus, Morna D. Hooker, in language remarkably similar to that of Athanasius, argues that the concept of interchange "is a vital clue" to understanding Pauline soteriology (1977–1978:481). For Paul, "Christ is identified with us in order that—in him—we might share in what he is" (1977–1978:463). And, again, "to be in Christ is to be identified with what he is" (1977-1978:476). Besides Paul, the Johannine concept of mutual indwelling in God also bears similarities to this doctrine (Pinnock 1996:151). Though the term *theosis* does not explicitly occur in Scripture, strong biblical warrant for this doctrine does exist.

Theosis *and 2 Peter*

The work of Jerome Neyrey illuminates the biblical link with the doctrine of *theosis*. Specifically, it is in his examination of 2 Peter 1:4, the biblical text most basic to the formulation of the doctrine, that Neyrey also provides a suggestive connection between the doctrine of *theosis* and the concepts of face, honor, and shame. Neyrey takes great pains to explicate the symbolic world in which both the author and the addressees lived. This was a world dominated by patron-client relationships and by issues of honor and shame. It is such issues that pervade the entire opening section of the letter of 2 Peter.

The author applies to himself the two terms "apostle" and "servant" (2 Pet 1:1). Rather than the traditional notions of humble service, however, Neyrey contends that the proper sense is that of servant as an esteemed ambassador of King Jesus.⁴ By doing so, the author formally identifies

---

3. For example, Exod 7:1; 34:30; Matt 17:4; John 3:8; 14:21–23; 15:4–8; 17:21–23; 1 Cor 6:5; 2 Cor 8:9; Col 3:1; Heb 4:15; Titus 2:13; 1 John 3:2; 4:12.

4. The tradition of special agents designated as "servants" in this sense, that is, as servants of the king, was well established in both the ancient and biblical worlds. Thus servant here has connotations of hierarchy and power. Combined with the term "apostle"

himself as one with honorable status (Neyrey 1993:145). Yet he also locates his audience in the same honor sphere by describing their faith as *isotime*, a term formed from *iso* (equal) and *time* (value, honor), meaning essentially "precious," "honorable," or "equal in value."[5] Such is part of the author's rhetorical strategy of *captatio benevolentiae*, asserting the addressees' own significant status. God calls the audience by his own *doxa kai arete*, likely a hendiadys meaning "famous valor" (1993:156). He is the supremely honorable Divine One[6] whose decree of salvation is framed in terms of resources (e.g., power, salvation, and promises), honor, and excellence. The force of such language designates God and Jesus as heavenly patrons whose generosity yields blessings that honor and enrich their clients (viz. believing Christians) (1993:145–46).

The section also resonates deeply with the patron-client dynamics so common in the ancient world. Thus, the catalog of virtues reflects the types of honorable behavior expected from loyal clients. He calls believers to add to their "faith" several qualities. More than simply an assent to the information of the gospel, this is likely "faithfulness" or "loyalty," which is the proper response of a client towards a benefactor or patron (Neyrey 1993:158–59). Such behaviors are those virtues that would normally constitute a faithful patron-client relationship. Those who do not respond is such manner the author describes as having "forgotten." This too is an important dynamic in patron-client relationships. "Honorable clients remember and thus manifest piety (*eusebia*), whereas dishonorable clients forget and shame their patron" (1993:162). Indeed, the entire section of 1:3–11 is framed in terms of a decree of honor to patrons or benefactors (1993:151). Frederick W. Danker notes twenty-seven phrases in these verses that parallel typical language used in such honor decrees (Danker 1982:467–68). The rhetorical force of the section then is to exhort God's clients (Christians) to honor their patron (God) by the type of lives (loyalty constituted by honorable virtue) appropriate for such a relationship.

If such is a true regarding of the general context, what about the particular verse from which the notion of *theosis* is frequently drawn? In such a context, verse 4 undoubtedly carries a sense of elevated status and

---

and the genitive of possession "of Jesus Christ," this designation heightens the author's sense of authority, honor, and status (Neyrey 1993:144).

5. Philo, in writing of the uniqueness of God, uses the term to assert that "no existing being is of equal honor to God" (Neyrey 1993:147).

6. Note 1 Peter 1:17, where the author designates God as "Supreme Honor."

honor. Believers are sharers and partners in the very status of God himself. To socially dislocated believers, such positive feelings and esteem derived from this new relationship and mode of being would no doubt contribute to a positive reconceptualizing of their own identity. Salvation from this perspective is about sharing in honor, majesty, and glory, the very virtues that characterize God. Salvation, in this mode of honor, is about the God who re-honors those who become part of his clientele, his family of believers. In contrast to their previous condition of shamed face-loss due to their fallen condition, believers gain a new face, one that derives from God's own divine face. Through Christ, God redeems our faces, restoring them to the original honorableness that was characteristic of the *imago Dei* as it existed in the pre-fall world. If through salvation Christians become partakers in the divine nature, then we must assert that such involves the believer's appropriation of nothing less than the glory and face of God.

Glory, Theosis, and Face

There are particular advantages for linking the notions of face and *theosis*. Though he does not significantly develop the idea, Mantzaridis notes that the glory (honor) of God is fundamental to the experience of *theosis* (Mantzaridis 1984:29–30). It is this link that provides a vital connection between the idea of honor and that of *theosis*. Such is especially the case if we understand "glory" not in essentialist terms provided by traditional interpretation but rather along the lines of interpretation offered by a sociocultural interpretation. Many have challenged modern readers to understand glory language in terms of the notion of honor.[7] Rather than a nebulous concept relating to the essence of God, these scholars argue that we must understand terms within this semantic domain (honor, glory, majesty, greatness) from the perspective of the ancient Mediterranean systems of honor.

If we view glory in this way, then the link between face, honor, glory, and *theosis* is clear. One may legitimately posit honorableness or glory as a primary characteristic of the *imago Dei*, understood as the pinnacle of God's created world. That is, humankind's original state was one of honor and dignity. God's destiny for humankind was participation in the divine life, which is true honor and glory. Loss of the image, falling short of

---

7. Such a view contends that the terms "honor" and "glory" point to the same reality and that the modern essentialist notions of the glory of God are misreadings. See, for example, DeSilva (1999a), Malina and Rohrbaugh (1998:122), and Piper (2001).

God's honorable designs, results in loss of this honor, viz., original shame. Salvation, viewed in this vein, is a re-honoring that is accomplished by a restoration of that image and the accompanying honor that comes from being included in the fellowship of Trinitarian life.

The notion of *theosis* involves divinizing grace that transforms a person to be like God. Yet, we must ask what constitutes these characteristics of God. Considering how frequently biblical writers describe God in terms of glory and honor, *theosis* seems a potentially fruitful way of correlating the notion of God's honor with the human experience of salvation. That is, part of the transformation that results from the infusion of divine life is our becoming truly honorable, filled with the life of God and bearing his characteristics. As Saint Theodore the Studite confesses, "Indeed an unheard of exchange! Life instead of death, incorruptibility instead of corruption, glory instead of dishonor" (Theodori Studitæ 1860:696:B).[8] The theological impulses present in the doctrine of *theosis* represent potentially fruitful resources for talking about honor/face and shame/loss of face as concepts central to salvation and atonement.

Another distinct benefit for considering the doctrine of *theosis* is its decidedly non-legal orientation that avoids a Western legal view of sin and salvation as essentially remission of guilt (Clendenin 1994:367). *Theosis* views sin in a much more holistic and relational way as a life in the world without reference to God or his ways. Such leads to a quite positive notion of salvation as a renewal and replenishment of a depleted and shamed self. By detaching notions of atonement and salvation from a traditional legal framework, it is more possible to tap into local spiritualities, religious notions, and cultural values in framing issues of salvation (Schönherr 1983:160; Norris 1996:413, 425). This is particularly the case as it relates to the issue of face, face loss, and face recovery.

Shults and Sandage note the need in the shame-saturated modern contexts of the Western world for a view of forgiveness and salvation that brings wholeness and not simply juridical absolution.

> A punitive concept of salvation may help a person who feels guilt about an activity, but for the deeper existential dread that accompanies repeated shaming, we need a complementary concept of forgiveness than is oriented toward wholeness and reconciliation. We need our sins remitted not only in a juridical sense, but

---

8. "Τὰ ἀνταλλάγματα ξένα! Ἀντὶ θανάτου ζωὴ, ἀντὶ φθορᾶς ἀφθαρσία, ἀντ' ὀνείδους δόξα!"

also in a medical sense: we want to be healed and made whole. (2003:215–16)

How much more the case is such for the relational face-logic of the Thai context.

God accomplishes such a transformation of the self by the filling of our shamed, depleted selves and broken faces by the honoring of divine presence and fellowship by God's own self. Instead of a legal transgression that results in personal guilt, *theosis* views sin as a falling from the honorable state of God, deprivation of divine glory, corruption of the God's "likeness" in us, and lost communion with and a forfeiture of participation in the life of God (Mantzaridis 1984:22). As Pinnock observes, Christ's work on the cross "was not primarily a legal transaction but a power event. Eastern theology grasps this point" (1996:99).

Viewing salvation along these lines helps counter the reductionist version of sin and human predicament often part of traditional Western theological approaches. As Paul R. Hinlicky notes, the traditional Reformation doctrine of justification can become simply a "declaration of divine favor that hangs in mid-air, without providing any vision of who the human person is and what he or she is to become" (1997:41). *Theosis*, in contrast, is itself a kind of "theological anthropology" that not only provides an account of salvation but also a real *telos* for the person (1997:41). We need an account of salvation that is integrative and highlights our transformation into God's own life.

> However, if the origin, condition, and goal of salvation is essentially relational (the eternal knowing and being-known of the Father, Son, and Holy Spirit), and if the eternal life into which humans are called involves an intensification of creaturely sharing in this knowledge, then . . . Christians are finding their personal identity (are being saved) as they know themselves and others in relation to God-as they are drawn into a more intense sharing (koinonia) in the eternal communal knowing and being know that is the divine life. (Shults 2003:188)

The doctrine of *theosis* demands a real change in the life of the person who experiences salvation (Kärkkäinen 2002:86). Such avoids the tendency of much soteriological thinking that focuses on the experience of the individual's personal salvation, avoiding the critical issues of discipleship and true "deeds of repentance."

The notion of *theosis* provides a fruitful way of discussing the nature of salvation vis-à-vis face because of its emphasis on Trinitarian relationality. Face lies at the core of our human selves and all sociality. It is not an adjunct to our personhood but truly constitutive of our selves. Face is inherently a function of our relationality though viewed from the vantage point of the individual it represents an instantiation of individual identity goals and the projection of such into social space. Yet, face as I have described it here, both from the theoretical literature and from my interview data, represents, as Arundale notes, a "conjoint co-creation" between the individual and others. As such, face forces us to see, in a specific fashion, that our selves are inherently and inescapably social entities.

The doctrine of *theosis* resonates deeply with such a notion of socially formed individuals-in-community. From this perspective, to be saved is to be included as a part of the community of the Face. It is the giving and supporting of the face of others that constitutes the Trinitarian mode of loving, ecstatic community into which the salvation experience draws us. Indeed, as God makes us share in his divine life, it is this very Trinitarian life into which he moves us.

It is the goal of the ongoing missional work of the triune God to bring about "bonded community . . . the ecclesial self, the new humanity in communion with the triune God" (Grenz 2001:305). This view of salvation, as conceived through the notion of reintegration into the divine life and honor/glory, is a renewing into the *imago Dei*. As I have argued, the *imago Dei* is connected to human relationality through the experience of face. In this way, *theosis* provides a framework by which face may function as a critical consideration of our soteriological description.

Again, a significant component of this discussion involves how *theosis*, at its core, is about honorification and glorification. Salvation, in a *theosis* framework, is about participation in the glory and honor of God. This is so since the dynamic in the Trinitarian life is none other than "the glorification entailed in the reciprocal sharing of love" (Grenz 2001:327). As God draws us into this divine life (which is simply another way of describing the process of "being saved") we participate in this eternal glorification (2001:327).

As individuals, our self-identity is reconstituted through this new acceptance and esteem which is a new face. This is at the same time a new self-face and also a result of the corporate face of the ecclesial community, which the Face of God in Christ creates. This participation in a bonded community constituted by Trinitarian glorification and love, is the true relationality that God intended at creation and the eschatological *telos* that drives the *missio Dei*. Following Zizioulas, we become true persons, ecclesial beings, as we participate in this Trinitarian honorification. In the process, God renews our faces, and the facework-laden modes of relationality that constitute our shared life in the church.

A Prototype Scenario of "Face Salvation"

I shall now restate the prototype model of Thai face that I developed in chapter 6. In particular, I wish to make use of the narrative logic and distinct stages within this prototype (see Figure 1) as a framework for guiding consideration of salvation in the Thai face context.

Face Gain and Face Possession

God's address to us as a valuable and esteemed part of the creation constitutes the primal face-granting activity of God. More than this, however, God grants us true honor and face by virtue of our being made in the image of God. Thus, through goodness and grace, God grants humankind authentic face. This face is a result of fellowship with God, and is formed by the acceptance and esteem of true relationality. Here, in this pre-fall life, the existential anxiety that drives much of the post-fall face game, is satisfied completely by the acceptance and affirmation that comes from pre-fall human-divine relationality. The subsequent human preoccupation of seeking face and honor from one another without reference to God rests upon the fundamental human yearning, given to us in our original pre-fall state, of a completely loving and affirming face that will not go away. Yet, a level of universal personal face, which is characteristic of the *imago Dei*, persists even after human sin distorts this image and face.

Offending Event(s)

As Thais see human actions as causing face loss, so humankind rebels against God's intentions, listening to the Deceiver rather than God. It is this sin that results in a loss of a state of honor, a total loss of face before God. Human ingratitude, which we demonstrate by our persistent rejection of God, constitutes the ultimate offense. Such is more than simply the infractions of individual agents. By our rebellion, humankind becomes complicit in constituting a world that ignores God's goodness, that impugns God's honor, and that perpetuates the primal face loss our ancestors imitated in the garden. It is our shameful rejection of God that continually reconstitutes the world of rebellion in which we live. It is our perpetual engagement in destructive modes of relationality and behavior that leads to lives quagmired in shame and sin.

Our sin has an even greater consequence than the shame it brings upon us. That is, by rejecting God's ways we also cause God to lose face. This loss of face brings shame on the name and character of the God who created us. By our own sin, we contribute to the making and remaking of a world that scorns God and the healing grace he offers.

Calculation

Thais calculate numerous factors in determining whether, and to what extent, a given action should be considered face depleting. So, too, there is a divine calculus for face consideration. It is here that we must acknowledge an audience that is of greater significance than any human assessment. That is, the judgments of the various "courts of reputation" that have guided our face assessments now give way to recognition of an eternal Court of Reputation. Thus, a face-scenario framed not by the dimensions given by the surrounding culture but by the gospel story relativizes the typical sources of face (personal evaluation, societal estimation). It replaces these former sources with the Face of God revealed through Jesus and the community that lives with the narrative of this God at the center of its existence.

Such is a familiar experience for most Thais. That is, most Thai people daily live with the ever-present potential of face loss, constantly pressed upon by the factors of face calculus (e.g., personal standing, nature of the offending event(s), audience evaluation, level of face attachment). This face calculus no doubt often exists as pre-critical and at a tacit level of awareness. Yet, such is an essential mechanism in the overall face game that most Thai people play.

Biblically, it is God's calculation that is ultimate and determinative. To the extent that we agree with God's assessment of what we have become in our face-fallen state, we will likely experience shame, fear, and estrangement. Thus, this stage is critical for our growing awareness of alienation from God's ways. Indeed, the acknowledgment of true face loss before God may constitute the starting point of the self turning back toward God. This, Scripture calls repentance. We begin to relinquish our cherished claim-rights as God's view of us and our state of rebellion erode the face claim-right logic gained from our surrounding culture.

This issue of face attachment becomes a critical issue here. On the one hand, our face attachment is relativized as we being to see how vacuous are the humanly formed sources of face. It is the gospel that now qualifies our face attachment. This does not mean, as some might suppose, that we therefore care nothing for face. To the contrary, such a reorientation remakes our attachment, now based upon God's own concern for our face. God loves us and is concerned with our face. He is particularly concerned with our face as it derives from our relationship with him. The evaluative criteria for calculation now come not from the dominant face modes the cultures around us dictate; the good news of God revealed in Jesus is our new standard for face evaluation.

Face Depletion

Face depletion results from a negative assessment of our behavior. Since God is the ultimate audience, and the ultimate reliable standard, it is divine judgment that establishes ultimate face loss. Such is not the facile loss of surface-level social acceptance that can be a part of the mundane face loss experience. Indeed, we have lost honor before God. If we view God as granting us face on righteous grounds, the revocation of such constitutes a face loss of incomparable gravity. We stand before God as creatures who have delighted in shame rather than virtue, honor, and seeking after God's approval. Our faces are broken by the loss of acceptance and esteem, which are the possessions of those who live by God's virtues. Such depletion of face is no mere embarrassment before some human audience but constitutes a loss of face in the presence of the eternal God.

The Christian story asserts that, by rejection of God's honorable ways, humankind exists in a state of face loss. In contrast to the similar experience in the Thai context, one's refusal to accept another's negative evaluation of the offending events does not prevent such from constituting a loss of face. God, whose face evaluation is eternal and true, judges our compromised state as truly face depleting. If we take the view of *theosis* seriously, this face loss involves our human mortality and corrupted states. Such involves taking a beautiful gift (the life God has given us) and dishonoring the Giver by polluting our selves with corrupt mortality, sin, and death.

Whereas in the Thai social context, face loss need not be absolute, the face loss the Christian account asserts is of a kind which there can be no greater. This is so since our rejection of the honorable and good ways of God is not partial but complete. Additionally, the magnitude of our loss of honor and face before the eternal God is incalculable in human terms. With another of similar social status, we may experience serious loss of face. Likewise, before another of greater status and face (e.g., the prime minister or the king) the potential for loss increases considerable. With God, of whom a being more noble, honorable, pure, righteous, and mighty cannot be conceived, our loss of face and honor and the extent of our true shame simple defies human categories.

The primeval experience of face loss in the garden of Eden forms the prototype of which our individual face depletion is a reflection. Such is not true in a platonic sense of eternal forms and earthly shadows. All subsequent human face loss (whether before a human or divine audience) is a recapitulation of the same dynamics and results as we continue to perpetuate the folly that is sin, that is, loss of face and honor. Though some may not experience conscious awareness as such, refusal to accept God's evaluation only confirms and perpetuates the loss of true honor and face that separation from God involves. Such is indeed both an eternal and a universal face loss.

Reaction(s)

A frequent reaction to face depletion in Thai culture is avoidance. Because we hold the esteem and acceptance that forms face to be important, we expend considerable energy to avoid such a painful experience. Like our ancestors in the garden, our tendency may be to try to hide, disengage, deny, or avoid the truth about us. Yet, the only proper reaction to a true estimation of our loss of face and honor before God must be one of sorrow and contrition. Here the poles of objective and subjective shame and face loss are important considerations. If we accept that God constitutes the ultimate standard for evaluation, then there always exists an objective level of shame irrespective of any subjective experience of it. Ideally, we should experience subjective shame because of the objective truth of our shameful face loss before God.

The affective and behavioral dimensions of our reaction resulting from our realization of this epic face loss should be congruent. That is, along with a true sorrow flowing from our realization of our own broken faces and the shame we have brought upon God, the gospel calls for a change of direction. This "about face" (a Godward turning of the self) will result in those acts that constitute true repentance.

Such godly repentance (2 Cor 7:10) cannot derive from a facile or shallow desire to "save face." That is, much human facework is corrupted by motivation and strategies that ultimately seek to fill these deepest needs without reference to the divine Face. Such may be only an attempt to look good, to put on a good face. Yet, understood properly, the post-fall existential anxiety that drives much face concern is actually the correct impulse. For when we reference God's acceptance and esteem as primary and our related desire to gain fellowship and true face from God, such constitute an authentic base for our emotional and behavior reactions to our loss of face before God.

Face Recovery

What does it mean for God to redeem our faces? At the most basic level, it surely means that God moves us to a new place where he accepts us fully and grants us divine distinction and affirmation. It in response to our total shame and loss of face that God "steps in" (of course, not implying that God is inactive or absent prior to this point) and initiates that which we may adequately describe only as transformative face. Just as Christ died, was raised, and was given the name that is above every name, so too we die and are raised, now seated in the heavenly realms with Christ (Col 3).

Thais engage in the face recover, not only for themselves, but also on behalf of others. Such is a beneficent gesture of restored relationality with individuals and, potentially, a group. That which seems to drive Thais at the human level to respond with help in redeeming another's face is care, love, and relational proximity. Yet, God's love is so incredible that Christ died for us while we were still full of shame because of our sins, at enmity with God, and unable to do anything about our compromised state (Rom 5). It is such a move to restore the faces of his own enemies that distinguishes the love of God in Christ as something amazing and unparalleled.

What God does for us here parallels something implicit in the experience of Thai face. This I term the dynamic of transformative face.[9] In Thai culture, a social inferior giving respect or honor to one who is superior

---

9. This dynamic appeared in several interviews, though I did not identify it as a specific area of investigation. The notion is compelling, though it deserves greater attention and research to understand properly its character. I suggest it here as a possible area for further investigation.

is usually said to "give honor" and not to "give face." Such constitutes a granting of honor that is a normal paying of the "debt" inherent in the legitimate face claim-right the superior possesses. It does not change the status or condition of the higher, as it is only what is appropriately due. It is an appropriate payment in the normal social currency that the face differential requires.

Yet, if the "higher" grants honor and respect, such is often termed "giving face." Such, if indeed granted, works outside the logic of the normal face claim-right. It is not a repayment of any face debt since the socially superior is under no such obligation. In different ways, this may transform the state of the lesser. Because of the recognition and favor given to them, the social inferior may actual increase in status, face, and honor as a result of this honoring and giving of face. In such a case, we may properly term this "transformative face." This represents a different type of face altogether. By nature of it coming not as a condition of the claim-right, such comes as the gracious favor of the socially superior. Such is indeed a free gift, a serendipitous bestowal of respect that may have lasting effect on the one who benefits from such a transformative act.

Such seems to parallel in important ways what happens to us in Christ. The new self with a new face comes as a gift. Our faces impose no clam-right upon God. God is under no obligation to recognize our human groping for acceptance and affirmation. Yet, in an act of unparalleled munificence, God reaches out to us, adopting us into his family, freeing us from our sin and shame, and redeeming our faces.

The quality of face that God grants us is an important issue. We must posit that the One whose judgments are completely true and right, whose honor and acceptance are the reality of which human honor and acceptance are shadows, grants a qualitatively different kind of face. It is, in fact, God's own face that he extends to us. By being drawn into the divine life and being remade according to the original *imago Dei*, we come to share in God's own face.

Face Preservation

Finally, for Thai face, the activity relating to face preservation or maintenance is absolutely critical. It safeguards that which is precious and, likely, has come by great personal and group effort. Such involves the important activities that allow people to continue enjoying that which is the goal of the face game, that is, possessing face.

Though we may experience temporary or lesser types of face loss because of our shameful activities of sin, such does not constitute total face loss before God or the community. Our lives, which are hidden with Christ, reflect the honor and glory of God as we look into the face of Christ. As we live "in Christ," we maintain the face granted to us by God. It is, indeed, the face of Christ that he gives to us by virtue of our adoption as children, that preserves our status of honorable favor and true face. Provided that we hold firm until the end, our assurance of God's esteem and acceptance, the true face God grants to those in his eternal family, is a secure possession. The face anxiety, so typical of the Thai face game, is alleviated for the believer, whose status as beloved child or God and brother or sister is secure.

The Christian community, which upholds the specific Christian virtues that lead to true face and honor, functions as another dimension of face preservation. God endeavors to protect our faces provided that we constitute them upon the proper virtues that are basic to the gospel narrative. Indeed, the church, God's bonded face community, functions as the visible and real-world broker of the face of God. We image and reflect back to the world God's honor and face. As such, God is invested in a church that faithfully follows and represents to the world the loving Face of God that comes in the face of Christ.

Summary

This chapter has provided an overview of important elements to consider for a more authentic soteriology in the Thai context. Since soteriological construction is inherently dynamic, contextual, and missional it is incumbent upon those in new contexts to explore how this nature of soteriological construction necessitates new metaphorical descriptions of salvation. Such will follow specific cultural logic and rest upon contextually relevant notions of the basic human problematic state.

Toward this end, I have proposed that the notions of shame, honor, and *theosis*, together with the cultural model and prototypical scenario of Thai face, hold great potential for reassessing contemporary Thai descriptions of salvation and atonement.

It would of course be the height of naïveté and totally counter to the entire proposal I have advanced simply to offer the Eastern version of *theosis* or any other theory, for that matter, as a cut-and-paste solution for the Thai context. Yet, the basic impulses of the doctrine of *theosis* provide an opportunity for bringing honor, shame, and face to the center of soteriological reflection. This is so since *theosis* conceives of the human predicament, the fall, and salvation in a decidedly non-Western and non-legal manner that parallels the basic logic of face and also follows the narrative flow of the face prototype scenario.

I wish to emphasize that here I do not attempt to write Thai theology or propose a developed Thai soteriology. Rather, what I offer in outline form is meant as provisional and suggestive, a catalyst for the substantive work of filling this out in the life and theology of the Thai Christian community. Thai Christians themselves must engage in their own study of Scripture, questioning existing models of interpretation and theological construction that Western missionary influence has established as normative in contemporary Thai theology. By doing so, the Thai church may find its own theological voice and establish new metaphors and narratives that will provide the contextual clarity Thai soteriology needs.

11

Conclusions and Recommendations

I CONCLUDE BY RECOUNTING the major contributions I propose. First, I have surfaced important issues that grow out of missionary mishandling of the gospel in the midst of Thai culture. Missionaries have superimposed Western legal notions of salvation, without significant modification, onto a culture for which the Western legal narrative logic appears feeble and lacks compelling force. The same asymmetrical strategies prevent missionaries from understanding or developing a proper appreciation for the issue of face. Undoubtedly, this is not uncommon in other lands, particularly those of Southeast and East Asia. The disconnect between the gospel of the Western missionaries and Thai culture is a specific manifestation of a more general pattern. In this sense, the lessons learned from this disconnect are likely generalizable to missionary activity in other Asian cultures.

Second, I have identified two important sources of prosopagnosia (both of the face-averse and face-oblivious kind). The first originates in deep misunderstandings regarding the nature of guilt and shame and the associated issues of honor and face. The other source I have highlighted flows from the modern Western configuration of the human self. Such a self, I have argued, essentially precludes any healthy appreciation for the universal phenomenon of face. Instead, I have argued for a social or narrative self that does not admit to the same face-averse tendencies. The theoretical perspectives that I have engaged will enlarge, within the missiological community, the understanding of face and face-related concepts.

Third, I have presented original work, drawing on actual discourse from Thai people, that has expanded the parameters of discussions about Thai face. Through ethnographic interviews, I have developed a cultural model of Thai face that illustrates the meaning and function of face in Thai culture. The prototypical scenario of face also constitutes original research that should augment the still underspecified issue of Thai face.

Fourth, my work in the area of metaphor, narrative, and atonement demonstrates that each theory of atonement or soteriological model must necessarily assume specific cultural logic. This points to the radically contextual nature of the critical task of soteriological construction. The framework I suggest for the soteriological task highlights the dynamic, contextual, and missional nature of all human descriptions of the effect of the cross on humankind.

Fifth, I explore Thai face as a theological issue, seeking to discern its implications for theology and missiology. In particular, I suggest that the areas of honor, shame, and Eastern Orthodox soteriology (*theosis*) provide valuable resources for the Thai Christian community to construct a relevant theology of salvation. I also highlight the potential value the narrative logic of the prototypical scenario of Thai face holds for a contextually appropriate Thai soteriology.

The most significant implication of this study, however, is the compelling case I believe I have made for face to gain a legitimate place in the Thai theological vocabulary. Such has not been the case due to disconnect the dominant face-averse and face-oblivious postures have generated in the Thai Christian community. This prosopagnosia has essentially immunized the Thai Christian community against face and face-related issues. Even when there does not exist a face-averse attitude, a lack of commentary on this basic cultural issue communicates that face is not an issue about which Christians need be concerned. Face theory and self-presentation theory help us understand how face and facework are essential components of all human relationality. Study of face in the Thai context highlights the salience of the logic of Thai face. A Trinitarian anthropology of the self together with biblical material that relates to face increase our awareness of the deep resonance face finds with primary matters in Scripture. The cumulative effect of these different components of this study requires us, I believe, to recognize face as a valid and worthy issue for Christian reflection in the Thai context.

Since in Thai culture face concerns are more explicitly "on the table," this recognition may prove an important and potentially freeing insight for the Thai Christian community. This account could encourage believers in such contexts to engage the issue of face as a positive source for local theological reflection. Taking the "about face" route this chapter suggests would require God's people to "face up" to the faceless theology that pervades the current theological landscape. This type of conversation might significantly counteract the unfortunate disconnect with face that has long been a part of the life of the Thai Christian community.

Additional Implications

The "about face" proposal of this study intends to legitimate face as an issue of explicit theological reflection in the Thai context. This remains the critical first-order task. The important second-order task is to seek ways of assessing face from a Christian perspective and put this understanding to use in the life of the Thai Christian community. I have proposed practical implications of an "about face" primarily in terms of a contextualized soteriology. Yet, an engagement with the issue of face as I am suggesting has a wider application for the life of the Thai church. Such critical work is, of course, the proper possession of the Thai church, yet I would be remiss to not hint at how this could potentially influence the work of missionaries, church planters, and church leaders in Thailand.

Face must form a more intentional and explicit focus in the work of Christian discipleship. How does a Christian "do" face? Without making face an area of intentional focus, new believers will either default into face dynamics they have received from the culture around them or will assume that silence equals censure (i.e., since we do not talk about face as Christians it must be something inappropriate). Neither of these is acceptable. To engage face Christianly is to seek to bring God into the very midst of the face game and ask, "Now that God is here, how are things different (or the same)?" This is to inquire how God makes Thai face into the kind of face that brings God true honor. To ask it another way, we may say that to engage Thai face as Christian believers is to discern how the honor/glory of God in the face of Christ transforms our faces.

To bring issues of face to the center of discipleship in the Thai context must surely mean understanding the shape of the prevalent Thai cultural model of face, the specific logic of face, and the specific dynamics of face claim-rights. These must be set aside the orienting motifs of the *imago Dei*, the Face of God/Christ, and biblical honor dynamics. We must investigate the ways Jesus himself engaged in the face game, sometimes upholding his and others' face, sometimes challenging others' face, sometimes even losing face in the various courts of reputation. The dialogue that ensues must discern through the guidance of the Holy Spirit the ways we should affirm, reorient, or subvert the various dimensions of Thai face.

The reorientation of honor we saw in the chapter 7 parallels the creative work done by early Christians. Theologian Kathryn Tanner notes how the early Christian community took the culture-specific notions of honor and shame given to them by the surrounding culture and transformed them by infusing a new cultural difference. This meant that, though incorporating much of what these notions entailed, early Christians changed the goal of the dominant honor codes (now the goal is to do the will of God), substituted new Scriptural warrants for engaging in such practices, made unexpected content substitutions (humility, service, and suffering are now honorable), and "by seeing moral achievement on those terms not as the individual accomplishment of the philosopher but something requiring sustenance from a particular religious community and guaranteed only by God" (Tanner 1997:109).

This important point cannot be underemphasized. That is, the early Christian response to honor was not a categorical rejection but a creative reformulation and reorientation through the new lenses of God's salvific activity in Jesus through the power of the Holy Spirit. Honor, though it is fundamentally reoriented, clearly occupies a crucial place in the early Christian lexicon.

Such is the case regarding the two fundamental sources of face, that is, esteem, and acceptance. At its core, honor trades upon the currency of esteem. Esteem exists, however, not purely in the realm of private values but values that operate in relationality and community. For the Christian, honor framed in terms of God's new creation may function as a foundational truth for Christian living. This is certainly true for honor and face from God given to the individual believer. It is equally the case that face is a corporate reality. The Christian community is unavoidably a face-generating community because we hold certain virtues and practices to be honorable, excellent. Such is not an unfortunate or adverse affect of human sinfulness but rather functions as part of the divine creational intention. The new community within which the face-formed ecclesial self exists is structured after the loving fellowship and the face-generating practices of mutual honoring and acceptance inherent in the life of the Trinity. Also, legitimate face and facework frame and support Christian community in its ongoing practices of virtue.

Yet, in becoming a part of the Christian community, the person who is being remade in the likeness and image of God, the ecclesial self, receives a new account of face. That is, what might count as legitimate generating, saving, or giving of face is given new substance. The older dominant narrative and *telos* that formed the social life of the self prior to being in Christ is now replaced by the narrative and *telos* of the Trinity in the midst of a community that structures its life around this new narrative.

This new self is a part of a new narrative that forms out facework strategies. In particular, this new face in Christ sets new terms for Christian face claim-rights. Does such imply no more claim-rights? No. The "I yet not I" dialectic of Galatians 2:19–20 must remain central in face related discipleship considerations. That is, we may possess legitimate contextual face claim-rights but these are always relative and circumscribed by the new identity, new face of Christ, into which we are being transformed every day (2 Cor 3:18; 4:6). If face is an enactment between the self and others based upon the specific logic of a claim-right, the new narrative into which our selves are drawn transforms all three of these dimensions. We are different now as God's honored children who have left the face logic and face claims of our old lives and have received the very face of God.

Such a reorientation must also take into account that human sin taints much of what falls under the rubric of face. That is, face, although a good, is always susceptible to being taken over by human sin. Face, by its connection to fallen humanity, is a face taken over by the flesh. Face may become a mask behind which pride, selfishness, and abusive power operate. In certain contexts face may be intertwined with unhealthy notions of male ideology, involve outright deception, or involve modes of self-aggrandizement. Because of this, it is critical to make a fundamental assertion that certain attitudes and practices are inherently antithetical to the Christian story and thus any Christian account of face. A Christian account of face must necessarily reject out of hand many of the dominant face codes that are a part of the worldly dimensions of the surrounding culture. C. S. Lewis recognizes an inherent goodness in the concept of honor. Yet, as he aptly notes,

> I am not forgetting how horribly this most innocent desire is parodied in our human ambitions, or how very quickly, in my own

> experience, the lawful pleasure of praise from those whom it was my duty to please turns into the deadly poison of self-admiration. (1980:12)

The same grave potential also exists for face.

This again reminds us of the Aristotelian critique of inappropriate honor and "honor lovers." That is, social honor is a great human good, yet many fall prey to desiring the thing itself rather than aspiring to the virtues upon which the claim to honor is made legitimate. By doing so, such people actually subvert their legitimate quest for honor since this amounts to crass public recognition they desire and not true virtue. This is an every-present danger with face. If those basic values upon which a proper attribution or affirmation of face is based remain in focus as that toward which a person truly aspires, the resultant face is legitimate. Yet, to desire the face as the real goal is to circumvent the very virtues upon which true face must rest. In the end, such a pursuit is nothing but bald egoism, a desire for public recognition that lacks an attachment to the virtuous practices upon which recognition would be proper.

This, it turns out, is the very thing against which Jesus warned his disciples (Matt 6:1–5). The same rejection of seeking approval for its own sake is also implied in Matthew 23:5–12. Here Jesus singles out the motivation of doing things *in order to be seen*. He associates such face aggrandizement with the use of and posturing for honorific titles (e.g., Rabbi, father, and teacher). The point seems to be less about abolishing any distinction such appellations might create within the disciple community and more about this human penchant for face seeking that involves a "love" of places of honor, prestigious titles, and face-seeking public greetings (Matt 23:6–7).

The author of the book of Hebrews also highlights this dynamic (Heb 5:5–10). He notes that Jesus did not seek out the honor of being high priest. Rather, it was given to him because of his exceptional virtuous life of faith and sacrifice. Likewise, the ethical call Paul extends, based upon the example of Jesus in the Christ hymn of Philippians 2, is to eschew "vainglory," that is, honor based on pretense or upon improper sources. One who is full of vain honor sees himself as "above" others. The example of Jesus subverts such moral elitism, which a face-seeking posture clearly implies.

Paul again points to this foundational dimension of Christian behavior in Romans 2:7–10. First, Paul establishes honor as a legitimate Christian goal (2:7). This Christian pursuit of honor, however, is bounded by "doing good." That is, the proper mode of the pursuit of honor is virtuous living, not in a blatant quest for honor itself. Such must also be a virtuous pursuit of honor not one based upon selfish motives that seek to elevate oneself in competitive rivalry (2:8).[1] God cannot be fooled and is not concerned with face that is devoid of virtue (Rom 2:11).[2] The proper reward for those who follow the proper honor course will ultimately receive a reward of true and eternal face.

Although not a focus of my research and thinking, it strikes me that those involved in leadership training and development must give consideration to the issue of face. It should be rather clear to any student of Thai culture that the issue of face and the role of leader are intimately and necessarily connected. The mere possession and use of face necessitated by leadership yields inherent tensions for Thai Christian leaders who must navigate potentially hazardous dimensions of the face game.

A rather common face valence, to which leaders seem particularly vulnerable, but one that a Christian account must reject categorically, is inappropriate behavior, which results from the possession of "big face." Those who acquire a high level of face status may use their face to leverage themselves into avoiding moral responsibility. That is, having a "big face" can function as a type of moral shield behind which people may attempt to hide from or simply evade commonly accepted codes of behavior. Accumulated honor and face can lead people to an invulnerable position where their "face" disallows others to question actions or decisions. Face then functions as entitlement and a pretense for engaging in or avoiding responsibility for morally questionable activity. In essence, such involves the creation of an improper face claim-right and logic that defies normal face accounting.

This is clear in a recent incident recorded in the *Los Angeles Times*. The author of an article on Palestinian leader Yasser Arafat asked Arafat in a private session in his Ramallah compound about alleged violations by Palestinians of the Oslo Peace Accords.

> Arafat grew visibly agitated and stammered: "Be careful when you are speaking to me! Be careful, you are speaking to Arafat!" The threat of violence hung in the air as we left. Clearly Arafat had not quite mastered the art of being a politician or, rather, he was a politician in the mold of Mugabe or Mao. (Boot 2004:B13)

1. Also compare 2 Cor 12:20; Gal 5:20; Phil 1:17; and Jas 3:14, 16, in which the same Greek term ἐριθεία appears.

2. Literally, "there is no accepting of face before God." The term προσωπολημψία carries the meaning of favoritism or partiality.

In contrast to a face-seeking or face-shielding posture, Christians are to follow the example of Jesus. Rather than hold on to exalted and honorable status (in this case the unparalleled face status of equality with God) Jesus pours himself out and takes not only a position lacking in social face (a slave) but also endures the most inglorious of all deaths (the face-losing death of the cross). It is upon this humble, non-face-seeking posture, however, that Jesus is granted ultimate honor and face, exalted to the highest place (a position of face and honor) and given a name that is superior to all names. The ethical injunction, based upon a self-effacing kenotic Christology, calls for a subversion of the dominant face-seeking game that controls much of human societies. Christ transforms the dominant modes of face calculation and face attachment. Such a call is rooted in Christian narrative of Trinitarian love. It requires a posture of active service, not one of passively being served. Such a face posture cannot but impact leadership development in the Thai church.

If we accept such a relational account, then, we must necessarily enlarge our theological vocabulary to make a place for face and begin a new theological exploration into this potentially rich area. Yet, it is clear that cultures may indeed distort true and legitimate face by association with any number of false, impure, or unjust conceptions. Face, when offered by societies based upon such inglorious criteria and dishonorable values, is of no consequence for those who claim to know God. Face may not become an end to pursue divorced from virtuous living. It must never function as a way to shield people from responsibility or moral living.

This does not mean, however, to naïvely dispose of face. Rather, such an approach seeks to reorient face. What this means is that somewhere between a basic acceptance of the necessity and goodness of face, on the one hand, and the subversion of certain modes of face and face behavior, on the other hand, there should exist a reappraisal of face. Face, in such an account then, must undergo a reorientation, an "about face."

Indeed, we must frame the notion of Christian face and facework in terms of a cruciform face attachment. This parallels what Paul contends about the new self which is now living in the realm of the Messiah. To paraphrase Galatians 2:19–20 with face in view, we might say, "My face has been crucified with Christ—my face no longer lives. Yet, it is not my face but Christ's face that I possess. And the face and facework I now enact I do by faith in the Son of God who loved me (and my face) and gave himself for me."

There are significant face-related questions that subsequent research should probe. For example, how does face function in the Thai context as a resource over which leaders compete? How does face attachment among leaders hinder the emergence of new leaders? In what way(s) is face necessary for effective Thai leadership? How might face provide a proper motivation, as the "crown of virtue," in the development of leadership training curriculum and systems?

Thai leaders may need to learn to hold their own face claim-rights loosely. A significant task for Christian leadership in Thailand, and thus for leadership training, may be to learn more fully the honorable virtues of a cruciform face attachment and Christ-like face claim-rights.

The "about face" toward which this project aims represents a vital task for the Thai Christian community. Face is so important, so pervasive a component of Thai culture, that it is incumbent upon the Thai church to make this issue a point of deep and thoughtful reflection. The damaging condition of cultural and theological prosopagnosia must give way to a new engagement of face. Missionaries and Thai leaders must urge upon the Thai Christian community a focal engagement with face. Such, I believe, will enable the Thai church to live and witness more faithfully within its face-formed cultural context.

Recall the concerned Thai believer I mentioned in the introduction. She expressed hope that I could help "solve the problem" of face. Such a "solution," if it is to exist, must begin with the concrete acknowledgment that Christians possess face and engage in facework. It is the redeeming of our faces by the Face of the honorable God in the face of Christ by which God brings us into his new face community. It is in this new community, which provides a new court of reputation and face logic, that we now "do" face in the "about face" way of the living and triune God.

Appendix A

Interviewee Demographic Information

Gender	Total	Percent
Female	38	56.72 %
Male	29	43.28 %

Present Occupation	Total	Percent
Non-Student	28	56.72 %
Student	38	41.79 %
Unassigned	1	1.49 %

Religion	Total	Percent
Buddhist	52	77.61 %
Christian	14	20.90 %
Unassigned	1	1.49 %

Geographical Identity	Total	Percent
Bangkok	5	7.46 %
Central	4	5.97 %
North	47	70.15 %
Northeast	7	10.45 %
South	4	5.97 %

Appendix A

Highest Level Of Education	Total	Percent
Associates Degree	1	1.49 %
Grade 6	2	2.99 %
Grade 10	1	1.49 %
Grade 11	4	5.97 %
Grade 12	2	2.99 %
Masters	6	8.96 %
Unassigned	2	2.99 %
Undergraduate	46	68.66 %
Vocational School	3	4.48 %

Age	Total	Percent
19	3	4.48%
20	9	13.43 %
21	9	13.43 %
22	11	16.42 %
23	5	7.46 %
24	4	5.97 %
25	1	1.49 %
26	3	4.48 %
28	1	1.49 %
29	1	1.49 %
31	1	1.49 %
32	1	1.49 %
33	1	1.49 %
34	1	1.49 %
36	3	4.48 %
37	2	2.99 %
38	1	1.49 %
40	1	1.49 %
41	1	1.49 %
42	2	2.99 %
46	1	1.49 %
47	1	1.49 %
49	1	1.49 %
50	1	1.49 %
53	1	1.49 %
64	1	1.49 %

Appendix B

Thai Facework Terms

1.	ออกหน้า (*òk nâ*)	"Display face"
2.	ให้หน้า (*hâi nâ*)	"Give face"
3.	กู้หน้า (*kû nâ*)	"Redeem face"
4.	แก้หน้า (*kâe nâ*)	"Fix face"
5.	เสนอหน้า (*sà-noe nâ*)	"Promote face"
6.	เอาหน้า/ทำเอาหน้า (*ao nâ/thám ao nâ*)	"Take face"
7.	ได้หน้า (*dâi nâ*)	"Gain face"
8.	มีหน้า/มีตา (*mi nâ/mi ta*)	"Possess face/eyes"
9.	นับหน้า/ถือตา (*náp nâ/thue ta*)	"Respect face/eyes"
10.	เป็นหน้า/เป็นตา (*pen nâ/pen ta*)	"Be face/be eyes"
11.	ตบหน้า (*tòp nâ*)	"Slap face"
12.	อยากได้หน้า (*yàk dâi nâ*)	"Want to get face"
13.	แคร์หน้า (*khâe nâ*)	"Care about face"
14.	ห่วงหน้า (*h`wong nâ*)	"Worry about face"
15.	สนใจหน้า (*son chai nâ*)	"Show interest in face"
16.	ตัดหน้า (*tàt nâ*)	"Cut off face"
17.	ตีหน้า (*ti nâ*)	"Strike face"
18.	หักหน้า (*hàk nâ*)	"Snap off face"
19.	ตอกหน้า (*tòk nâ*)	"Hammer face"

20.	บากหน้า (bàk nâ)	"Carry face"
21.	หยามหน้า/น้ำหน้า (yam nâ/nám nâ)	"Impugn face"
22.	เห็นแก่หน้า (hen kàe nâ)	"Heed face"
23.	ไว้หน้า/เอาหน้าไว้ (wai nâ/ao nâ wái)	"Preserve face"
24.	รักษาหน้า/รักษ์หน้า (rák-sa nâ/rák nâ)	"Maintain/save face"
25.	เชิดหน้าชูตา/เทิดหน้า (chôet nâ chu ta/thôet nâ)	"Enhance face/eyes"
26.	หน้าแตก (nâ tàek)	"Face breaks"
27.	ขายหน้า (khai nâ)	"Sell face"
28.	เสียหน้า (sia nâ)	"Lose face"
29.	ฉีกหน้า (chìk nâ)	"Tear off face"

Appendix C

Reasons for Avoiding Face Loss

Others think-speak negative about us	28
Shame	11
Feels bad	8
Lose credibility-believability	7
Impacts situation-utility-ability to act properly	4
Lose respect from others	4
Negative to being in society	4
Lose confidence	4
Negatively impacts honor-dignity	3
Lose acceptance from others	3
Negatively impacts relationships	3
Others gossip	3
Want to stand out	2
Hurts friendships	2
Lose your form	1
Exposure	1
Others rub it in	1
Negatively impacts others	1
Causes uncertainty	1
Hurts self pride	1

Lose value in society	1
Hassle	1
Fear	1
Cannot accept the truth	1
Lose sense of self	1
Others lose face too	1
Become a bad person	1
Desire former face level	1

Appendix D

Positive Ways of Gaining Face

STATUS	
Be a representative	3
Have a desirable job	2
Unique work	1

PERFORMANCE	
Help others	12
Benefit society	9
Unique work	8
Do good	6
Doing something exceptional	3
Doing something heroic	2
Do good to others	2
Give to others	2
Help blind cross road	2
Personal sacrifice	2
Make merit	2
Ability in school	2
Win competition	2
Contribute to building a temple	1

APPENDIX D

Build orphanage	1
Do good work	1
Do work others see	1
Experience success	1
Find something and return it	1
Give to the needy	1
Give clothing to others	1
Provide knowledge to others	1
Help catch criminals	1
Help fix homes	1
Help others with money	1
Help others by working	1
Host large party	1
Love others	1
Positive moral accomplishment	1
Prepare food for others	1
Significant work	1
Speak first	1
Treat others to food	1
Tutor	1
Volunteer work	1
Watch neighbor's home	1
Ability in athletics	1
Ability in work	1
Demonstrate ability	1
Perform well in school	1
Successful children	1
Top in grades	1

PERSONAL CHARACTERISTICS	
be good person'	2
Personal ability	1
be good citizen	1

Diligent	1
Do not cause others problems	1

RECOGNIZED BY OTHERS	
Significant other admire us	4
Honored	2
Admired	1
Interviewed by reporter	1

PROPER MOTIVES	
Do good/help others without expecting any return	5
Need proper motivation	3
Must be sincere	2
Doing things not thinking about personal gain	1
Help others while not desiring face	1

Appendix E

Positive Consequences of Face

RELATIONSHIPS	
Others respect-fear us	16
Others desire relationship	11
Easy to relate-build relationships	10
Others trust us	6
Others treat-speak of us well	6
Others accept us	4
Socially useful	4
Associative face-look good	4
Others depend upon us	3
Others love us	3
Others want to help-work with us	3
Able-must help others	3
Able to associate	2
Others listen to us	2
Others interested in us	2
Others follow us	1
Others do not contradict us	1
Others speak well of us	1
Cooperation from others	1

OTHER	
Easy to accomplish things	5
Brings happiness	3
Able to control things	1
Can boast to others	1
Beautiful appearance	1
Brings peacefulness	1
Gain social preference	1

Appendix F

Characteristics of a Face-Person

STATUS	
Status	12
Wealthy	6
Work-job	3
Lineage	3
Education-knowledge	3
Influence-power	2
High society	1

PERSONAL CHARACTERISTICS	
Ability	4
Positive personal qualities	4
Speak politely-gently	3
Attractive	2
Carries self-walks well	2
Nice dress	2
Charisma	1
Personal success	1
Wary of mistakes	1

DISTINCTION	15

ACCEPTANCE	7

RECOGNITION	
Known	18
Name	7
Self promoter-wants others to see	4
Important	3
Others desire to be close	1
Others follow-imitate	1
Reputable places	1

MORALITY	
Does good-moral	8

HONOR	
Respected-praised	9
Possesses honor-dignity	5
Prideful-cocky	2
Personal pride	1

Appendix G

Characteristics of a Person with Honor

ACCEPTANCE	10

HONOR	
Respect from and to others	26
Self respect	2
No one looks down on us	2
Respectable	1
Loves own dignity	1
Not inferior to others	1

DISTINCTION	1

STATUS	
Status	5
Leader	3
Good job	3
Has money	3
Has position	3
Has work	2

Social standing-status	1
Older age	1
Family lineage	1
Appropriateness with status	1
High education	1

PERSONAL CHARACTERISTICS	
Has a sense of self definition	3
Graceful	3
Well dressed	3
Trustworthy speech	3
Polite	2
Knows how to act	2
Personal successes	2
Composed	1
Calm	1
Loves self	1
Not use power wrongly	1
Loves self worth	1
Clean	1
Nice personality	1
Upbeat	1
Self confidence	1
Accept others ideas	1
Speaks little	1
Has something to say	1
Has others confidence	1
Adjusts with situation	1
Knows appropriate speech	1
Speaks politely	1
Manners	1
Responsible	1
Others can depend on them	1

Got it together	1
Gets along with others	1
Wears expensive things	1
Accepts self	1
Forthright	1

MORALITY	
Positive morality	16
Helps society-others	9
Not prideful	5
Faithful	3
Good motives	2
Respects others	2
No spotted history-impure	2
Life consistent with words	2
Does not look down on others	2
Does not take advantage of others	1
Takes care of others	1
Not selfish	1
Does not oppress others	1
Does not cause others trouble	1
Empathizes with others	1
Does not discriminate among social class	1
Sincere	1

RECOGNITION	
Known	5
Reputation	2
Others desire relationship	2
Others listen	1
Others listen/obey	1

Appendix H

Characteristics of a Person with Dignity

SELF	
Self-awareness or definition	31
Self-pride	23
Real self	10
Self reliant	8
Self-confidence	4

IMPRACTICAL	7

VALUABLE	7

RESOLUTE	19

MORAL	13

OTHER	
Ability-knowledge	2
Possession	2
Standard of groupness	2

Appendix H

Lasting	1
Ability-knowledge-success	1

STATUS	3

WILL NOT BE INSULTED	13

Appendix I

Metaphors of Face

ACCEPTANCE–APPROVAL	
Acceptance	3
Approval	1

POSSESSION	246

SELF	
Reflects expresses self	11
(Self) confidence	2
Self-enhancement	1

VALUABLE	
Utility	19
Valuable	7
Power	3

VARIABLE	
Variable	12
Beauty-attractive	11

Ambiguous	8
Loss	4
Requires care	3
Impermanent	2
Requires effort	1

DISTINCTION	
Social honor	16
Distinction	10
Goodness	3
Status	1
Addictive	1

VISIBLE	
Visible	21
Obscuring-covers	8
Deceptive	1
Inviting	1
False	1

Bibliography

Acocella, Joan. 2001. *Mission to Siam: The Memoirs of Jessie MacKinnon Hartzell*. Honolulu: University of Hawaii Press.

Adeyemo, Tokunboh. 1983. The Idea of Salvation in Contemporary World Religions. *East African Journal of Evangelical Theology* 2.1:4–12.

Aquino, Frederick D. 2000. The Incarnation: The Dignity and Honor of Human Personhood. *Restoration Quarterly* 42.1:39–46.

Aristotle. 1934. *The Nichomachean Ethics*. H. Racham, trans. Loeb Classical Library 73. Cambridge, MA: Harvard University Press.

———. 1952. *The Eudemian Ethics*. H. Racham, trans. Loeb Classical Library 285. Cambridge, MA: Harvard University Press.

Arundale, Robert B. 2004. Constituting Face in Conversation: An Alternative to Brown & Levinson's Politeness Theory. Paper presented at the 90th Conference of the National Communication Association, Chicago, November 2004.

Athanasius. 1978. *On the Incarnation of the Word*. In *NPNF* vol. 4, ed. Archibald Robertson. Grand Rapids: Eerdmans.

Atkinson, David. 1995. What Difference Does the Cross Make to Life? In *Atonement Today*, ed. John Goldingay, 253–271. London, UK: SPCK.

Augsburger, David W. 1992. *Conflict Mediation across Cultures*. Louisville: Westminster John Knox.

Augustine. 1984. *Concerning the City of God against the Pagans*. Trans. Henry Bettenson. London: Penguin.

Backus, Mary, ed. 1884. *Siam and Laos as Seen by Our American Missionaries*. Philadelphia: Presbyterian Board of Publication.

Bailey, Kenneth E. 1983. *Poet and Peasant and through Peasant Eyes: A Literary-Cultural Approach to the Parables in Luke*. Grand Rapids: Eerdmans.

Balás, David L., and O. Cist. 1997. Divinization. In *Encyclopedia of Early Christianity*, ed. Everett Ferguson, 338–40. New York: Garland.

Barnett, Milton L. 1966. Hiya, Shame and Guilt: Preliminary Consideration of the Concepts as Analytical Tools for Philippine Social Science. *Philippine Sociological Review* 14.4:271–82.

Barrett, Karen C. 1995. A Functionalist Approach to Shame and Guilt. In *Self-Conscious Emotions: The Psychology of Shame, Guilt, Embarrassment, and Pride*, eds. June Price Tangney and Kurt W. Fischer, 25–63. New York: Guilford.

Bartlett, Anthony W. 2001. *Cross Purposes: The Violent Grammar of Christian Atonement*. Harrisburg, PA: Trinity.

Baumeister, Roy F. 1987. How the Self Became a Problem: A Psychological Review of Historical Research." In *Journal of Personality and Social Psychology* 52:163–76.

———. 1998. The Self. In *The Handbook of Social Psychology*, eds. Daniel T. Gilbert, Susan T. Fiske, and Gardner Lindzey, 1:680–40. New York: McGraw-Hill.

Bavinck, Johan H. 1960. *An Introduction to the Science of Missions*. Trans. David Hugh Freeman. Philadelphia: Presbyterian and Reformed.

Bebbington, David W. 1989. *Evangelicalism in Modern Britain: A History from the 1730s to the 1980s*. London: Unwin Hyman.

Beker, J. Christiaan. 1990. *The Triumph of God: The Essence of Paul's Thought*. Trans. Loren T. Stuckenbruck. Minneapolis: Fortress.

Benedict, Ruth. 1946. *The Chrysanthemum and the Sword*. Boston: Houghton Mifflin.

Benson, Steven R. 1995. By One Man's Obedience Many Will Be Made Righteous: Christian Understanding of the Atonement in the Context of Asian Religious Pluralism. *Asia Journal of Theology* 9.1:101–22.

Bernard, H. Russell. 2002. *Research Methods in Anthropology*. Walnut Creek, CA: Altamira.

Bilmes, Leela. 2001. Sociological Aspect of Thai Politeness. PhD diss., University of California, Berkeley.

Boethius, Ancius Manlius Severinus. 1847. *De Persona*. PL 64:1371D. Paris, France.

Boff, Leonardo. 1988. *Trinity and Society*. Maryknoll, NY: Orbis.

Boot, Max. 2004. How Arafat Got Away with It. *Los Angeles Times*, November 11:B13.

Booth, Wayne C., Gregory G. Colomb, and Joseph M. Williams, eds. 1995. *The Craft of Research*. Chicago: University of Chicago Press.

Bosch, David. 1991. *Transforming Mission: Paradigm Shifts in Theology of Mission*. Maryknoll, NY: Orbis.

Botterweck, Johannes, and Helmer Ringgren, eds. 1974. *Addereth*. In *The Theological Dictionary of the Old Testament*, vol. 1. Grand Rapids: Eerdmans.

Bowen, Nancy R. 1991. Damage and Healing: Shame and Honor in the Old Testament. *Koinonia* 3.1:29–36.

Brackett, K. P. 2000. Facework Strategies among Romance Fiction Readers. *The Social Science Journal* 37:347–60.

Bradley, Dan Beach. 1841a. General Letter from the Mission, Dated Dec. 1st, 1839. *The Missionary Herald* 37.5:199–202.

———. 1841b. How Christianity Is Regarded by the Rulers (Letter from Doct. Bradley, Dated Bangkok, 24th August, 1840). *The Missionary Herald* 37.4:176–78.

Bradley, William L. 1981. *Siam Then: The Foreign Colony in Bangkok before and after Anna*. Pasadena, CA: William Carey Library.

Brandes, Stanley. 1987. Reflections on Honor and Shame in the Mediterranean. In *Honor and Shame and the Unity of the Mediterranean*, ed. David D. Gilmore, 121–34. Washington, DC: American Anthropological Association.

Brown, Penelope, and Stephen C. Levinson. 1978. *Politeness: Some Universals in Language Usage*. Cambridge, UK: Cambridge University Press.

Bultmann, Rudolf. 1951. *Theology of the New Testament*. New York: Scribner's.

Carson, D. A., ed. 1992. *Right with God: Justification in the Bible and the World*. Grand Rapids: Baker.

Carroll, John T., and Joel B. Green. 1995. *The Death of Jesus in Early Christianity*. Peabody, MA: Hendrickson.

Caswell, Jesse. 1848. Communications from the Missions. Siam. Annual Report of the Mission. *The Missionary Herald* 44.1:15–18.
Chaiyan Ukosakul. 1994. A Study in the Patterns of Detachment in Interpersonal Relationships in a Local Thai Church. PhD diss., Trinity Evangelical Divinity School.
Chance, John K. 1994. The Anthropology of Honor and Shame: Culture, Values, and Practice. *Semeia* 68:139–51.
Chang, H., and R. Holt. 1994. A Chinese Perspective on Face as Inter-Relational Concern. In *The Challenge of Facework: Cross-Cultural and Interpersonal Issues*, ed. Stella Ting-Toomey, 95–132. Albany: State University of New York Press.
Charmaz, Kathy. 1994. The Grounded Theory Method: An Explication and Interpretation. In *More Grounded Theory Methodology: A Reader*, ed. Barney G. Glaser, 95–115. Mill Valley, CA: Sociology Press.
Cheng, C. 1986. The Concept of Face and its Confucian Roots. *Journal of Chinese Philosophy* 13:329–48.
Christensen, Michael J. 1996. Theosis and Sanctification: John Wesley's Reformulation of a Patristic Doctrine. *Wesleyan Theological Journal* 31.2:71–94.
Chryssides, George D. 1985. Meaning, Metaphor and Meta-Theology. *Scottish Journal of Theology* 38.2:145–53.
Clark, William N. 2000. Face and Cross-Cultural Interaction in the Thai Classroom. MA thesis, St. Cloud State University.
Clendenin, Daniel B. 1994. Partakers of the Divinity: The Orthodox Doctrine of Theosis. *Journal of the Evangelical Theological Society* 37.3:365–79.
Cohen, Erik. 1990. The Missionary as Stranger: A Phenomenological Analysis of Christian Missionaries' Encounter with the Folk Religions of Thailand. *Review of Religious Research* 31.4:337–350.
Christian Conference Committee of South Siam for all Siamese Christians. 1929. *Findings of the Bangkok Conference*. Report of the conference held at Bangkok, Siam, July 19–23, 1928. N.p. Chiang Mai, Thailand: Payap University Archives.
Cooke, Joseph R. 1978. *The Gospel for Thai Ears*. Chiang Mai, Thailand: Payap College.
Creighton, Millie R. 1990. Revisiting Shame and Guilt Cultures: A Forty-Year Pilgrimage. *Ethos* 18:279–307.
Crutcher, Timothy J. 2003. The Christocentric Community: An Essay toward a Relational Ecclesiology. In *Theology and Conversation: Towards a Relational Theology*, eds. Jacques Haers and P. De Mey, 547–56. Bibliotheca Ephemeridum Theologicarum Lovaniensium 172. Leuven, Belgium: Leuven University Press.
Cunningham, David S. 1998. *These Three Are One: The Practices of Trinitarian Theology*. Malden, MA: Blackwell.
Cupach, William R., and Sandra Metts. 1994. *Facework*. Thousand Oaks, CA: Sage.
D'Andrade, Roy G. 1995. *The Development of Cognitive Anthropology*. Cambridge, UK: Cambridge University Press.
D'Andrade, Roy G., and Claudia Strauss. 1992. *Human Motives and Cultural Models*. Cambridge, UK: Cambridge University Press.
Danker, Frederick W. 1982. *Benefactor: Epigraphic Study of a Graeco-Roman and New Testament Semantic Field*. St. Louis: Clayton.
Davis, John R. 1993. *Poles Apart?* Bangkok: Kanok Bannasan.
Delin, Judy. 1998. Facework and Instructor Goals in the Step Aerobics Workout. In *Language at Work*, ed. S. Hunston, 56–71. British Studies in Applied Linguistics 13. Clevedon, England: BAAL/Multilingual Matters.

DeSilva, David A. 1995. *Despising Shame: Honor Discourse and Community Maintenance in the Epistle to the Hebrews.* Atlanta: Scholars.

———. 1996. The Wisdom of Ben Sira: Honor, Shame, and the Maintenance of the Values of a Minority Culture. *The Catholic Biblical Quarterly* 58:433–35.

———. 1998. *The Credentials of an Apostle: Paul's Gospel in 2 Corinthians 1–7.* North Richland Hills, TX: Bibal.

———. 1999a. *Bearing Christ's Reproach: The Challenge of Hebrews in an Honor Culture.* North Richland Hills, TX: Bibal Press.

———. 1999b. *The Hope of Glory: Honor Discourse and New Testament Interpretation.* Collegeville, MN: Liturgical.

———. 2000a. *Honor, Patronage, Kinship and Purity: Unlocking New Testament Culture.* Downers Grove, IL: InterVarsit.

———. 2000b. *Perseverance in Gratitude: A Socio-Rhetorical Commentary on the Epistle "to the Hebrews."* Grand Rapids: Eerdmans.

Dodd, W. Clifton. 1888. Twenty-Eight Years Between. *The Church at Home and Abroad* 3:493–94.

Downing, F. Gerald. 1999. "Honor" among Exegetes. *Catholic Biblical Quarterly* 61(1): 53–73.

Driver, John. 1986. *Understanding the Atonement for the Mission of the Church.* Scottsdale, PA: Herald.

Dunn, James D. G. 1988. *Romans 1–8.* WBC 38a. Dallas: Word.

———. 1996. *Paul and the Mosaic Law.* Tübingen: Mohr.

Dunn, James D. G., and Alan M. Suggate. 1994. *The Justice of God: A Fresh Look at the Old Doctrine of Justification by Faith.* Grand Rapids: Eerdmans.

Edelmann, Robert J. 1994. Embarrassment and Blushing: Factors Influencing Face-Saving Strategies. In *The Challenge of Facework: Cross-Cultural and Interpersonal Issues*, ed. Stella Ting-Toomey, 231–67. Albany: State University of New York Press.

Ek Thabping, Joseph. 1974. The Conversion of Thai Buddhists: Are Christianity and Thai Culture Irreconcilable? MA thesis, Ateneo de Manila University.

Elliott, John H. 198. *A Home for the Homeless: A Sociological Exegesis of I Peter, Its Situation and Strategy.* Philadelphia,: Fortress.

Ervin-Tripp, Susan, Kei Nakamura, and Jiansheng Guo. 1995. Shifting Face from Asia to Europe. In *Essays in Semantics and Pragmatics: In Honor of Charles J. Fillmore*, eds. Masayoshi Shibatani and Sandra Thompson, 43–71. Amsterdam/Philadelphia: John Benjamins.

Esler, Philip F. 1994. *The First Christians in their Social Worlds: Social-Scientific Approaches to New Testament Interpretation.* London: Routledge.

Feltus, George H. 1936. *Abstract of the Journal of Rev. Dan Beach Bradley: Medical Missionary in Siam 1835–1873.* Oberlin, OH: Multigraph Department of Pilgrim Church. Quoted in Nantachai Mejudhon, Meekness: A New Approach to Christian Witness to the Thai People. DMiss diss., Asbury Theological Seminary, 1997.

Fiddes, Paul S. 1989, *Past Event and Present Salvation: The Christian Idea of Atonement.* Louisville: Westminster John Knox.

Fowler, James W. 1996. *Faithful Change: The Personal and Public Challenges of Postmodern Life.* Nashville: Abingdon.

Freeman, David N., ed. 1992. *The Anchor Bible Dictionary.* New York: Doubleday.

Geertz, Clifford. 1984. "From the Native's Point of View": On the Nature of Anthropological Understanding. In *Cultural Theory: Essays on Mind, Self, and Emotion*, eds. Richard A. Shweder and Robert A. Levine, 123–36. Cambridge, UK: Cambridge University Press.

Gergen Kenneth J. 1971. *The Concept of Self.* New York: Holt Rinehart and Winston.
Gilbert, Paul. 1998. What Is Shame? Some Core Issues and Controversies. In *Shame: Interpersonal Behavior, Psychopathology, and Culture,* 3–38. New York: Oxford University Press.
Gilbert, Paul, and Bernice Andrews, eds. 1998. *Shame: Interpersonal Behavior, Psychopathology, and Culture.* New York: Oxford University Press.
Ginkel, Eric van. 2004, The Mediator as Face-Giver. *Negotiation Journal* 20:475–87.
Goffman, Erving. 1955. On Face-Work: An Analysis of Ritual Elements in Social Interaction. *Psychiatry* 18(3):213–31.
Goldingay, John. 1995a. Old Testament Sacrifice and the Death of Christ. In *Atonement Today,* ed. John Goldingay, 3–20. London: SPCK.
———, ed. 1995b. *Atonement Today.* London: SPCK.
Green, Joel B., and Mark D. Baker. 2000. *Recovering the Scandal of the Cross: Atonement in New Testament and Contemporary Contexts.* Downers Grove, IL: InterVarsity.
Greenwald, Deborah F., and David W. Harder. 1998. Domains of Shame: Evolutionary, Cultural, and Psychotherapeutic Aspects. In *Shame: Interpersonal Behavior, Psychopathology, and Culture,* eds. Paul Gilbert and Bernice Andrews, 225–45. New York: Oxford University Press.
Grenz, Stanley J. 1994. *Theology for the Community of God.* Grand Rapids: Eerdmans.
———. 1996. *A Primer on Postmodernism.* Grand Rapids: Eerdmans.
———. 2000. *Renewing the Center: Evangelical Theology in a Post-Theological Era.* Grand Rapids: Baker.
———. 2001. *The Social God and the Relational Self: A Trinitarian Theology of the Imago Dei.* Louisville: Westminster John Knox.
———. 2004. *Rediscovering the Triune God: The Trinity in Contemporary Theology.* Minneapolis: Fortress.
Grenz, Stanley J., and John R. Franke. 2001. *Beyond Foundationalism: Shaping Theology in a Postmodern Context.* Louisville: Westminster John Knox.
Gross, Jules. 2002. *The Divinization of the Christian According to the Greek Fathers.* Trans. Paul A. Onica. Anaheim, CA. A and C.
Gunton, Colin E. 1985. Christus Victor Revisited: A Study in Metaphor and the Transformation of Meaning. *Journal of Theological Studies* 36(1):129–45.
———. 1989. *The Actuality of Atonement: A Study of Metaphor, Rationality and the Christian Tradition.* Grand Rapids: Eerdmans.
———. 1997. *The Promise of Trinitarian theology.* Edinburgh: T. & T. Clark.
Gustafson, James W. 1987. Syncretistic Rural Thai Buddhism. MA thesis, Fuller Theological Seminary.
Haers, Jacques. 2003. *Defensor vinculi et conversationis*: Connectedness and Conversation as a Challenge to Theology. In *Theology and Conversation: Towards a Relational Theology,* eds. Jacques Haers and P. De Mey, 1–40. Bibliotheca Ephemeridum Theologicarum Lovaniensium 172. Leuven, Belgium: Leuven University Press.
Haers, Jacques, and P. De Mey, eds. 2003. *Theology and Conversation: Towards a Relational Theology.* Bibliotheca Ephemeridum Theologicarum Lovaniensium 172. Leuven, Belgium: Leuven University Press.
Hanson, K. C. 1994. How Honorable! How Shameful! A Cultural Analysis of Matthew's Makarisms and Reproaches. *Semeia* 68:81–111.
Heyer, C. J. den. 1998. *Jesus and the Doctrine of the Atonement: Biblical Notes on a Controversial Topic.* Harrisburg, PA: Trinity.

Ho, David Yau-Fai. 1976. On the Concept of Face. *American Journal of Sociology* 81(4):867–84.

———. 1994. Face Dynamics: From Conceptualization to Measurement. In *The Challenge of Facework: Cross-Cultural and Interpersonal Issues*, ed. Stella Ting-Toomey, 269–86. Albany: State University of New York Press.

Holifield, E. Brooks. 2003. *Theology in American: Christian Thought from the Age of the Puritans to the Civil War*. New Haven, CT: Yale University Press.

Holland, Dorothy, and Naomi Quinn. 1987. *Cultural Models in Language and Thought*. Cambridge, UK: Cambridge University Press.

Hooker, Morna D. 1977–78. Interchange and Atonement. *Bulletin of the John Rylands University Library* 60:462–81.

Houts, Margo G. 1993. Classical Atonement Imagery: Feminist and Evangelical Challenges. *Catalyst* 19(3):1, 5–6.

Hu, Hsien Chin. 1944. The Chinese Concepts of "Face." *American Anthropologist* 46(1):45–64.

Hughes, Philip J. 1982. *Proclamation and Response: A Study of the History of the Christian Faith in Northern Thailand*. Chiang Mai, Thailand: Payap College.

———. 1984a. The Assimilation of Christianity in the Thai Culture. *Religion* 14:313–36.

———. 1984b. The Use of Actual Beliefs in Contextualizing Theology. *East Asia Journal of Theology* 2(2):251–58.

———. 1994. Dialogue and Identity in the Protestant Church of Northern Thailand. *Australian Religious Studies Review* 7(1):31–37.

———. 1996. Accepting the Christian Faith in Thailand. *Christian Research Association Bulletin* 6(4):6–9.

Hultgren, Arland J. 1985. *Paul's Gospel and Mission: The Outlook from His Letter to the Romans*. Philadelphia: Fortress.

Hunston, S., ed. 1998. *Language at Work*. British Studies in Applied Linguistics 13. Clevedon, UK: BAAL/Multilingual Matters.

Hwa, Yung. 1989. Theories of Atonement and the Mission of the Church. *Asia Journal of Theology* 3(2):540–57.

Hwang, Kwang-Kuo. 1987. Face and Favor: The Chinese Power Game. *American Journal of Sociology* 92(4):944–74.

Jewett, Robert. 1999. *Saint Paul Returns to the Movies: Triumph over Shame*. Grand Rapids: Eerdmans.

Kao, Samson S. 1990. The Historical Development of the Sixth District Church and the Strategies for Its Growth. ThM thesis, Fuller Theological Seminary.

Karen, Robert. 1992. Shame. *The Atlantic Monthly*, February:40–70.

Kärkkäinen, Veli-Matti. 2002. *Pneumatology: The Holy Spirit in Ecumenical, International, and Contextual Perspective*. Grand Rapids: Baker Academic.

———. 2004. *One With God: Salvation as Deification and Justification*. Collegeville, MN: Liturgical.

Kaufman, Gershen. 1974. The Meaning of Shame: Towards a Self-Affirming Identity. *Journal of Counseling Psychology* 21:568–74.

Kerr, Fergus. 1986. *Theology after Wittgenstein*. Oxford: Blackwell.

Keyes, Charles F. 1993. Why the Thai Are Not Christians: Buddhist and Christian Conversion in Thailand. In *Conversion to Christianity: Historical and Anthropological Perspectives on a Great Transformation*, ed. R. W. Hefner, 259–83. Berkeley: University of California Press.

———. 1996. Being Protestant Christians in Southeast Asian Worlds. *Journal of Southeast Asian Studies* 27(2):280–92.
Kim, Samuel I. 1980. *The Unfinished Mission in Thailand*. Seoul: East-West Center for Missions Research and Development.
Kitayama, Shinobu, Hazel Markus, and Hisaya Matsumoto. 1995. Culture, Self, and Emotion: A Cultural Perspective on "Self-Conscious" Emotions. In *Self-Conscious Emotions: The Psychology of Shame, Guilt, Embarrassment, and Pride*, ed. June Price Tangney and Kurt W. Fischer, 439–64. New York: Guilford.
Klausner, William. 1993. *Reflections on Thai Culture*. Bangkok: Siam Society.
Klein, C. 1978. *Anti-Judaism in Christian Theology*. Philadephia: Fortress.
Koehler, Walter, and Ludwig Baumgartner, eds. 1995. פ-ע. In *The Hebrew and Aramaic Lexicon of the Old Testament*, ed. M. E. J. Richardson, trans. W. Baumgartner and Johann Jakob Stamm, vol. 2. Rev. ed. Leiden: Brill.
Koyama, Kosuke. 1974. *Water Buffalo Theology*. Maryknoll, NY: Orbis.
Kraus, Norman C. 1990. *Jesus Christ Our Lord: Christology from a Disciple's Perspective*. Rev. ed. Scottsdale, PA: Herald.
Kressel, Gideon M. 1994. An Anthropologist's Response to the Use of Social Science Models in Biblical Studies. *Semeia* 68:153–61.
Kressel, Gideon M., and Unni Wikan. 1988. More on Honour and Shame. *Man*, n.s., 23(1):167–70.
Kuyper, L. J. 1977. Righteousness and Salvation. *Scottish Journal of Theology* 30(3):233–52.
LaCugna, Catherine Mowry. 1991. *God for Us: The Trinity and Christian Life*. San Francisco: HarperCollins.
Lakoff, George. 1987. *Women, Fire, and Dangerous Things: What Categories Reveal about Mind*. Chicago: University of Chicago Press.
Lakoff, George, and Mark Johnson. 1999. *Philosophy in the Flesh: The Embodied Mind and Its Challenge to Western Thought*. New York: Basic Books.
———. 2003. *Metaphors We Live By*. Chicago: University of Chicago Press.
Lawrence, Louise J. 2003. *An Ethnography of the Gospel of Matthew*. Tübingen: Mohr/Siebeck.
Leary, Mark R., and June Price Tangney, eds. 2003. *Handbook of Self and Identity*. New York: Guilford.
Lebra, Takie Sugiyama. 1971. The Social Mechanism of Guilt and Shame: The Japanese Case. *Anthropological Quarterly* 44(4):241–55.
———. 1983. Shame and Guilt: A Psychocultural View of the Japanese Self. *Ethos* 11(3):192–209.
Lewis, C. S. 1952. *Mere Christianity*. New York: Macmillan.
———. 1980. *The Weight of Glory*. New York: Macmillan.
Lewis, Michael. 1995. *Shame: The Exposed Self*. New York: Free Press.
Lienhard, Ruth. 2000. Restoring Relationships: Theological Reflection on Shame and Honor among the Raba and Bana of Cameroon. PhD diss., Fuller Theological Seminary.
———. 2001. A "Good Conscience": Differences between Honor and Justice Orientation." *Missiology* 39(2):131–41.
Lim, Tae-Sop. 1994. Facework and Interpersonal Relationships. In *The Challenge of Facework: Cross-Cultural and Interpersonal Issues*, ed. Stella Ting-Toomey, 209–29. Albany: State University of New York Press.
Loder, James E. 1998. *The Logic of the Spirit: Human Development in Theological Perspective*. San Francisco: Jossey-Bass.

Loder, James E., and W. Jim Neidhardt. 1992. *The Knight's Move: The Relational Logic of the Spirit in Theology and Science*. Colorado Springs, CO: Helmers and Howard.

Loewen, Jacob A. 1970. The Social Context of Guilt and Forgiveness. *Practical Anthropology* 17:80–96.

Longenecker, Richard N. 1999. The Focus of Romans: The Central Role of 5:1—8:39 in the Argument of the Letter. In *Romans and the People of God: Essays in Honor of Gordon D. Fee on the Occasion of His 65th Birthday*, eds. Sven K. Soderlund and N. T. Wright, 49–69. Grand Rapids: Eerdmans.

Lord, Donald C. 1969. *Mo Bradley in Thailand*. Grand Rapids: Eerdmans.

Lu, Hsün (Chou, Shü-jen). 1960. On "Face." In *Selected Works of Lu Hsün*, 4:129–32. Peking: Foreign Language Press.

Lyall, Francis. 1984. *Slaves, Citizens, Sons: Legal Metaphors in the Epistles*. Grand Rapids: Academic.

Lynd, Helen Merrell. 1958. *On Shame and the Search for Identity*. New York: Science Editions.

MacIntyre, Alasdair C. 1985. *After Virtue: A Study in Moral Theory*. Notre Dame, IN: University of Notre Dame Press.

Maen, Pongudom. 1979. Apologetic and Missionary Proclamation Exemplified by American Presbyterian Missionaries to Thailand (1828–1978), Early Church Apologists: Justin Martyr, Clement of Alexandria and Origen, and the Venerable Buddhadasa Bhikku, A Thai Buddhist Monk-Apologist. PhD diss., University of Otago.

Malina, Bruce J. 1993. *The New Testament World: Insights from Cultural Anthropology*. Louisville: Westminster John Knox.

Malina, Bruce J., and Jerome H. Neyrey. 1991. Honor and Shame in Luke-Acts: Pivotal Values of the Mediterranean World. In *The Social World of Luke-Acts: Models for Interpretation*, ed. Jerome H. Neyrey, 24–46. Peabody, MA: Hendrickson.

Malina, Bruce J., and Richard L. Rohrbaugh. 1998. *Social Scientific Commentary on the Gospel of John*. Minneapolis: Fortress.

Mantzaridis, Georgios I. 1984. *The Deification of Man: St. Gregory Palamas and the Orthodox Tradition*. Trans. Liadain Sherrard, trans. Crestwood, NY: St. Vladimir's Seminary Press.

Markus, Hazel Rose, and Shinobu Kitayama. 1991. Culture and the Self: Implications for Cognition, Emotion, and Motivation." *Psychological Review* 98(2):224–53.

Marshall, I. Howard. 1990. *Jesus the Saviour: Studies in New Testament Theology*. London: SPCK.

Matsumoto, Yoshiko. 1988. Reexamination of the Universality of Face: Politeness Phenomenon in Japanese. *Journal of Pragmatics* 12:403–26.

Mattoon, Mrs. S. 1884. Missionary Ladies in the King's Palace. In *Siam and Laos as Seen by Our American Missionaries*, ed. Mary Backus, 320–37. Philadelphia: Presbyterian Board of Publication.

McClendon, James William. 1994. *Doctrine: Systematic Theology*. Vol. 2. Nashville: Abingdon.

McCord Adams, Marilyn. 1999. *Horrendous Evils and the Goodness of God*. Ithaca, NY: Cornell University Press.

McFadyen, Alistair. 1990. *The Call to Personhood: A Christian Theory of the Individual in Social Relationships*. New York: Cambridge University Press.

McFarland, Bertha Blount. 1932. Personal letter to Rev. C. B. McAfee, Bangkok, Siam, April 12.

McFarland, George B., ed. 1999. *Historical Sketch of Protestant Missions in Siam 1828–1928*. Bangkok: White Lotus. Originally published by Bangkok Times Press, 1928.
McGilvary, Daniel. 1894. Mission Work among the Laos. *Missionary Review of the World*, n.s., 7[17 o.s.](5):373–77.
———. 1904. The Buddha or Christ. *The Laos News* 1(4):109. Chiang Mai, Thailand: Payap University Archives.
———. 1912. *A Half Century among the Siamese and the Lao*. New York: Revell.
McGrath, Alister E. 1993a. Atonement. In *The Blackwell Encyclopedia of Modern Christian Thought*, ed. Alister E. McGrath, 20. Oxford: Blackwell.
———. 1993b. Soteriology. In *The Blackwell Encyclopedia of Christian Thought*, ed. Alister E. McGrath, 616–26. Oxford: Blackwell.
Mead, George Herbert. 1964. *On Social Psychology*. Chicago: University of Chicago Press.
Meakin, J. E. B. 1896. Gospel Work in Siam. *Missionary Review of the World*, n.s., 9 [19 o.s.](1):43–46.
Mischel, Walter, and Carolyn C. Morf. 2003. The Self as a Psycho-Social Dynamic Processing System: A Meta-Perspective on a Century of the Self in Psychology. In *Handbook of Self and Identity*, eds. Mark R. Leary and June Price Tangney, 3–14. New York: Guilford.
Mole, Robert L. 1973. *Thai Values and Behavior Patterns*. Rutland, VT: C. E. Tuttle.
Moreau, A. Scott, ed. 2000. *Evangelical Dictionary of World Missions*. Grand Rapids: Baker.
Morisaki, Seiichi, and William B. Gudykunst. 1994. Face in Japan and the United States. In *The Challenge of Facework: Cross-Cultural and Interpersonal Issues*, ed. Stella Ting-Toomey, 47–93. Albany: State University of New York Press.
Mühlhäusler, Peter, and Rom Harré. 1990. *Pronouns and People: The Linguistic Construction of Social and Personal Identity*. Oxford: Oxford University Press.
Mulder, Niels. 1985. *Everyday Life in Thailand: An Interpretation*. Bangkok: Editions Duang Kamol.
———. 1997. *Thai Images: The Culture of the Public World*. Chiang Mai, Thailand: Silkworm Books.
———. 2000. *Inside Thai Society: Religion, Everyday Life, Change*. Chiang Mai, Thailand: Silkworm Books.
Müller, Klaus. 1996. Elenktik: Die Lehre vom Scham-und Schuldorientierten Gewissen. *Evangelikale Missiologie* 4:98–110.
Muller, Roland. 2000. *Honor and Shame: Unlocking the Door*. Philadelphia: Xlibris.
Murdoch, Iris. 1971. *The Sovereignty of Good*. New York: Schocken.
Nantachai Mejudhon. 1997. Meekness: A New Approach to Christian Witness to the Thai People. DMiss Diss., Asbury Theological Seminary.
Neyrey, Jerome H. 1993. *2 Peter, Jude: A New Translation with Introduction and Commentary*. AB 37c. New York: Doubleday.
———. 1998. *Honor and Shame in the Gospel of Matthew*. Louisville: Westminster John Knox.
Neyrey, Jerome H., ed. 1991. *The Social World of Luke-Acts: Models for Interpretation*. Peabody, MA: Hendrickson.
Noble, Lowell Lappin. 1975. Naked and Not Ashamed: An Anthropological, Biblical, and Psychological Study of Shame. Jackson, MI: Jackson Printing.
Noll, Mark A. 2002. *America's God: From Jonathon Edwards to Abraham Lincoln*. Oxford: Oxford University Press.
Norris, F. W. 1996. Deification: Consensual and Cogent. *Scottish Journal of Theology* 49(4):411–28.

Packer, J. I. 1980. Sacrifice and Satisfaction. In *Our Savior God: Studies on Man, Christ, and the Atonement*, ed. James M. Boice, 125–37. Grand Rapids: Baker.

Penman, Robyn. 1994. Facework in Communication: Conceptual and Moral Challenges. In *The Challenge of Facework: Cross-Cultural and Interpersonal Issues*, ed. Stella Ting-Toomey, 15–45. Albany: State University of New York Press.

Peristiany, J. G., and Julian Pitt-Rivers. 1992. Introduction. In *Honor and Grace in Anthropology*, eds. J. Pitt-Rivers and J. G. Peristiany, 1–17. Cambridge Studies in Social and Cultural Anthropology 76. Cambridge, UK: Cambridge University Press.

Phillips, Herbert P. 1965. *Thai Peasant Personality: The Patterning of Interpersonal Behavior in the Village of Bang Chan*. Berkeley: University of California Press.

Piers, G., and M. B. Singer. 1953. *Shame and Guilt*. New York: Norton.

Pilch, John J., ed. 2000. *Social Scientific Models for Interpreting the Bible: Essays by the Context Group in Honor of Bruce J. Malina*. Leiden: Brill.

Pilch, John J., and Bruce J. Malina, eds. 1998. *Handbook of Biblical Social Values*. Peabody, MA: Hendrickson.

Pinnock, Clark H. 1996. *Flame of Love: A Theology of the Holy Spirit*. Downers Grove, IL: InterVarsity.

Piper, Ronald A. 2001. Glory, Honor, and Patronage in the Fourth Gospel: Understanding the *Doxa* Given to Disciples in John 17. In *Social Scientific Models for Interpreting the Bible*, eds. Bruce J. Malina and John J. Pilch, 281–309. Leiden: Brill.

Pitt-Rivers, Julian A. 1977. *The Fate of Shechem; or, The Politics of Sex: Essays in the Anthropology of the Mediterranean*. Cambridge Studies in Social Anthropology 19. Cambridge, UK: Cambridge University Press.

Plevnik, Joseph. 1998. Honor/Shame. In *Handbook of Biblical Social Values*, eds. John J. Pilch and Bruce J. Malina, 106–15. Peabody, MA: Hendrickson.

Potter, Jonathan, and Margaret Wetherell. 1987. *Discourse and Social Psychology: Beyond Attitude and Behavior*. London: Sage.

Quinn, Naomi, and Claudia Strauss. 1996. *A Cognitive Theory of Cultural Meanings*. Cambridge, UK: Cambridge University Press.

Rakestraw, Robert V. 1997. Becoming Like God: An Evangelical Doctrine of Theosis. *Journal of The Evangelical Theological Society* 40(2):257–69.

Robichaux, Kerry S. and Paul A. Onica. 2002. Introduction to the English Edition. In *The Divinization of the Christian According to the Greek Fathers*, by Jules Gross, trans. Paul A. Onica, viii–xvii. Anaheim, CA: A and C.

Rohrbaugh, Richard, ed. 1996. *The Social Sciences and New Testament Interpretation*. Peabody, MA: Hendrickson.

Root, Michael. 1989. The Narrative Structure of Soteriology. In *Why Narrative?: Readings in Narrative Theology*, eds. Stanley Hauerwas and L. Gregory Jones, 263–78. Grand Rapids: Eerdmans.

Rosaldo, Michelle Z. 1984. Does the Concept of the Person Vary Cross-Culturally? In *Culture Theory: Essays on Mind, Self, and Emotion*, eds. Richard A. Shweder and Robert A. LeVine, 137–57. Cambridge, UK: Cambridge University Press.

Sacks, Oliver. 1998. *The Man Who Mistook His Wife for a Hat and Other Clinical Tales*. New York: Touchstone.

Sandage, Steve J., and F. LeRon Shults. 2003. *The Faces of Forgiveness: Searching for Wholeness and Salvation*. Grand Rapids: Baker Academic.

Sanders, E. P. 1977. *Paul and Palestinian Judaism*. Philadelphia: Fortress.

Sanit Samarkan. 1975. Concerning the "Face" of Thai People: Analysis According to the Anthropological Linguistics Approach [In Thai]. *Thai Journal of Development Administration* 15(4):492–505.
Sawicki, Marianne. 2000. *Crossing Galilee: Architectures of Contact in the Occupied Land of Jesus*. Harrisburg, PA: Trinity.
Schlenker, Barry R. 2003. Self-Presentation. In *Handbook of Self and Identity*, eds. Mark R. Leary and June Price Tangney, 492–518. New York: Guilford.
Schönherr, Hartmut. 1983. Concepts of Salvation in Christianity. *Africa Theological Journal* 12(3):159–65.
Schrag, Calvin O. 1997. *The Self after Postmodernity*. New Haven, CT: Yale University Press.
Scollon, Ron, and Suzie Wong Scollon. 1994. Face Parameters in East-West Discourse. In *The Challenge of Facework*, ed. Stella Ting-Toomey, 133–57. Albany: State University of New York Press.
Shore, Alan N. 1998. Early Shame Experiences and Infant Brain Development." In *Shame: Interpersonal Behavior, Psychopathology, and Culture*. Paul Gilbert and Bernice Andrews, eds. Pp. 57–77. New York: Oxford University Press.
Shults, F. LeRon. 2003. *Reforming Theological Anthropology: After the Philosophical Turn to Relationality*. Grand Rapids: Eerdmans.
Shweder, Richard A. 1984. Preview: A Colloqy of Culture Theorists. In *Culture Theory: Essays on Mind, Self, and Emotion*, eds. Richard A. Shweder and Robert A. LeVine, 1–24. Cambridge, UK: Cambridge University Press.
Shweder, Richard A., and Robert A. LeVine, eds. 1984. *Culture Theory: Essays on Mind, Self, and Emotion*. Cambridge, UK: Cambridge University Press.
Siam Mission. 1909. *Siam Mission Annual Report, APM*. Chiang Mai, Thailand: Payap University Archives.
Sifianou, Maria. 1992. *Politeness Phenomena in England and Greece: A Cross-Cultural Perspective*. Oxford: Clarendon.
Smith, Alex G. 1982. *Siamese Gold: A History of Church Growth in Thailand 1816–1982*. Bangkok: Kanok Bannasan (OMF Publishers).
Southern, R. W. 1990. *Saint Anselm: A Portrait in a Landscape*. Cambridge, UK: Cambridge University Press.
Spiro, Melford E. 1958. *Children of the Kibbutz*. New York: Shocken.
Spradley, James P. 1979. *The Ethnographic Interview*. New York: Holt, Rinehart and Winston.
Stanley, Brian. 2001. Christian Missions and the Enlightenment: A Reevaluation. In *Christian Missions and the Enlightenment*, ed. Brian Stanley, 1–21. Grand Rapids: Eerdmans.
Stanley, Brian, ed. 2001. *Christian Missions and the Enlightenment*. Grand Rapids: Eerdmans.
Stauropoulos, Christoforos. 1995. Partakers of Divine Nature. In *Eastern Orthodox Theology: A Contemporary Reader*, ed. Daniel B. Clendenin, 183–92. Grand Rapids: Baker.
Stendahl, Krister. 1977. *Paul among Jews and Gentiles*. Philadelphia: Fortress.
Stets, Jan E., and Peter J. Burke. 2003. A Sociological Approach to Self and Identity. In *Handbook of Self and Identity*, eds. Mark R. Leary and June Price Tangney, 128–52. New York: Guilford.
Stewart, Frank H. 1994. *Honor*. Chicago: University of Chicago Press.
Stockitt, Robin. 1998. "Love Bade Me Welcome; But My Soul Drew Back"—Towards an Understanding of Shame. *Anvil* 15(2):111–19.

Sumithra, Sunand. 1992. Justification by Faith: Its Relevance in Hindu Context. In *Right with God: Justification in the Bible and the World*, ed. D. A. Carson, 216–27. Grand Rapids: Baker.

Sunquist, Scott, ed. 2001. *A Dictionary of Asian Christianity*. Grand Rapids: Eerdmans.

Suntaree Komin. 1991. *Psychology of the Thai People: Values and Behavioral Patterns*. Bangkok: Research Center, National Institute of Development Administration.

———. 1998. The Thai World View Through Thai Value Systems. In *Traditional and Changing Thai Worldview*, ed. A. Pongsapich, 207–29. Bangkok: Chulalongkorn University Press.

Swanson, Herbert R. 1984. *Khrischak Muang Nua: A Study in Northern Thai Church History*. Bangkok: Chuan.

———. 1991. *Towards a Clean Church: A Case Study in 19th Century Thai Church History*. Chiang Mai, Thailand: Office of History, Church of Christ in Thailand.

———. 1999. Introduction. In *Historical Sketch of Protestant Missions in Siam 1828–1928*, ed. George Bradley McFarland. Bangkok: White Lotus. Originally published by Bangkok Times Press Ltd., 1928.

———. 2002a. *HeRB*. March 1. Online: http://www.herbswanson.com/herb/herb1/7.php#1.

———. 2002b. E-mail to the author. December 1.

———. 2003. Prelude to Irony: The Princeton Theology and the Practice of American Presbyterian Missions in Northern Siam, 1867–1880. PhD diss., University of Melbourne.

———. N.d. No Middle Ground: Christianity in the Context of Thai History. Unpublished manuscript.

Tambasco, Anthony J. 1991. *A Theology of Atonement and Paul's Vision of Christianity*. Collegeville, MN: Liturgical.

Tangney, June Price. 2003. Self-Relevant Emotions. In *Handbook of Self and Identity*, eds. Mark R. Leary and June Price Tangney, 384–400. New York: Guilford.

Tangney, June Price, and Ronda L. Dearing. 2002. *Shame and Guilt*. New York: Guilford.

Tangney, June Price, and Kurt W. Fischer, eds. 1995. *Self-Conscious Emotions: The Psychology of Shame, Guilt, Embarrassment, and Pride*. New York: Guilford.

Tanner, Kathryn. 1997. *Theories of Culture: A New Agenda for Theology*. Minneapolis: Fortress.

Taylor, Charles. 1989. *Sources of the Self: The Making of Modern Identity*. Cambridge, MA: Harvard University Press.

Taylor, Gabriele. 1985. *Pride, Shame, and Guilt: Emotions of Self-Assessment*. Oxford: Clarendon.

Thai Royal Institute Dictionary [in Thai]. 1995. 6th ed. Bangkok: Àksoncharoenthát.

Theodori Studitæ. 1860. Oratio II. PG 99:696. Paris.

Ting-Toomey, Stella. 1994. Face and Facework: An Introduction. In *The Challenge of Facework: Cross-Cultural and Interpersonal Issues*, ed. Stella Ting-Toomey, 1–14. Albany: State University of New York Press.

———. 2004. Translating Conflict Face-Negotiation Theory into Practice. In *Handbook of Intercultural Training*, eds. Dan Landis, Janet M. Bennett, and Milton J. Bennett, 217–48. Thousand Oaks, CA: Sage.

Ting-Toomey, Stella, ed. 1994 *The Challenge of Facework: Cross-Cultural and Interpersonal Issues*. New York: State University of New York Press.

Ting-Toomey, Stella, and Beth-Ann Cocroft. 1994. Face and Facework: Theoretical and Research Issues. In *The Challenge of Facework*, ed. Stella Ting-Toomey, 307–40. Albany: State University of New York Press.

Tracy, Karen. 1990. The Many Faces of Facework. In *Handbook of Language and Social Psychology*, eds. Howard Giles and W. Peter Robinson, 209–26. Chichester, UK: Wiley and Sons.

Tracy, Karen, and Sheryl Baratz. 1994. The Case for Case Studies of Facework. In *The Challenge of Facework: Cross-Cultural and Interpersonal Issues*, ed. Stella Ting-Toomey, 287–305. Albany: State University of New York Press.

Travis, Stephen H. 1995. Christ as Bearer of Divine Judgment in Paul's Thought About the Atonement. In *Atonement Today*, ed. John Goldingay, 21–38. London: SPCK.

Tuckett, C. M. 1992. Atonement in the NT. In *Anchor Bible Dictionary*, ed. David N. Freeman, 1:518–22. New York: Doubleday.

Uenuma, Masao. 1992. Justification by Faith: Its Relevance in a Buddhist Context. In *Right with God: Justification in the Bible and the World*, ed. D. A. Carson, 243–55. Grand Rapids: Baker.

Ukosakul, Margaret. 1999. Conceptual Metaphors Motivating the Use of Thai "Face." MA thesis, Payap University.

Ury, M. William. 2001. *Trinitarian Personhood: Investigating the Implications of a Relational Definition*. Eugene, OR: Wipf and Stock.

Virat, Koydul. 1990. The History and Growth of the Church of Christ in Thailand: An Evangelistic Perspective. ThM thesis, Fuller Theological Seminary.

Volf, Miroslav. 1998a. *After Our Likeness: The Church as the Image of the Trinity*. Grand Rapids: Eerdmans.

———. 1998b. "The Trinity Is Our Social Program": The Doctrine of the Trinity and the Shape of Social Engagement. *Modern Theology* 14(3):403–23.

Wachter, Egon. 1888. Personal Letter to Mitchell, February 1. Records of the Board of Foreign Missions, Presbyterian Church in the United States of America. Quoted in Herbert R. Swanson, *Towards a Clean Church: A Case Study in 19th Century Thai Church History*. Chiang Mai, Thailand: Office of History, Church of Christ in Thailand, 1991.

Wallbott Harald G., and Klaus R. Scherer. 1995. Cultural Determinants in Experiencing Shame and Guilt. In *Self-Conscious Emotions: The Psychology of Shame, Guilt, Embarrassment, and Pride*. Eds. June Price Tangney and Kurt W. Fischer, 465–87. New York: Guilford.

Walls, Andrew F. 1996. *The Missionary Movement in Christian History: Studies in the Transmission of the Faith*. Maryknoll, NY: Orbis.

Walsh, Sharon L., Ethel Gregory, Yvonne Lake, and Charlotte N. Gunawardena. 2003. Self-Construal, Facework, and Conflict Styles Among Cultures in Online Learning Environments. *Educational Technology Research and Development* 51(4):113–22.

Ware, Kallistos. 1980. *The Orthodox Way*. Crestwood, NY: St. Vladimir's Seminary Press.

Weaver, J. Denny. 2001. *The Nonviolent Atonement*. Grand Rapids: Eerdmans.

Webb, Tony. 2000. *Shame—A Salutogenic View: Some Ideas on Work in Progress Towards a PhD in Theories for Social Change—Towards a Mature Shame Culture*. Social Ecology Research Group, November 23. Online: http://sites.uws.edu.au/research/SERG/Spsych1_webb.htm.

Westerholm, Stephen. 1988. *Israel's Law and the Church's Faith: Paul and His Recent Interpreters*. Grand Rapids: Eerdmans.

Wikan, Unni. 1984. Shame and Honour: A Contestable Pair. *Man* 19:635–52.

Wilson, A. N. 1999. *The Ground of Union: Deification in Aquinas and Palamas*. Oxford: Oxford University Press.

Wilson, Steven R., and Adrianne W. Kunkel. 2000. Identity Implications of Influence Goals: Similarities in Perceived Face Threats and Facework across Sex and Close Relationships. *Journal of Language and Social Psychology* 19(2):195–221.

Wisely, Thomas Noel. 1984. Dynamic Biblical Christianity in the Buddhist/Marxist Context: Northeast Thailand. PhD diss., Fuller Theological Seminary.

Wright, N. T. 1991. Putting Paul Together Again. In *Pauline Theology*, ed. Jouette M. Bassler, 183–211. Minneapolis: Fortress.

———. 1992. *The New Testament and the People of God*. Minneapolis: Fortress.

———. 1997. *What Saint Paul Really Said*. Grand Rapids: Eerdmans.

Yoder, John Howard. 2002. *Preface to Theology: Christology and Theological Method*. Grand Rapids: Brazos.

Zehner, Edwin R. 1991. Merit, Man and Ministry: Traditional Thai Hierarchies in a Contemporary Church. *Social Compass* 38(2):155–75.

———. 1996. Thai Protestants and Local Supernaturalism: Changing Configurations. *Journal of Southeast Asian Studies* 27:293–319.

———. 2003. Unavoidably Hybrid: Thai Buddhist Conversions to Evangelical Christianity. PhD diss., Cornell University.

Zimmerman, Carle C., and Mrs. George B. McFarland. 1931. *Extracts from Report on Siam*. Chiang Mai, Thailand: Payap University Archives.

Zizioulas, John D. 1985. *Being as Communion: Studies in Personhood and the Church*. Crestwood, NY: St. Vladimir's Seminary Press.

Index

Acocella, Joan, 16
Adeyemo, Tokunboh, 227, 228
Andrews, Bernice, 58
Anselm, 220, 224, 225, 226
Aquino, Frederick D., 178
Aristotle, 47, 48, 164, 165, 185, 186, 187, 214, 226
Arundale, Robert, 102, 254
Athanasius, 246, 249
Atkinson, David, 245
atonement, 2, 3, 8, 9, 10, 11, 34, 35, 73, 74, 210, 211, 212, 213, 214, 215, 216, 218–28, 233, 235, 236, 237, 238, 239, 240, 241, 242, 244, 245, 264
    penal substitution theory of, 8–10, 35, 73, 74, 213, 220, 225, 226, 227, 228, 233
    relational atonement, 11
    satisfaction theory of, 227
Augsburger, David W., 66
Augustine, 46, 49, 50, 51, 52, 55, 171, 172, 177, 187, 246

Balás, David L., 246, 248
Baratz, Sheryl, 5, 117
Barnett, Milton L., 58, 66
Barrett, Karen C., 58, 68
Bartlett, Anthony W., 213, 225, 226, 227
Baumeister, Roy F., 53, 67

Bavinck, Johann H., 72
Bebbington, David W., 20
Beker, J. Christiaan, 236
Benedict, Ruth, 58, 65, 69, 70, 71, 72
Benson, Steven R., 240, 244
Bernard, H. Russell, 119
Bilmes, Leela, 109, 110, 115, 116, 155, 156, 157
Boethius, 50, 51, 52, 55
Boff, Leonardo, 172, 183, 184
Boot, Max, 269
Booth, Wayne C., 7
Bosch, David, 20
Bowen, Nancy R., 245
Brackett, K. P., 78
Bradley, Dan Beach, 29, 32, 34, 39, 40
Brandes, Stanley, 66
Brown, Penelope, 84, 86, 87, 88, 89, 91, 93, 100, 109, 110, 115, 116, 156
Bultmann, Rudolf, 232, 234
Burke, Peter J., 170

Carroll, John T., 213, 214, 219, 222
Carson, D. A., 228
Caswell, Jesse, 34, 35, 41
Chaiyan Ukosakul, 115
Chance, John K., 202
Chang, H., 5, 96, 117
Charmaz, Kathy, 118
Cheng, C., 88

Christensen, Michael J., 246
Chryssides, George D., 215, 217
Cist, O., 246
Clark, William N., 4
Clendenin, Daniel B., 252
Cocroft, Beth-Ann, 6, 77, 91, 102, 117, 198
Cohen, Erik, 7, 15, 18, 28
Colomb, Gregory C., 7
Common Sense Realism, 20–23, 25, 27, 28
Cooke, Joseph R., 3, 7, 15, 37, 243
Creighton, Millie R., 58
Crutcher, Timothy J., 6
Cunningham, David S., 172
Cupach, William R., 85, 86, 101

Danker, Frederick W., 250
Davis, John R., 38, 70
Dearing, Ronda L., 58, 59, 60, 61, 62
Delin, Judy, 78
den Heyer, C. J., 214
deSilva, David A., 202, 203, 204, 205, 206, 207, 251
Dodd, W. Clifton, 19, 20, 32, 33
Downing, F. Gerald, 202
doxa, 204, 250
Driver, John, 9, 217
Dunn, James D. G., 229, 232, 233, 234, 235, 245

ecclesial self, 174, 178, 179, 180, 182, 183, 185, 188, 192, 193, 198, 199, 200, 201, 202, 254, 266, 267
Edelmann, Robert J., 87
Ek Thabping, Joseph, 15
Elliott, John H., 202
Ervin-Tripp, Susan, 77

face
    as claim right, 98, 99, 100, 102, 111, 256, 257, 260, 265, 267, 269, 271
    Chinese face, 94, 95, 96, 98
    competence face, 93, 100, 102, 111, 157
    face loss/depletion, viii, 11, 41, 43, 93, 94, 112, 115, 121, 122, 125, 126, 127, 128, 131, 133, 134, 137, 143, 146, 147, 148, 151, 152, 153, 154, 155, 156, 159, 251, 252, 255, 256, 257, 258, 261, 277
    fellowship face, 93, 100, 102, 110, 111, 157
    function of, 4, 8, 85, 97, 112, 135, 264
    independent face, 90, 91
    interdependent face, 90, 91
    Japanese face, 91, 92
    maintenance of, 11, 86, 108, 121, 132, 152
    of Christ, 190, 193, 194, 195, 197, 198, 209, 261, 265, 266, 267, 271
    of God, 190, 193, 194, 195, 196, 197, 198, 199, 200, 209, 251, 254, 256, 261, 266, 267
    personal face, 91, 94, 95, 100, 102, 124, 125, 126, 127, 128, 146, 152, 154, 156, 158, 159, 191, 201, 202, 255
    recovery of, 115, 121, 131, 151, 152, 154, 155, 252, 259
    social face, 85, 94, 95, 100, 102, 121, 125, 127, 134, 135, 146, 152, 153, 156, 158, 159, 191, 201, 202, 270
    Thai face, vii, viii, 1, 2, 3, 4, 6, 7, 8, 9, 11, 12, 38, 39, 92, 103–16, 117, 159, 163, 210, 242–61, 264, 265, 266, 275
    ubiquity of, 101, 191
facework, vii, viii, 4, 5, 6, 41, 42, 77–102, 104, 107, 109, 110, 113, 115, 116, 117, 119, 120, 121, 128, 129, 130, 131, 132, 138, 145, 146, 147, 148, 152, 154, 156, 159, 187, 190, 196, 198, 199, 255, 259, 264, 267, 270, 271, 275
Feltus, Georgy H., 32, 39
Fiddes, Paul S., 9, 212, 226
Fowler, James W., 64
Franke, John R., 178

Geertz, Clifford, 46
Gergen, Kenneth J., 46, 52

Gilbert, Paul, 58, 63, 64
Goffman, Erving, 57, 78, 85, 86, 87, 88, 89, 95, 98, 100, 104, 110, 185, 186, 187
Goldingay, John, 228
Green, Joel B., 9, 213, 214, 219, 222, 223, 225, 238, 239, 240, 244
Greenwald, Deborah F., 60, 64
Gregory, Ethel, 78, 182, 247
Grenz, Stanley J., 46, 49, 50, 51, 52, 55, 168, 171, 172, 174, 175, 177, 178, 179, 183, 184, 185, 224, 225, 254
grounded theory, 118
Gudykunst, William B., 77, 89, 91, 92, 94
guilt, vii, ix, 31–38, 46, 57–63, 65–74, 78, 111, 137, 153, 157, 171, 195, 220, 224, 227, 228, 231, 233, 236, 242, 243, 244, 245, 248, 252, 253, 263
guilt culture, 57, 58, 59, 66, 70
Gunawardena, Charlotte, 78
Gunton, Colin E., 9, 47, 50, 51, 171, 172, 173, 214–18, 223, 224, 226, 228, 237, 239, 240
Gustafson, James W., 7, 15, 18, 38

Haers, Jacques, 6
Hanson, K. C., 208
Harder, David W., 60, 64
Harré, Rom, 167, 170
Ho, David Yau-Fai, 88, 92, 94, 95, 96, 97
Holifield, E. Brooks, 21
Holland, Dorothy, 144
Holt, R., 5, 96, 117
honor, vii, viii, ix, 1, 3, 5, 6, 9, 11, 45, 57, 64, 67–74, 78, 88, 97, 98, 99, 102, 103, 106, 108, 109, 111, 113, 114, 115, 117, 118, 121, 122, 123, 125, 130, 131, 132, 135–43, 146, 148, 152, 153, 154, 156, 157, 174, 178, 179, 183, 184, 185, 186, 187, 190, 191, 192, 193, 196–209, 220, 224, 225, 226, 233, 242, 243, 244, 245, 246, 249, 250, 251, 252, 254–70, 277, 281, 285, 286, 287, 292

boasting related to, 206, 207, 234, 283
zeal related to, 207, 208, 232, 233
honor culture, 6, 46, 57, 68, 70, 71
honor discourse, 191, 204, 205, 206, 209
Hooker, Morna D., 249
Houts, Margo G., 238
Hu, Hsien Chin, 88, 95, 102
Hughes, Philip J., 7, 15, 19, 31, 36, 38
Hultgren, Arland J., 236
Hwa, Yung, 228
Hwang, Kwang-Kuo, 88, 97, 98

Jewett, Robert, 233, 242, 245
Johnson, Mark, 54, 144
justice culture, 46, 57, 70, 71

Kant, Emmanual, 52, 55, 164, 165, 215
Kao, Samson S., 38
Karen, Robert, 74
Kärkkäinen, Veli-Matti, 247, 248, 253
Kaufman, Gershen, 60
Kerr, Fergus, 46, 52
Keyes, Charles F., 7, 15, 18
Kim, Samuel I., 19, 38
Kitayama, Shinobu, 54, 55, 90, 91
Klausner, William, 107
Koehler, Walter, 203
Koyama, Kosuke, 15
Kraus, Norman C., 74, 242, 244, 245
Kressel, Gideon M., 57, 202, 208
Kunkel, Adrianne W., 98
Kuyper, L. J., 230

LaCugna, Catherine Mowry, 50, 171, 172
Lake, Yvonne, 78
Lakoff, George, 54, 114, 144, 149, 150
Lawrence, Louise J., 202
Lebra, Takie Sugiyama, 58, 65, 66
Levinson, Stephen C., 84, 86, 87, 88, 89, 91, 93, 100, 109, 110, 115, 116, 156
Lewis, C. S., 59, 62, 65, 196, 203, 204, 216, 267
Lewis, Michael, 59, 62, 65, 196, 203, 204, 216, 267

Lienhard, Ruth, 69, 70, 71
Lim, Tae-Sop, 92, 93, 96, 101
Loder, James E., 182, 194, 197
Loewen, Jacob A., 70
Longenecker, Richard N., 229
Lord, Donald C., 39
Lu, Hsün (Chou, Shü-jen), 77, 88,
Lyall, Francis, 216
Lynd, Helen Merrell, 58, 61, 63, 67

MacIntyre, Alasdair C., 52, 166, 185, 186, 187
Maen Pongudom, 16, 18, 40
makarisms, 208
Malina, Bruce J., 202, 206, 251
Mantzaridis, Georgios I., 247, 251, 253
Markus, Hazel Rose, 53, 54, 55, 90, 91
Marshall, I. Howard, 214
Matsumoto and Matsumoto, 88, 90, 91
Mattoon, Mrs. S., 40
McClendon, James William, 9, 211, 213, 221, 222, 223, 225, 239
McCord Adams, Marilyn, 201, 204
McFadyen, Alistair, 173, 178, 180, 185
McFarland, Bertha Blount, 17, 30, 36, 40, 42, 43
McFarland, George B., 17, 30, 36, 40, 42, 43
McGilvary, Daniel, 19, 20, 32, 33, 34, 39, 40, 41
McGrath, Alister, 213
Mead, George Herbert, 58, 168, 169, 170
Meakin, J. E. B., 35
metaphor, viii, 1, 6, 9, 10, 50, 77, 107, 108, 109, 114, 138, 144, 145, 146, 147, 150, 192, 194, 197, 213–22, 237, 238, 239, 261, 262, 264, 291
Metts, Sandra, 85, 86, 101
Mischel, Walter, 53, 54
missional space, 25, 26
missionary practice
  disconnect with Thai culture, 8, 19
  universalizing, 8, 22, 25, 28
Mole, Robert L., 107
Moreau, A. Scott, 69

Morf, Carolyn C., 53, 54
Morisaki, Seiichi, 77, 89, 91, 92, 94
Mühlhäusler, Peter, 167, 170
Mulder, Niels, 105, 106, 111, 112, 113, 157, 158
Müller, Klaus, 6, 70, 71, 72, 73
Muller, Roland, 68
Murdoch, Iris, 52, 53

Nakamura, Kei, 77
Nantachai Mejudhon, 18, 28, 32, 37, 39, 40
narrative, ii, 8, 9, 11, 83, 166, 185, 186, 187, 188, 198, 199, 211, 213, 220, 221, 222, 238, 239, 240, 242, 243, 256, 261, 262, 263, 264, 267, 270
Neidhardt, W. Jim, 197
New Perspective
  Hebrew law court, 228, 230
  righteousness, 228, 229, 230, 232–36, 245
Neyrey, Jerome H., 202, 206, 249, 250
Noble, Lowell Lappin, 115
Noll, Mark A., 21, 22
Norris, F. W., 246, 252

Onica, Paul A., 248
ontological anxiety, 195, 196

Packer, J. I., 226, 227
panim, 194
Penman, Robyn, 79, 84, 88, 97, 167, 168
Peristiany, J. G., 66
Phillips, Herbert, 103, 104, 105, 107, 112, 113, 157
Piers, G., 60, 62, 66, 67
Pilch, John J., 202
Pinnock, Clark H., 248, 249, 253
Piper, Ronald A., 204, 251
Pitt-Rivers, Julian, 66, 99
Plevnik, Joseph, 202
Potter, Jonathan 170
prosopagnosia, vii, 44–46, 57, 78, 163, 164, 188, 190, 263, 264, 271
prosopon, 44, 194

prototype, ix, 109, 149, 150, 151, 194, 255, 258, 262
prototype scenario, 149, 157, 255, 262

Quinn, Naomi, 114, 144, 145, 150

Rakestraw, Robert V., 246, 247, 248
relationality, 6, 8, 9, 11, 40, 48, 49, 52, 55, 74, 78, 79, 80, 84, 86, 87, 94, 105, 110, 112, 123, 124, 136, 155, 156, 163, 164, 165, 166, 168–74, 176–82, 184, 185, 187, 188, 189, 191, 192, 193, 194, 195, 197, 198, 199, 201, 202, 254, 255, 251, 259, 264, 266
retributive justice, 31, 74, 225, 236, 248,
Ringgren, Helmer, 203
Robichaux, Kerry S., 248
Rohrbaugh, Richard L., 202, 251
Root, Michael, 211, 220, 221, 239
Rosaldo, Michelle Z., 58

Sacks, Oliver, 44
Sandage, Steven J., 191, 195, 196, 199, 252
Sanders, E. P., 235, 249
Sanit Samarkan, 88, 106, 107, 109, 113, 157
Sawicki, Marianne, 202
Scherer, Klaus R., 65
Schlenker, Barry R., 79–83
Schönherr, Hartmut, 252
Schrag, Calvin O., 166, 168
Scollon, 79
self
    independent self, 52, 55, 90, 91, 92, 97, 111, 113
    interdependent self, 55, 90, 91, 92, 113, 157, 158
    modern Western self, vii, 44–55, 78, 163, 164, 168, 170, 177, 185, 187, 188
    relational self, 163, 164, 165, 174, 177, 185, 188
    social self, 54, 55, 89, 90, 96, 169, 170, 181, 191, 198

Self Presentation, 78–84, 87, 96, 102, 111, 112, 116, 130, 165, 185, 186, 187, 188, 264
    automatic response, 81
    controlled response, 81
shame, vii, ix, 3, 5, 6, 9, 11, 45, 46, 57–74, 78, 88, 94, 104, 109, 114, 115, 126, 127, 137, 148, 152, 153, 155, 159, 185, 192, 195, 196, 201, 202, 204, 205, 207, 208, 209, 242–46, 249, 250, 251, 252, 253, 256–64, 266, 277
shame culture, 6, 57, 58, 65, 6, 68, 70, 71, 73
Shore, Alan N., 68
Shults, F. LeRon, 47, 49, 50, 164, 165, 171, 177, 191, 195, 196, 199, 252, 253
Shweder, Richard A., 90
Siam Mission, 41
Sifianou, Maria, 91
Singer, M. B., 60, 62, 66, 67
Smith, Alex G., 38
soteriology
    construction of, 3, 6, 15, 31, 32, 43, 176, 210, 211, 212, 213, 220, 221, 225, 234, 236, 238–43, 246, 249, 261, 262, 264
    contextual, 4, 9, 10, 11, 242, 243, 265
Southern, R. W., 225
Spiro, Melford E., 59, 67, 68
Spradley, James P., 119
Stanley, Brian, 20, 23, 24, 26, 27
Stauropoulos, Christoforos, 248
Stendahl, Krister, 74, 234
Stets, Jan E., 170
Stewart, Frank H., 98, 99
Stockitt, Robin, 244
Strauss, Claudia, 114, 144, 150
Suggate, Alan M., 232, 233, 234, 235
Sumithra, Sunand, 228
Sunquist, Scott, 69
Suntaree Komin, 1, 106, 107, 108, 109, 113, 134, 157
Swanson, Herbert R., 7, 15–19, 29, 30

Tambasco, Anthony J., 224, 231
Tangney, June Price, 58, 59, 60, 61, 62
Tanner, Kathryn, 266
Taylor, Charles, 47, 48, 49, 51, 52, 55, 165, 168
Taylor, Gabriele, 57, 58, 61, 64
Thai face, vii, viii, 1, 2, 3, 4, 6, 7, 8, 9, 11, 12, 38, 39, 92, 103–62, 163, 210, 242–61, 264, 265, 266, 275
  as container of honor, 108, 113
  as ego-self, 106, 108, 109, 113, 158
  as façade, 54, 105, 106, 11, 112, 200
  as social capital, 94, 109, 110, 113, 115, 131, 147, 153, 156, 157, 159
  as social cosmetic, 103, 104, 105, 107, 111, 112, 113
  cultural model of, 4, 6, 7, 8, 117, 118, 143, 144, 145, 149, 150, 157, 158, 159, 243, 261, 164, 165
  non-players, 133, 134, 135, 154, 158
Thai Royal Institute Dictionary [in Thai], 138
Theodori Studitæ, 252
theological anthropology
  trinitarian, viii, 163, 164, 165–89, 247, 253
theory of culture, 20, 22, 24, 25, 29, 37, 43, 243, 244, 246–54, 257, 261, 262, 264
theosis, 243, 244, 246–54, 257, 261, 262, 264
Ting-Toomey, Stella, 1, 6, 77, 87, 89, 91, 98, 100, 101, 102, 117, 138, 191, 193
Tracy, Karen, 5, 78, 96, 97, 101, 117
Travis, Stephen H., 228
trinitarian identity, 178, 180
trinitarian theology, 163, 165, 170, 171, 172, 174, 180, 187
Tuckett, C. M., 218, 220

Ukosakul, Margaret, 106, 108, 109, 113, 114, 115, 116, 120, 154, 157
Ury, M. William, 47, 48, 49, 165, 171, 174, 178, 182, 289

Virat, Koydul, 38
Volf, Miroslav, 174, 176, 178, 180, 181, 182, 199

Wachter, Egon, 29, 30
Wallbott, Harald G., 65
Walls, Andrew F., 11, 12, 24
Walsh, Sharon L., 78
Ware, Kallistos, 247
Weaver, J. Denny, 223, 227
Webb, Tony, 64
Westerholm, Stephen, 67
Wetherell, Margaret, 170
Wikan, Unni, 57
Williams, Joseph M.,
Wilson, A. N., 98, 246
Wilson, Steven R., 98
Wisely, Thomas Noel, 15, 18
Wright, N. T., 179, 229, 230, 231, 232, 234, 236

Yoder, John Howard, 237

zeal, 201, 208, 232, 233
Zehner, Edwin R., 16, 18
Zimmerman, Carle C., 17, 30, 36, 42, 43
Zizioulas, John D., 171, 174, 175, 176, 178, 179, 255

www.ingramcontent.com/pod-product-compliance
Lightning Source LLC
Chambersburg PA
CBHW050620300426
44112CB00012B/1590